T0215905

Cloud Data Management

Liang Zhao • Sherif Sakr • Anna Liu
Athman Bouguettaya

Cloud Data Management

Foreword by Albert Y. Zomaya

 Springer

Liang Zhao
NICTA Kensington
NSW, Australia

Anna Liu
NICTA, Eveleigh
NSW, Australia

Sherif Sakr
Software Systems Research Group
NICTA, Eveleigh, NSW
Australia

Faculty of Computers and Information
Cairo University, Egypt

Athman Bouguettaya
School of Computer Science
    and Information Technology
RMIT University, Melbourne
VIC, Australia

ISBN 978-3-319-34776-9   ISBN 978-3-319-04765-2 (eBook)
DOI 10.1007/978-3-319-04765-2
Springer Cham Heidelberg New York Dordrecht London

Printed on acid-free paper

Springer is part of Springer Science+Business Media (www.springer.com)

Foreword

The rapidly expanding generation of Internet-based services such as e-mail, blogging, social networking, search, and e-commerce has substantially redefined the behavior and trends of web users when it comes to creating, communicating, accessing content, sharing information, and purchasing products. Information technology professionals are witnessing a proliferation in the scale of the data generated and consumed because of the growth in the number of these systems; this ever increasing need for scalability and new application requirements has created new challenges for traditional relational database management systems (RDBMS). Currently, the apparent goal of the system and tool manufacturers is to facilitate the job of implementing every application as a distributed, scalable, and widely accessible service on the web (e.g., services from Facebook, Flickr, YouTube, Zoho, and LinkedIn).

Cloud computing technology is a relatively new model for hosting software applications. The cloud model simplifies the time-consuming processes of hardware provisioning, hardware purchasing, and software deployment; therefore it revolutionizes the way computational resources and services are commercialized and delivered to customers. In particular, it shifts the location of this infrastructure to the network in order to reduce the costs associated with the management of hardware and software resources. This means that the cloud represents the long-held dream of envisioning computing as a utility, a dream in which the economy of scale principles help to effectively drive down the cost of the computing infrastructure. In practice, cloud computing promises a number of advantages for the deployment of software applications such as pay-per-use cost model, short time to market, and the perception of (virtually) unlimited resources and infinite scalability.

The rise of the cloud technology has been somewhat disruptive. The advantages of the cloud computing model open up new avenues for deploying novel applications that were not economically feasible in a traditional enterprise infrastructure setting. Therefore, the cloud has become an increasingly popular platform for hosting software applications in a variety of domains such as e-retail, finance, news, and social networking. The proliferation in the number of applications also delivers a tremendous increase in the scale of the data generated and consumed by these applications. This is why a cloud-hosted database system powering these applications forms a critical component in the software stack of these applications.

To meet the challenges posed by hosting databases on cloud computing environments there are a plethora of systems and approaches. This book is the first that approaches the challenges associated with hosting databases on cloud computing environments from different but integrated perspectives; it connects the dots. The authors deal with the problems that may be encountered in every cloud-based data hosting solution: NoSQL storage services, database-as-a-service (DaaS), virtualized database servers in addition to batch-based processing systems for big data. The book is useful for many database researchers or practitioners because the inherent change in hosting database in cloud environment is fundamental on many perspectives as it originates from new foundations and models of thinking.

I found the book to contain a lot of timely and useful information. The book has many gems that inspire the readers as they go through the different chapters which are covering an area that is currently changing the data management field in a fundamental way. It covers an impressive array of topics with great clarity that will excite any reader wishing to understand this emerging technology. It also provides extensive references which will help the interested reader find out more information about the discussed topics. All in all, this is an impressive piece of work and an invaluable source of knowledge for advanced students and researchers working in or wishing to explore this exciting field.

Darlington, NSW, Australia   Albert Y. Zomaya

Preface

Cloud computing technology represents a new paradigm for the provisioning of computing resources. Cloud computing is with us and for the foreseeable future. This paradigm shift allows for the outsourcing of computing resources to reduce the ownership costs associated with the management of hardware and software. Cloud computing simplifies the time-consuming processes of hardware provisioning, hardware purchasing, and software deployment.

Cloud computing is not a passing trend but a stubborn reality that is rooted on an emerging trend leading computing into a technological quantum leap. It builds on decades of research in virtualization, autonomic computing, grid computing, and utility computing, and ubiquity of the web as the network and delivery medium.

Central to the success of cloud computing is the ability to provision data using different quality of service requirements, including latency, performance, and reliability. Unfortunately, most cloud providers do not guarantee, and let alone, provide information about actual quality of service for data access. This is a complex exercise that depends on many factors, including the location of the data store, type of data, network congestion and data store platforms.

This book fills a gap in that it provides an in-depth analysis of major data cloud platforms using an exhaustive series of tests and experiments to unlock the unanswered questions surrounding the performance of each cloud data platform that is considered. The work presented in this book focuses on evaluating cloud databases in the presence of very little information from cloud providers. This can also be interpreted as reverse-engineering the performance of cloud databases with its own risks in interpretation.

The data cloud platforms considered in this book include the leaders in the field, including, Amazon, Microsoft, and Google. Amazon offers a collection of services, called Amazon Web Services, which includes Amazon Elastic Compute Cloud (EC2) as cloud hosting server, offering infrastructure as a service and Amazon SimpleDB and Simple Storage Service (S3) as cloud databases.

Microsoft Azure is recognized as a combination of infrastructure as a service and platform as a service. It features web role and worker role for web hosting tasks and computing tasks, respectively. It also offers a variety of database options including

Windows Azure Table Storage and Windows Azure Blob Storage as the NoSQL database options and Azure SQL Database as the relational database option.

Google App Engine supports a platform as a service model, supporting programming languages including Python and Java and Google App Engine Datastore as a Bigtable-based, non-relational, and highly sharable cloud database.

We propose a performance evaluation framework of cloud platforms as a uniform testing environment for all the cloud data environments. We describe novel frameworks and architectures to address the following issues: (1) the performance characteristics of different cloud platforms, including cloud hosting servers and cloud databases, (2) availability and reliability characteristics that cloud platforms typically exhibit, (3) type of faults and errors that may be encountered when services are running on different cloud platforms under high request volume or high stress situations, (4) reasons behind the faults and errors, (5) the architecture internal insights that may be deduced from these observations, and (6) the software engineering challenges that developers and architects could face when using cloud platforms as their production environment for service delivery.

Kensington, NSW, Australia   Liang Zhao
Eveleigh, NSW, Australia   Sherif Sakr
Eveleigh, NSW, Australia   Anna Liu
Melbourne, VIC, Australia   Athman Bouguettaya

Acknowledgements

I would like to thank my parents, Lijuan Chu and Dianchi Zhao, for their constant love, support, and encouragement during my Ph.D. study. I would also like to express my appreciation to my wife, Huan Wang, for her patience, understanding, and encouragement. The work would not have been possible without their support and care.

Liang Zhao

I would like to thank my parents, Ali Sakr and Amira Awad, for their encouragement and support. I want to thank my daughter, Jana, for the happiness and enjoyable moments she is always bringing to my life. My most special appreciation goes to my wife, Radwa Elshawi, for her everlasting support and deep love.

Sherif Sakr

I would like to sincerely thank the excellent hard work of my coauthors, without their dedication, commitment, and persistence, this book would not be here. I would also like to thank the wider NICTA Dependable Cloud Computing research team, who have provided wonderful companionship through our research journey. Lastly, many thanks go to our industry partners, who have provided much of the use inspiration for our work.

Anna Liu

I would like to thank my family for their love and understanding during my work on this book.

Athman Bouguettaya

The authors of this book would like to extend their sincere gratitude and appreciation to their collaborators for the contribution to this book; in particular, we would like to mention Alan Fekete, Jacky Keung, Kevin Lee, Hiroshi Wada, Xiwei Xu, Zhen Ye, Xiaofang Zhou, and Liming Zhu. Thank you all!

Contents

List of Figures

List of Tables

Chapter 1
Introduction

We live in the era of big data. Information from multiple sources is growing at a staggering rate. The number of Internet users reached 2.27 billion in 2012. Google estimates that the total number of web pages exceeds one trillion. Every day, Facebook generates more than 25 TB of log data, Twitter generates more than 12 TB of tweets, and the New York Stock Exchange captures 1 TB of trade information. Each minute, 15 h of video are uploaded to YouTube. About 30 billion radio-frequency identification (RFID) tags are created every day. Add to this mix the data generated by the hundreds of millions of GPS devices sold every year, and the more than 30 million networked sensors currently in use (and growing at a rate faster than 30 percent per year). Modern high-energy physics experiments, such as *DZero* [46], typically generate more than one TeraByte of data per day. These data volumes are expected to double every two years over the next decade.

The rapidly expanding generation of Internet-based services such as email, blogging, social networking, search, and e-commerce have substantially redefined the behavior and trends of web users when it comes to creating, communicating, accessing content, sharing information, and purchasing products. For example, we buy books on *Amazon*, sell thing on *eBay*, stay in contact with friends and colleagues via *Facebook* and *Linkedin*, start a blog using *WordPress*. share pictures via *Flickr*, and share videos via *YouTube*. These are just examples to name a few well-known internet-based services that we use in our everyday life. IT professionals are witnessing a proliferation in the scale of the data generated and consumed because of the growth in the number of these systems.

A company can generate up to petabytes of information in the course of a year: web pages, blogs, clickstreams, search indices, social media forums, instant messages, text messages, email, documents, consumer demographics, sensor data from active and passive systems, and more. By many estimates, as much as 80% of this data is semi-structured or unstructured. Companies are always seeking to become more nimble in their operations and more innovative with their data analysis and decision-making processes. And they are realizing that time lost in these processes can lead to missed business opportunities. The core of the big

L. Zhao et al., *Cloud Data Management*, DOI 10.1007/978-3-319-04765-2_1,
© Springer International Publishing Switzerland 2014

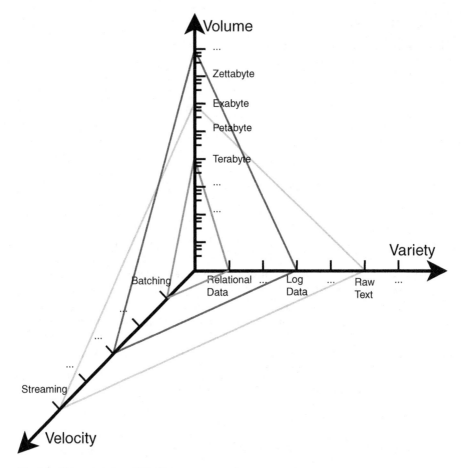

Fig. 1.1 Characteristics of Big Data

data challenge is for companies to gain the ability to analyze and understand Internet-scale information just as easily as they can now analyze and understand smaller volumes of structured information.

As shown in Fig. 1.1, the characteristics of these overwhelming flows of data which are produced at multiple sources are currently subsumed under the notion of *Big Data* with 3Vs (volume, variety and velocity) defining properties as follows:

- *Volume*: refers to the scale of data, from terabytes to zettabytes.
- *Velocity*: reflects streaming data and large-volume data movements.
- *Variety*: refers to the complexity of data in many different structures, ranging from relational to logs to raw text.

In general, the continuous increase of computational power, in the last two decades, has been behind producing this overwhelming flow of data which called for a paradigm shift in the computing architecture and large scale data processing mechanisms. Jim Gray, a database software pioneer and a Microsoft researcher, called the shift a *"fourth paradigm"* [151]. The first three paradigms were *experimental, theoretical* and, more recently, *computational science*. Gray argued that the only way to cope with this paradigm is to develop a new generation of computing tools to manage, visualize and analyze the data flood. In general, the current computer architectures are increasingly imbalanced where the latency gap between multi-core CPUs and mechanical hard disks is growing every year which makes the challenges of data-intensive computing harder to overcome [76].

Recently, there has been a great deal of hype about cloud computing. Cloud computing is associated with a new paradigm for the provision of computing infrastructure. This paradigm shifts the location of this infrastructure to the network to reduce the costs associated with the management of hardware and software resources. Hence, businesses and users become able to access application services from anywhere in the world on demand. Therefore, it represents the long-held dream of envisioning computing as a utility [68] where the economy of scale principles help to drive the cost of computing infrastructure effectively down. Big players such as Amazon, Google, IBM, Microsoft and Sun Microsystems have established new data centers for hosting Cloud computing applications in various locations around the world to provide redundancy and ensure reliability in case of site failures.

In principle, one of the main reasons for the success of cloud computing is the role it has played in eliminating the size of an enterprise as a critical factor in its economic success. An excellent example of this change is the notion of *data centers* which provide clients with the physical infrastructure needed to host their computer systems, including redundant power supplies, high bandwidth communication capabilities, environment monitoring, and security services. In practice, on-premise data centers are often under-utilized due to over-provisioning, as well as the time-varying resource demands of typical enterprise applications. Multi-tenancy is an optimization mechanism for hosted services in which multiple customers are consolidated onto the same operational system (a single instance of the software runs on a server, serving multiple clients) and thus the economy of scale principles help to effectively drive down the cost of computing infrastructure. In particular, multi-tenancy allows pooling of resources which improves utilization by eliminating the need to provision each tenant for their maximum load. This makes multi-tenancy an attractive mechanism for both: Cloud providers (who are able to serve more customers with a smaller set of machines) and Customers of cloud services (who do not need to pay the price of renting the full capacity of a server). Therefore, Public data centers have helped to eliminate the need for small companies to make a large capital expenditure in building an infrastructure to create a global customer base [62]. The data center model has been effective since it allows an enterprise of any size to manage growth with the popularity of its product or service while at the same time also allows the enterprise to cut its losses if the launched product or service does not succeed.

In general, the concept of renting computing power goes back decades to the days when companies would share space on a single mainframe with big spinning tape drives and it has been envisioned that computing facilities will be provided to the general public like a utility [191]. Recently, the technology industry has matured to the point where there is now an emerging mass market for this rental model. Hence, cloud computing is not a revolutionary new development. However, it is an evolution that has taken place over several decades and different technologies such as virtualization, grid computing, utility computing and autonomic computing.

From the data management and processing point of view, there are two general archetypes of data-intensive applications:

1. *On-Line Analytical Processing (OLAP)*: is characterized by relatively low volume of transactions. Queries are often complex, involve aggregations. and require accessing historical and multi-dimensional data with the purpose of analyzing it and reporting certain figures. For OLAP systems, queries usually runs in a batch processing mode.
2. *On-line Transaction Processing (OLTP)*: is characterized by a large number of short transactions. The main emphasis for OLTP systems is put on very fast query processing, maintaining data integrity in multi-access environments and an effectiveness measured by number of transactions per second.

In general, successful cloud data management systems are normally designed to satisfy as much as possible from the following *wish list* [58, 110]:

- *Availability*: They must be always accessible even on the occasions where there is a network failure or a whole datacenter has gone offline. Towards this goal, the concept of Communication as a Service (CaaS) emerged to support such requirements, as well as network security, dynamic provisioning of virtual overlays for traffic isolation or dedicated bandwidth, guaranteed message delay, communication encryption, and network monitoring [235].
- *Scalability*: They must be able to support very large databases with very high request rates at very low latency. They should be able to take on new tenants or handle growing tenants without much effort beyond that of adding more hardware. In particular, the system must be able to automatically redistribute data to take advantage of the new hardware.
- *Elasticity*: They must be able to satisfy changing application requirements in both directions (scaling up or scaling down). Moreover, the system must be able to gracefully respond to these changing requirements and quickly recover to its steady state.
- *Performance*: On public cloud computing platforms, pricing is structured in a way such that one pays only for what one uses, so the vendor price increases linearly with the requisite storage, network bandwidth, and compute power. Hence, the system performance has a direct effect on its costs. Thus, efficient system performance is a crucial requirement to save money.
- *Multitenancy*: They must be able to support many applications (tenants) on the same hardware and software infrastructure. However, the performance of these tenant must be isolated from each another. Adding a new tenant should require little or no effort beyond that of ensuring that enough system capacity has been provisioned for the new load.

- *Load and Tenant Balancing*: They must be able to automatically move load between servers so that most of the hardware resources are effectively utilized and to avoid any resource overloading situations.
- *Fault Tolerance*: For transactional workloads, a fault tolerant cloud data management system needs to be able to recover from a failure without losing any data or updates from recently committed transactions. Moreover, it needs to successfully commit transactions and make progress on a workload even in the face of worker node failures. For analytical workloads, a fault tolerant cloud data management system should not need to restart a query if one of the nodes involved in query processing fails.
- *Ability to run in a heterogeneous environment*: On cloud computing platforms, there is a strong trend towards increasing the number of nodes that participate in query execution. It is nearly impossible to get homogeneous performance across hundreds or thousands of compute nodes. Part failures that do not cause complete node failure, but result in degraded hardware performance become more common at scale. A cloud data management system should be designed to run in a heterogeneous environment and must take appropriate measures to prevent performance degrading due to parallel processing on distributed nodes.

However, deploying data-intensive applications on cloud environment is not a trivial or straightforward task. Armbrust et al. [68] and Abadi [56] argued a list of obstacles to the growth of cloud computing applications as follows.

- *Availability of a Service*: In principle, a distributed system is a system that operates robustly over a wide network. A particular feature of network computing is that the network links can potentially disappear. Organizations worry about whether cloud computing services will have adequate availability. High availability is one of the most challenging goals because even the slightest outage can have significant financial consequences and impacts customer trust.
- *Data Confidentiality*: In general, moving data off premises increases the number of potential security risks and appropriate precautions must be made. Transactional databases typically contain the complete set of operational data needed to power mission-critical business processes. This data includes detail at the lowest granularity, and often includes sensitive information such as customer data or credit card numbers. Therefore, unless such sensitive data is encrypted using a key that is not located at the host, the data may be accessed by a third party without the customer's knowledge.
- *Data Lock-In*: APIs for cloud computing have not been, yet, subject of active standardization. Thus, customers cannot easily extract their data and programs from one site to run on another. The concerns about the difficulties of extracting data from the cloud is preventing some organizations from adopting cloud computing. Customer lock-in may be attractive to cloud computing providers but cloud computing users are vulnerable to price increases, to reliability problems, or even to providers going out of business.

- *Data Transfer Bottlenecks*: Cloud users and cloud providers have to think about the implications of placement and traffic at every level of the system if they want to minimize costs.
- *Application Parallelization*: Computing power is elastic but only if workload is parallelizable. Getting additional computational resources is not as simple as just upgrading to a bigger and more powerful machine on the fly. However, the additional resources are typically obtained by allocating additional server instances to a task.
  Performance Unpredictability: Many HPC applications need to ensure that all the threads of a program are running simultaneously. However, today's virtual machines and operating systems do not provide this service.

Throughout the book, we will dive into detail with respect to the requirements, characteristics an challenges of deploying data-intensive applications in cloud computing platforms. Chapter 2 provides an overview of cloud computing technology and also discusses the state-of-the-art of a few public cloud platforms. Chapter 3 provides an overview of cloud-hosted data storage systems. It starts with concepts, challenges, and trade-offs of cloud databases in general, and ends with a broad survey of the state-of-the-art of public cloud databases in three categorizations. Part two also pays extra attentions on the NoSQL movement and the stat-of-the-art of NoSQL database systems.

Chapter 4 addresses the performance evaluation problem on cloud platforms. There have been a number of research efforts that specifically evaluated the Amazon cloud platform. However, there has been little in-depth evaluation research conducted on other cloud platforms, such as Google App Engine and Microsoft Windows Azure. But more importantly, these work lack a more generic evaluation method that enables a fair comparison between the various cloud platforms. Motivated by this, in this book, a novel approach called CARE, Cloud Architecture Runtime Evaluation, is developed to perform four test set methods with different load stresses against cloud hosting servers or cloud databases from the perspective of the end-user or the cloud host. The framework is capable to address performance, availability, and reliability characteristics of various cloud platforms. The overall data analysis of faults and errors based on intensive collected data, for deducing architecture internal insights, is also another contribution.

Chapter 5 investigates the replication evaluation on NoSQL database as a service. NoSQL database as a service is part of the database as a service offering to complement traditional database systems by rejecting of general ACID transactions as one common feature. NoSQL database as a service has been supported by many service providers that offer various consistency options, from eventual consistency to single-entity ACID. With different consistency options, the correlated performance gains are unclear to many customers. Therefore, in this book, a simple benchmark is proposed for evaluating replication delay of NoSQL database as a service from the customers' perspective. The detailed measurements over several NoSQL database as a services offerings show how frequently, and in what circumstances, different inconsistency situations are observed, and to what impact the customers sees on performance characteristics from choosing to operate with weak consistency mechanisms. The overall methodology of experiments, for measuring consistency from a customer's view, is also another contribution.

Chapter 6 describes a solution to replication evaluation on virtualized database servers. In addition to the two widespread approaches, namely NoSQL database as a service and relational database as a service, virtualized database servers is the third approach for deploying data-intensive applications in cloud platforms. It takes advantages of virtualization technologies by taking an existing application designed for a conventional data center and then porting it to virtual machines in the public cloud. Such migration process usually requires minimal changes in the architecture or the code of the deployed application. In this book, the limits to scaling for an application that itself manages database replicas in virtualized database servers in the cloud is explored. A few important limits are characterized in the load on the master copy, the workload imposed on each slave copy when processing updates from the master, and also from the increasing staleness of replicas.

Chapter 7 introduces a SLA-driven framework for managing database replication. Cloud-hosted database systems, such as virtualized database servers, powering cloud-hosted applications form a critical component in the software stack of these applications. However, the specifications of existing SLA for cloud services are not designed to flexibly handle even relatively straightforward performance and technical requirements of customer applications. Motivated by this, in this book, a novel adaptive approach for SLA-based management of virtualized database servers from the customer perspective is presented. The framework is database platform-agnostic, supports virtualized database servers, and requires zero source code changes of the cloud-hosted software applications. It facilitates dynamic provisioning of the database tier in software stacks based on application-defined policies for satisfying their own SLA performance requirements, avoiding the cost of any SLA violation and controlling the monetary cost of the allocated computing resources. Therefore, the framework is able to keep several virtualized database replica servers in different data centers to support the different availability, scalability and performance improvement goals. The experimental results confirm the effectiveness of the SLA-based framework in providing the customer applications with the required flexibility for achieving their SLA requirements.

Chapter 8 presents a genetic-algorithm-based service composition approach cloud computing. In particular, a coherent way to calculate the QoS values of services in cloud computing is presented. In addition, comparisons between the proposed approach and other approaches show the effectiveness and efficiency of the proposed approach. Chapter 9 provides a comprehensive overview for modern approaches and mechanisms of large scale data processing mechanisms and systems. Chapter 10 concludes the contents of this books and sheds the lights on a set of research challenges that have been introduced by the new wave of cloud-hosted data storage and big data processing systems.

Chapter 2
Cloud Computing

Cloud computing technology represents a new paradigm for the provisioning of computing resources. This paradigm shifts the location of resources to the network to reduce the costs associated with the management of hardware and software resources. It represents the long-held dream of envisioning computing as a utility [68] where the economy of scale principles help to effectively drive down the cost of computing resources. Cloud computing simplifies the time-consuming processes of hardware provisioning, hardware purchasing and software deployment. Therefore, it promises a number of advantages for the deployment of data-intensive applications, such as elasticity of resources, pay-per-use cost model, low time to market, and the perception of unlimited resources and infinite scalability. Hence, it becomes possible, at least theoretically, to achieve unlimited throughput by continuously adding computing resources if the workload increases.

To take advantage of cloud-hosted data storage systems, it is important to well understand the different aspects of the cloud computing technology. This chapter provides an overview of cloud computing technology from the perspectives of key definitions (Sect. 2.1), related technologies (Sect. 2.2), service models (Sect. 2.3) and deployment models (Sect. 2.4), followed by Sect. 2.5 which analyzes state-of-the-art of current public cloud computing platforms, with focus on their provisioning capabilities. Section 2.6 summarizes the business benefits for building software applications using cloud computing technologies.

2.1 Definitions

Cloud computing is an emerging trend that leads to the next step of computing evolution, building on decades of research in virtualization, autonomic computing, grid computing, and utility computing, as well as more recent technologies in networking, web, and software services [227]. Although cloud computing is widely accepted nowadays, the definition of cloud computing has been arguable, due to the diversity of technologies composing the overall view of cloud computing.

L. Zhao et al., *Cloud Data Management*, DOI 10.1007/978-3-319-04765-2_2,
© Springer International Publishing Switzerland 2014

From the research perspective, many researchers have proposed their definitions of cloud computing by extending the scope of their own research domains. From the view of service-oriented architecture, Dubrovnik [227] implied cloud computing as *"a service-oriented architecture, reduced information technology overhead for the end-user, greater flexibility, reduced total cost of ownership, on-demand services, and many other things"*. Buyya et al. [91] derived the definition from clusters and grids, acclaiming for the importance of service-level agreements (SLAs) between the service provider and customers, describing that cloud computing is *"a type of parallel and distributed system consisting of a collection of interconnected and virtualized computers that are dynamically provisioned and presented as one or more unified computing resource(s) based on SLAs"*. Armbrust et al. [68] from Berkeley highlighted three aspects of cloud computing including illusion of infinite computing resources available on demand, no up-front commitment, and pay-per-use utility model, arguing that cloud computing *"consists of the service applications delivered over the Internet along with the data center hardware and systems software that provide those services"*. Moreover, from the industry perspective, more definitions and excerpts by industry experts can be categorized from the perspectives of scalability, elasticity, business models, and others [225].

It is hard to reach a singular agreement upon the definition of cloud computing, because of not only a fair amount of skepticism and confusion caused by various technologies, but also the prevalence of marketing hype. For that reason, National Institute of Standards and Technology has been working on proposing a guideline of cloud computing. The definition of cloud computing in the guideline has received fairly wide acceptance. It is described as [181]:

"a model for enabling convenient, on-demand network access to a shared pool of configurable computing resources (e.g., networks, servers, storage, applications, and services) that can be rapidly provisioned and released with minimal management effort or service provider interaction"

According to this definition, cloud computing has the following essential characteristics:

1. *On-demand self-service.* A consumer can unilaterally provision computing capabilities, such as server time and network storage, as needed automatically without requiring human interaction with each service's provider.
2. *Broad network access.* Capabilities are available over the network and accessed through standard mechanisms that promote use by heterogeneous thin or thick client platforms (e.g., mobile phones, laptops, and PDAs).
3. *Resource pooling.* The provider's computing resources are pooled to serve multiple consumers using a multi-tenant model, with different physical and virtual resources dynamically assigned and reassigned according to consumer demand. There is a sense of location independence in that the customer generally has no control or knowledge over the exact location of the provided resources but may be able to specify location at a higher level of abstraction (e.g., country, state, or datacenter). Examples of resources include storage, processing, memory, network bandwidth, virtual networks and virtual machines.

4. *Rapid elasticity*. Capabilities can be rapidly and elastically provisioned, in some cases automatically, to quickly scale out and rapidly released to quickly scale in. To the consumer, the capabilities available for provisioning often appear to be unlimited and can be purchased in any quantity at any time.
5. *Measured Service*. Cloud systems automatically control and optimize resource use by leveraging a metering capability at some level of abstraction appropriate to the type of service (e.g., storage, processing, bandwidth, and active user accounts). Resource usage can be monitored, controlled, and reported providing transparency for both the provider and consumer of the utilized service.

2.2   Related Technologies for Cloud Computing

Cloud computing has evolved out of decades of research in different related technologies from which it has inherited some features and functionalities such as virtualized environments, autonomic computing, grid computing, and utility computing. Figure 2.1 illustrates the evolution towards cloud computing in hosting software applications [214]. In fact, cloud computing is often compared to the following technologies, each of which shares certain aspects with cloud computing. Table 2.1 provides a summary of the feature differences between those technologies

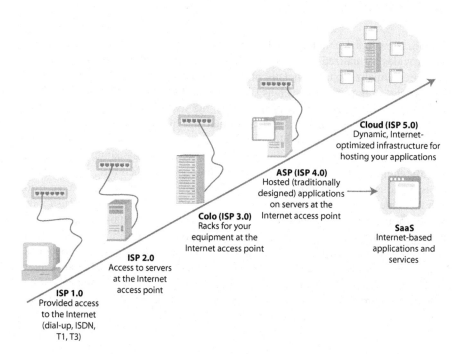

Fig. 2.1 The evolution towards cloud computing in hosting software applications

Table 2.1 Feature similarities and differences between related technologies and cloud computing

Technologies	Differences	Similarities
Virtualization	Cloud computing is not only about virtualizing resources, but also about intelligently allocating resources for managing competing resource demands of the customers.	Both isolate and abstract the low-level resources for high-level applications.
Autonomic computing	The objective of cloud computing is focused on lowering the resource cost rather than to reduce system complexity as it is in autonomic computing.	Both interconnect and integrate distributed computing systems.
Grid computing	Cloud computing however also leverages virtualization to achieve on-demand resource sharing and dynamic resource provisioning.	Both employ distributed resources to achieve application-level objectives.
Utility computing	Cloud computing is a realization of utility computing.	Both offer better economic benefits.

and cloud computing in short, while details of related technologies are discussed as following [239]:

Virtualization

Virtualization is a technology that isolates and abstracts the low-level resources and provides virtualized resources for high-level applications. In the context of hardware virtualization, the details of physical hardware can be abstracted away with support of hypervisors, such as Linux Kernel-based Virtual Machine [33] and Xen [48]. A virtualized server managed by the hypervisor is commonly called a virtual machine. In general, several virtual machines can be abstracted from a single physical machine. With clusters of physical machines, hypervisors are capable of abstracting and pooling resources, as well as dynamically assigning or reassigning resources to virtual machines on-demand. Therefore, virtualization forms the foundation of cloud computing. Since a virtual machine is isolated from both the underlying hardware and other virtual machines. Providers can customize the platform to suit the needs of the customers by either exposing applications running within virtual machines as services, or providing direct access to virtual machines thereby allowing customers to build services with their own applications. Moreover, cloud computing is not only about virtualizing resources, but also about intelligent allocation of resources for managing competing resource demands of the customers. Figure 2.2 illustrates a sample exploitation of virtualization technology in the cloud computing environments [214].

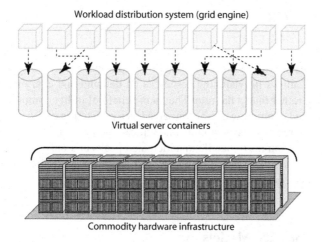

Fig. 2.2 Exploitation of virtualization technology in the architecture of cloud computing

Autonomic computing aims at building computing systems capable of self-management, which means being able to operate under defined general policies and rules without human intervention. The goal of autonomic computing is to overcome the rapidly growing complexity of computer system management, while being able to keep increasing interconnectivity and integration unabated [161]. Although cloud computing exhibits certain similarities to automatic computing the way that it interconnects and integrates distributed data centers across continents, its objective somehow is to lower the resource cost rather than to reduce system complexity.

Grid Computing

Grid computing is a distributed computing paradigm that coordinates networked resources to achieve a common computational objective. The development of grid computing was originally driven by scientific applications which are usually computation-intensive, but applications requiring the transfer and manipulation of a massive quantity of data was also able to take advantage of the grids [142, 143, 171]. Cloud computing appears to be similar to grid computing in the way that it also employs distributed resources to achieve application-level objectives. However, cloud computing takes one step further by leveraging virtualization technologies to achieve on-demand resource sharing and dynamic resource provisioning.

Utility Computing

Utility computing represents the business model of packaging resources as a metered services similar to those provided by traditional public utility companies. In particular, it allows provisioning resources on demand and charging customers based on usage rather than a flat rate. The main benefit of utility computing is better economics. Cloud computing can be perceived as a realization of utility computing. With on-demand resource provisioning and utility-based pricing, customers are able to receive more resources to handle unanticipated peaks and only pay for resources they needed; meanwhile, service providers can maximize resource utilization and minimize their operating costs.

2.3 Cloud Service Models

The categorization of three cloud service models defined in the guideline are also widely accepted nowadays. The three service models are namely *Infrastructure as a Service* (IaaS), *Platform as a Service* (PaaS), and *Software as a Service* (SaaS).

As shown in Fig. 2.3, the three service models form a stack structure of cloud computing, with Software as a Service on the top, Platform as a Service in the middle, and Infrastructure as a Service at the bottom, respectively. While the inverted triangle shows the possible proportion of providers of each model, it is worth mentioning that definitions of three service models from the guideline paid more attentions to the customers' view. In contrast, Vaquero et al. [225] defined

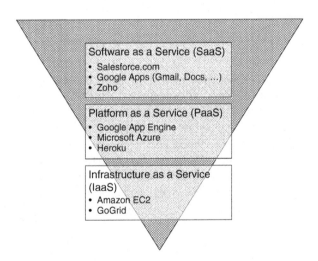

Fig. 2.3 The service models of cloud computing

the three service models from the perspective of the providers' view. The following definitions of the three models combines the two perspectives [181,225], in the hope of showing the whole picture.

1. *Infrastructure as a Service*: Through virtualization, the provider is capable of splitting, assigning, and dynamically resizing the cloud resources including processing, storage, networks, and other fundamental computing resources to build virtualized systems as requested by customers. Therefore, the customer is able to deploy and run arbitrary operating systems and applications. The customer does not need to deploy the underlying cloud infrastructure but has control over which operating systems, storage options, and deployed applications to deploy with possibly limited control of select networking components. The typical providers are Amazon Elastic Compute Cloud (EC2) [4] and GoGrid [17].

2. *Platform as a Service*: The provider offers an additional abstraction level, which is a software platform on which the system runs. The change of the cloud resources including network, servers, operating systems, or storage is made in a transparent manner. The customer does not need to deploy the cloud resources, but has control over the deployed applications and possibly application hosting environment configurations. Three platforms are well-known in this domain, namely Google App Engine [19], Microsoft Windows Azure Platform [37], and Heroku [28] which is a platform built on top of Amazon EC2. The first one offers Python, Java, and Go as programming platforms. The second one supports languages in .NET Framework, Java, PHP, Python, and Node.js. While the third one is compatible with Ruby, Node.js, Clojure, Java, Python, and Scala.

3. *Software as a Service*: The provider provides services of potential interest to a wide variety of customers hosted in its cloud infrastructure. The services are accessible from various client devices through a thin client interface such as a web browser. The customer does not need to manage the cloud resources or even individual application capabilities. The customer could, possibly, be granted limited user-specific application configuration settings. A variety of services, operating as Software as a Service, are available in the Internet, including Salesforce.com [43], Google Apps [21], and Zoho [55].

2.4 Cloud Deployment Models

The guideline also defines four types of cloud deployment models [181], which are described as follows:

1. *Private cloud.* A cloud that is used exclusively by one organization. It may be managed by the organization or a third party and may exist on premise or off premise. A private cloud offers the highest degree of control over performance, reliability and security. However, they are often criticized for being similar to traditional proprietary server farms and do not provide benefits such as no up-front capital costs.

2. *Community cloud.* The cloud infrastructure is shared by several organizations and supports a specific community that has shared concerns (e.g., mission, security requirements, policy, and compliance considerations).
3. *Public cloud.* The cloud infrastructure is made available to the general public or a large industry group and is owned by an organization selling cloud services (e.g. Amazon, Google, Microsoft). Since customer requirements of cloud services are varying, service providers have to ensure that they can be flexible in their service delivery. Therefore, the quality of the provided services is specified using Service Level Agreement (SLA) which represents a contract between a provider and a consumer that specifies consumer requirements and the provider's commitment to them. Typically an SLA includes items such as uptime, privacy, security and backup procedures. In practice, Public clouds offer several key benefits to service consumers such as: including no initial capital investment on infrastructure and shifting of risks to infrastructure providers. However, public clouds lack fine-grained control over data, network and security settings, which may hamper their effectiveness in many business scenarios.
4. *Hybrid cloud.* The cloud infrastructure is a composition of two or more clouds (private, community, or public) that remain unique entities but are bound together by standardized or proprietary technology that enables data and application portability (e.g., cloud bursting for load-balancing between clouds). In particular, cloud bursting is a technique used by hybrid clouds to provide additional resources to private clouds on an as-needed basis. If the private cloud has the processing power to handle its workloads, the hybrid cloud is not used. When workloads exceed the private cloud's capacity, the hybrid cloud automatically allocates additional resources to the private cloud. Therefore, Hybrid clouds offer more flexibility than both public and private clouds. Specifically, they provide tighter control and security over application data compared to public clouds, while still facilitating on-demand service expansion and contraction. On the down side, designing a hybrid cloud requires carefully determining the best split between public and private cloud components.

Table 2.2 summarizes the four cloud deployment models in terms of ownership, customership, location, and security.

2.5   Public Cloud Platforms: State-of-the-Art

Key players in public cloud computing domain including Amazon Web Services, Microsoft Windows Azure, Google App Engine, Eucalyptus [16], and GoGrid offer a variety of prepackaged services for monitoring, managing, and provisioning resources. However, the techniques implemented in each of these clouds do vary.

For Amazon EC2, the three Amazon services, namely Amazon Elastic Load Balancer [5], Amazon Auto Scaling [2], and Amazon CloudWatch [3], together expose functionalities which are required for undertaking provisioning of application

Table 2.2 Summary of cloud deployment models

Deployment model	Ownership	Customership	Infrastructure location to customers	Security	Examples
Public cloud	Organization(s)	General public customers	Off-premises	No fine-grained control	Amazon Web Services
Private cloud	An organization/ A third party	Customers within an organization	On/Off-premises	Highest degree of control	Internal cloud platform to support business units in a large organization
Community cloud	Organization(s) in a community/ A third party	Customers from organizations that have shared concerns	On/Off-premises	Shared control among organizations in a community	Healthcare cloud for exchanging health information among organizations
Hybrid cloud	Composition of two or more from above	Composition of two or more from above	On/Off-premises	Tighter control, but require careful split between distinct models	Cloud bursting for load balancing between cloud platforms

services on EC2. The Elastic Load Balancer service automatically provisions incoming application workload across available EC2 instances while the Auto Scaling service can be used to dynamically scale-in or scale-out the number of EC2 instances for handling changes in service demand patterns. Finally the CloudWatch service can be integrated with the above services for strategic decision making based on collected real-time information.

Eucalyptus is an open source cloud computing platform. It is composed of three controllers. Among the controllers, the *cluster controller* is a key component that supports application service provisioning and load balancing. Each cluster controller is hosted on the *head node* of a cluster to interconnect the outer public networks and inner private networks together. By monitoring the state information of instances in the pool of server controllers, the cluster controller can select any available service/server for provisioning incoming requests. However, as compared to Amazon services, Eucalyptus still lacks some of the critical functionalities, such as auto scaling for its built-in provisioner.

Fundamentally, Microsoft Windows Azure *fabric* has a weave-like structure, which is composed of node including servers and load balancers, and edges including power and Ethernet. The *fabric controller* manages a *service node* through a built-in service, named Azure Fabric Controller Agent, running in the background, tracking the state of the server, and reporting these metrics to the controller. If a fault state is reported, the controller can manage a reboot of the server or a migration of services from the current server to other healthy servers. Moreover, the controller also supports service provisioning by matching the VMs that meet required demands.

GoGrid Cloud Hosting offers developers the F5 Load Balancer [18] for distributing application service traffic across servers, as long as IPs and specific ports of these servers are attached. The load balancer provides the round robin algorithm and least connect algorithm for routing application service requests. Additionally, the load balancer is able to detect the occurrence of a server crash, redirecting further requests to other available servers. But currently, GoGrid only gives developers a programmatic set of APIs to implement their custom auto-scaling service.

Unlike other cloud platforms, Google App Engine offers developers a scalable platform in which applications can run, rather than providing direct access to a customized virtual machine. Therefore, access to the underlying operating system is restricted in App Engine where load-balancing strategies, service provisioning, and auto scaling are all automatically managed by the system behind the scenes where the implementation is largely unknown. Chohan et al. [105] have presented initial efforts of building App Engine-like framework, *AppScale*, on top of Amazon EC2 and Eucalyptus. Their offering consists of multiple components that automate deployment, management, scaling, and fault tolerance of an App Engine application. In their design and implementation, a single *AppLoadBalancer* exists in AppScale for distributing initial requests of users to the *AppServer*s of App Engine applications. The users initially contact AppLoaderBalancer to request a login to an App Engine application. The AppLoadBalander then authenticates the login and redirects request to a randomly selected AppServer. Once the request is redirected, the user can start contact the AppServer directly without going through the AppLoaderBalancer during the current session. The *AppController* sit inside the AppLoadBalancer is also in charge of monitoring the AppServers for growing and shrinking as the AppScale deployments happen over the time.

There is no single cloud infrastructure provider has their data centers at all possible locations throughout the world. As a result, all cloud application providers currently have difficulty in meeting SLA expectations for all their customers. Hence, it is logical that each would build bespoke SLA management tools to provide better support for their specific needs. This kind of requirements often arises in enterprises with global operations and applications such as Internet service, media hosting, and Web 2.0 applications. This necessitates building technologies and algorithms for seamless integration of cloud infrastructure service providers for provisioning of services across different cloud providers.

2.6   Business Benefits of Cloud Computing

With cloud computing, organizations can consume shared computing and storage resources rather than building, operating, and improving infrastructure on their own. The speed of change in markets creates significant pressure on the enterprise IT infrastructure to adapt and deliver. In principle, cloud computing enables organizations to obtain a flexible and cost-effective IT infrastructure in much the same way that national electric grids enable homes and organizations to plug into a centrally managed, efficient, and cost-effective energy source. When freed from creating their own electricity, organizations were able to focus on the core competencies of their business and the needs of their customers. In particular, cloud computing technologies have provided some clear business benefits for building software applications. Examples of these benefits are:

1. *No upfront infrastructure investment*: Building a large-scale system may cost a fortune to invest in real estate, hardware (racks, machines, routers, backup power supplies), hardware management (power management, cooling), and operations personnel. Because of the high upfront costs, it usually takes several rounds of management approvals before the project could even get started. With cloud computing, there is no fixed cost or startup cost to start your project.
2. *Just-in-time Infrastructure*: In the past, if your system got famous and your infrastructure could not scale well at the right time, your application may became a victim of its success. On the other hand, if you invested heavily and did not get famous, your application became a victim of your failure. By deploying applications in cloud environments, your application can smoothly scale as you grow.
3. *More efficient resource utilization*: System administrators usually worry about hardware procuring (when they run out of capacity) and better infrastructure utilization (when they have excess and idle capacity). With cloud technology,

they can manage resources more effectively and efficiently by having the applications request resources only what they need on-demand according to the *pay-as-you-go* philosophy.

4. *Potential for shrinking the processing time*: Parallelization is the one of the well-known techniques to speed up processing. For example, if you have a compute-intensive or data-intensive job that can be run in parallel takes 500 h to process on one machine. Using cloud technology, it would be possible to spawn and launch 500 instances and process the same job in 1 h. Having available an elastic infrastructure provides the application with the ability to exploit parallelization in a cost-effective manner reducing the total processing time.

Chapter 3
Cloud-Hosted Data Storage Systems

Over the past decade, rapidly growing Internet-based services such as e-mail, blogging, social networking, search and e-commerce have substantially redefined the way consumers communicate, access contents, share information and purchase products. Relational database management systems (RDBMS) have been considered as the *one-size-fits-all* solution for data persistence and retrieval for decades. However, ever increasing need for scalability and new application requirements have created new challenges for traditional RDBMS. Recently, a new generation of low-cost, high-performance database software, aptly named as *NoSQL* (Not Only SQL), has emerged to challenge the dominance of RDBMS. The main features of these systems include: ability to horizontally scale, supporting weaker consistency models, using flexible schemas and data models and supporting simple low-level query interfaces. In this chapter, we explore the recent advancements and the state-of-the-art of Web scale data management approaches. We discuss the advantages and the disadvantages of several recently introduced approaches and its suitability to support certain class of applications and end-users.

3.1 Introduction

The recent advances in the Web technology has made it easy for any user to provide and consume content of any form. For example, we buy books on *Amazon*, sell thing on *eBay*, stay in contact with friends and colleagues via *Facebook* and *Linkedin*, start a blog using *WordPress* or *LiveJournal*, share pictures via *Picasa* or *Flickr*, and share and comment on videos via *YouTube*. These are just examples to name a few well-known internet-based services that we use in our everyday life. Arguably, the main goal of the next wave is to facilitate the job of implementing every application as a distributed, scalable and widely-accessible service on the Web like these example services. In practice, common features of these applications include that they are both *data-intensive* and very *interactive* applications. For example, the Facebook social network has announced that it has more than a

L. Zhao et al., *Cloud Data Management*, DOI 10.1007/978-3-319-04765-2__3,
© Springer International Publishing Switzerland 2014

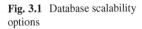

Fig. 3.1 Database scalability options

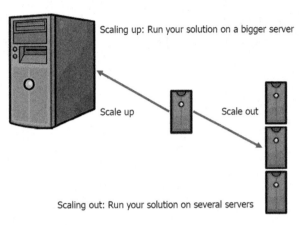

billion of monthly active users and more than 140 billion friendship relationships. Moreover, there are about 900 million objects that registered users interact with such as: pages, groups, events and community pages. Other smaller scale social networks such as Linkedin which is mainly used for professionals has more than 120 million registered users. Twitter has also claimed to have over 500 million users. Therefore, it becomes an ultimate goal to make it easy for every application to achieve such high scalability and availability goals with minimum efforts.

Nowadays, the most common architecture to build enterprise Web applications is based on a 3-tier approach: the Web server layer, the application server layer and the data layer. In practice, data partitioning [189] and data replication [160] are two well-known strategies to achieve the availability, scalability and performance improvement goals in the distributed data management world. In particular, when the application load increases, there are two main options for achieving scalability at the database tier that enables the applications to cope with more client requests (Fig. 3.1) as follows:

1. *Scaling up*: aims at allocating a bigger machine to act as database servers.
2. *Scaling out*: aims at *replicating* and *partitioning* data across more machines.

In fact, the scaling up option has the main drawback that large machines are often very expensive and eventually a physical limit is reached where a more powerful machine cannot be purchased at any cost. Alternatively, it is both extensible and economical—especially in a dynamic workload environment—to scale out by adding storage space or buying another commodity server which fits well with the new *pay-as-you-go* philosophy of cloud computing paradigm.

This chapter explores the recent advancements and the new approaches of the Web scale data management. We discuss the advantages and the disadvantages of each approach and its suitability to support certain class of applications and end-users. Section 3.2 describes the NoSQL systems which are introduced and used internally in the key players: Google, Yahoo and Amazon respectively. Section 3.3 provides an overview of a set of open source projects which have been designed following the main principles of the NoSQL systems. Section 3.4

discusses the notion of providing database management as a services and gives an overview of the main representative systems and their challenges. In Sect. 3.5, we briefly describe the approach of deploying database servers on cloud-hosted virtual machine environments. The Web scale data management trade-offs and open research challenges are discussed in Sect. 3.6 before we conclude the chapter in Sect. 3.7.

3.2 NoSQL Key Systems

In general, relational database management systems (e.g. MySQL, PostgreSQL, SQL Server, Oracle) have been considered as the *one-size-fits-all* solution for data persistence and retrieval for decades. They have matured after extensive research and development efforts and very successfully created a large market and solutions in different business domains. However, ever increasing need for scalability and new application requirements have created new challenges for traditional RDBMS. Therefore, recently, there has been some dissatisfaction with this *one-size-fits-all* approach in some Web scale applications [216].

Recently, a new generation of low-cost, high-performance database software has emerged to challenge the dominance of relational database management systems. A big reason for this movement, named as *NoSQL* (*Not only SQL*), is that different implementations of Web, enterprise, and cloud computing applications have different database requirements (e.g. not every application requires rigid data consistency). For example, for high-volume Web sites (e.g. eBay, Amazon, Twitter, Facebook), scalability and high availability are essential requirements that can not be compromised. For these applications, even the slightest outage can have significant financial consequences and impacts customers' trust.

In general, the *CAP* theorem [86, 138] and the *PACELC* model [57] describe the existence of direct tradeoffs between consistency and availability as well as consistency and latency. For example, the *CAP* theorem shows that a distributed database system can only choose at most two out of three properties: *Consistency*, *Availability* and *tolerance to Partitions*. Therefore, there is a plethora of alternative consistency models which have been introduced for offering different performance trade-offs such as *session guarantees, causal consistency* [70], *causal+consistency* [178] and *parallel snapshot isolation* [212]. In practice, the new wave of NoSQL systems decided to compromise on the strict consistency requirement. In particular, they apply a relaxed consistency policy called *eventual consistency* [226] which guarantees that if no new updates are made to a replicated object, eventually all accesses will return the last updated value. If no failures occur, the maximum size of the inconsistency window can be determined based on factors such as communication delays, the load on the system, and the number of replicas involved in the replication scheme. In particular, these new NoSQL systems have a number of design features in common:

- The ability to horizontally scale out throughput over many servers.
- A simple call level interface or protocol (in contrast to a SQL binding).

- Supporting weaker consistency models in contrast to ACID guaranteed properties for transactions in most traditional RDBMS. These models are usually referred to as *BASE* models (*B*asically *A*vailable, *S*oft state, *E*ventually consistent) [196].
- Efficient use of distributed indexes and RAM for data storage.
- The ability to dynamically define new attributes or data schema.

These design features are made in order to achieve the following system goals:

- *Availability*: They must always be accessible even on the situations of having a network failure or a whole datacenter is went offline.
- *Scalability*: They must be able to support very large databases with very high request rates at very low latency.
- *Elasticity*: They must be able to satisfy changing application requirements in both directions (scaling up or scaling down). Moreover, the system must be able to gracefully respond to these changing requirements and quickly recover its steady state.
- *Load Balancing*: They must be able to automatically move load between servers so that most of the hardware resources are effectively utilized and to avoid any resource overloading situations.
- *Fault Tolerance*: They must be able to deal with the situation that the rarest hardware problems go from being freak events to eventualities. While hardware failure is still a serious concern, this concern needs to be addressed at the architectural level of the database, rather than requiring developers, administrators and operations staff to build their own redundant solutions.
- *Ability to run in a heterogeneous environment*: On scaling out environment, there is a strong trend towards increasing the number of nodes that participate in query execution. It is nearly impossible to get homogeneous performance across hundreds or thousands of compute nodes. Part failures that do not cause complete node failure, but result in degraded hardware performance become more common at scale. Hence, the system should be designed to run in a heterogeneous environment and must take appropriate measures to prevent performance degradation that are due to parallel processing on distributed nodes.

In the following subsections, we provide an overview of the main NoSQL systems which has been introduced and used internally by three of the key players in the Web scale data management domain: *Google*, *Yahoo* and *Amazon*.

Google: Bigtable

Bigtable is a distributed storage system for managing structured data that is designed to scale to a very large size (petabytes of data) across thousands of commodity servers [99]. It has been used by more than sixty Google products and projects such as: Google search engine, Google Finance, Orkut, Google Docs and Google Earth. These products use Bigtable for a variety of demanding workloads which

Row Id	Column Id	Timestamp	Column Value
com.cnn.www	anchor:cnnsi.com	t9	CNN
com.cnn.www	anchor:my.look.ca	t8	CNN.com

Row Id	Column Id	Timestamp	Column Value
com.cnn.www	contents:	t6	<html>...
com.cnn.www	contents:	t5	<html>...
com.cnn.www	contents:	t3	<html>...

Fig. 3.2 Sample BigTable structure

range from throughput-oriented batch-processing jobs to latency-sensitive serving of data to end users. The Bigtable clusters used by these products span a wide range of configurations, from a handful to thousands of servers, and store up to several hundred terabytes of data.

Bigtable does not support a full relational data model. However, it provides clients with a simple data model that supports dynamic control over data layout and format. In particular, a Bigtable is a sparse, distributed, persistent multidimensional sorted map. The map is indexed by a row key, column key, and a timestamp. Each value in the map is an uninterpreted array of bytes. Thus, clients usually need to serialize various forms of structured and semi-structured data into these strings. A concrete example that reflects some of the main design decisions of Bigtable is the scenario of storing a copy of a large collection of web pages into a single table. Figure 3.2 illustrates an example of this table where *URLs* are used as row keys and various aspects of web pages as column names. The contents of the web pages are stored in a single column which stores multiple versions of the page under the timestamps when they were fetched.

The row keys in a table are arbitrary strings where every read or write of data under a single row key is atomic. Bigtable maintains the data in lexicographic order by row key where the row range for a table is dynamically partitioned. Each row range is called a *tablet* which represents the unit of distribution and load balancing. Thus, reads of short row ranges are efficient and typically require communication with only a small number of machines. BigTables can have an unbounded number of columns which are grouped into sets called *column families*. These column families represent the basic unit of access control. Each cell in a Bigtable can contain multiple versions of the same data which are indexed by their timestamps. Each client can flexibly decide the number of n versions of a cell that need to be kept. These versions are stored in decreasing timestamp order so that the most recent versions can be always read first.

The Bigtable API provides functions for creating and deleting tables and column families. It also provides functions for changing cluster, table, and column family metadata, such as access control rights. Client applications can write or delete values in Bigtable, look up values from individual rows, or iterate over a subset of the data in a table. At the transaction level, Bigtable supports only *single-row* transactions which can be used to perform atomic read-modify-write sequences on data stored under a single row key (i.e. no general transactions across row keys).

At the physical level, Bigtable uses the distributed Google File System (GFS) [137] to store log and data files. The Google *SSTable* file format is used internally to store Bigtable data. An SSTable provides a persistent, ordered immutable map from keys to values, where both keys and values are arbitrary byte strings. Bigtable relies on a distributed lock service called *Chubby* [90] which consists of five active replicas, one of which is elected to be the *master* and actively serve requests. The service is live when a majority of the replicas are running and can communicate with each other. Bigtable uses Chubby for a variety of tasks such as: (1) ensuring that there is at most one active master at any time. (2) storing the bootstrap location of Bigtable data. (3) storing Bigtable schema information and to the access control lists. The main limitation of this design is that if Chubby becomes unavailable for an extended period of time, the whole Bigtable becomes unavailable. At the runtime, each Bigtable is allocated to one master server and many tablet servers which can be dynamically added (or removed) from a cluster based on the changes in workloads. The master server is responsible for assigning tablets to tablet servers, balancing tablet-server load, and garbage collection of files in GFS. In addition, it handles schema changes such as table and column family creations. Each tablet server manages a set of tablets. The tablet server handles read and write requests to the tablets that it has loaded, and also splits tablets that have grown too large.

Yahoo: PNUTS

The *PNUTS* system (renamed later to Sherpa) is a massive-scale hosted database system which is designed to support Yahoo!'s web applications [111,209]. The main focus of the system is on data serving for web applications, rather than complex queries. It relies on a simple relational model where data is organized into tables of records with attributes. In addition to typical data types, *blob* is a main valid data type which allows arbitrary structures to be stored inside a record, but not necessarily large binary objects like images or audio. The PNUTS system does not enforce constraints such as referential integrity on the underlying data. Therefore, the schema of these tables are flexible where new attributes can be added at any time without halting any query or update activity. In addition, it is not required that each record have values for all attributes.

Figure 3.3 illustrates the system architecture of PNUTS. The system is divided into regions where each region contains a full complement of system components

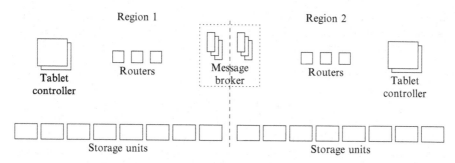

Fig. 3.3 PNUTS system architecture

and a complete copy of each table. Regions are typically, but not necessarily, geographically distributed. Therefore, at the physical level, data tables are horizontally partitioned into groups of records called *tablets*. These tablets are scattered across many servers where each server might have hundreds or thousands of tablets. The assignment of tablets to servers is flexible in a way that allows balancing the workloads by moving a few tablets from an overloaded server to an under-loaded server.

The query language of PNUTS supports selection and projection from a single table. Operations for updating or deleting existing record must specify the primary key. The system is designed primarily for online serving workloads that consist mostly of queries that read and write single records or small groups of records. Thus, it provides a *multiget* operation which supports retrieving multiple records in parallel by specifying a set of primary keys and an optional predicate. The *router* component (Fig. 3.3) is responsible of determining which storage unit need to be accessed for a given record to be read or written by the client. Therefore, the primary-key space of a table is divided into intervals where each interval corresponds to one tablet. The router stores an interval mapping which defines the boundaries of each tablet and maps each tablet to a storage unit. The query model of PNUTS does not support join operations which are too expensive in such massive scale systems.

The PNUTS system does not have a traditional database log or archive data. However, it relies on a pub/sub mechanism that act as a redo log for replaying updates that are lost before being applied to disk due to failure. In particular, PNUTS provides a consistency model that is between the two extremes of general serializability and eventual consistency [226]. The design of this model is derived from the observation that web applications typically manipulate one record at a time while different records may have activity with different geographic locality. Thus, it provides *per-record timeline* consistency where all replicas of a given record apply all updates to the record in the same order. In particular, for each record, one of the replicas (independently) is designated as the master where all updates to that record are forwarded to the master. The master replica for a record is adaptively changed to suit the workload where the replica receiving the majority of write requests for a particular record is selected to be the master for that record. Relying on the per-record timeline consistency model, the PNUTS system supports the following range of API calls with varying levels of consistency guarantees:

- *Read-any*: This call has a lower latency as it returns a possibly stale version of the record.
- *Read-critical (required version)*: This call returns a version of the record that is strictly newer than, or the same as the *required version*.
- *Read-latest*: This call returns the latest copy of the record that reflects all writes that have succeeded. It is expected that the *read-critical* and *read-latest* can have a higher latency than *read-any* if the local copy is too stale and the system needs to locate a newer version at a remote replica.
- *Write*: This call gives the same ACID guarantees as a transaction with a single write operation in it (e.g. blind writes).
- *Test-and-set-write (required version)*: This call performs the requested write to the record if and only if the present version of the record is the same as required version. This call can be used to implement transactions that first read a record, and then do a write to the record based on the read, e.g. incrementing the value of a counter.

Since the system is designed to scale to cover several worldwide replicas, automated failover and load balancing is the only way to manage the operations load. Therefore, for any failed server, the system automatically recover by copying data from a replica to other live servers.

Amazon: Dynamo

Amazon runs a world-wide e-commerce platform that serves tens of millions customers at peak times using tens of thousands of servers located in many data centers around the world. In this environment, there are strict operational requirements on Amazon's platform in terms of performance, reliability and efficiency, and to support Amazon's continuous growth the platform needs to be highly scalable. Reliability is one of the most important requirements because even the slightest outage has significant financial consequences and impacts customer trust.

The Dynamo system [121] is a highly available and scalable distributed key/value based datastore built for supporting *internal* Amazon's applications. Dynamo is used to manage the state of services that have very high reliability requirements and need tight control over the tradeoffs between availability, consistency, cost-effectiveness and performance. There are many services on Amazons platform that only need primary-key access to a data store. The common pattern of using a relational database would lead to inefficiencies and limit the ability to scale and provide high availability. Thus, Dynamo provides a simple primary-key only interface to meet the requirements of these applications. The query model of the

Fig. 3.4 Partitioning and
replication of keys in
dynamo ring

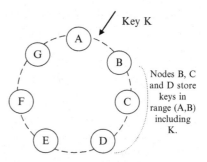

Nodes B, C
and D store
keys in
range (A,B)
including
K.

Dynamo system relies on simple read and write operations to a data item that is
uniquely identified by a key. State is stored as binary objects (blobs) identified by
unique keys. No operations span multiple data items.

Dynamo's partitioning scheme relies on a variant of consistent hashing mechanism [158] to distribute the load across multiple storage hosts. In this mechanism,
the output range of a hash function is treated as a fixed circular space or "ring"
(i.e. the largest hash value wraps around to the smallest hash value). Each node
in the system is assigned a random value within this space which represents its
"position" on the ring. Each data item identified by a key is assigned to a node by
hashing the data item's key to yield its position on the ring, and then walking the
ring clockwise to find the first node with a position larger than the item's position.
Thus, each node becomes responsible for the region in the ring between it and its
predecessor node on the ring. The principle advantage of consistent hashing is that
departure or arrival of a node only affects its immediate neighbors and other nodes
remain unaffected.

In the Dynamo system, each data item is replicated at N hosts where N is a
parameter configured "per-instance". Each key k is assigned to a coordinator node.
The coordinator is in charge of the replication of the data items that fall within
its range. In addition to locally storing each key within its range, the coordinator
replicates these keys at the $(N - 1)$ clockwise successor nodes in the ring. This
results in a system where each node is responsible for the region of the ring between
it and its Nth predecessor. As illustrated in Fig. 3.4, node B replicates the key k at
nodes C and D in addition to storing it locally. Node D will store the keys that fall
in the ranges $(A, B]$, $(B, C]$, and $(C, D]$. The list of nodes that is responsible for
storing a particular key is called the preference list. The system is designed so that
every node in the system can determine which nodes should be in this list for any
particular key.

3.3 NoSQL Open Source Projects

In practice, most NoSQL data management systems which are introduced by the
key players (e.g. BigTable, Dynamo, PNUTS) are meant for their internal use only
and are thus, not available for public users. Therefore, many open source projects

have been built to implement the concepts of these systems and make it available for public users [94, 205]. Due to the ease in which they can be downloaded and installed, these systems have attracted a lot of interest from the research community. There are not much details that have been published about the implementation of most of these systems. In general, the NoSQL open source projects can be broadly classified into the following categories:

- *Key-value stores*: These systems use the simplest data model which is a collection of objects where each object has a unique key and a set of attribute/value pairs.
- *Document stores*: These systems have the data models that consists of objects with a variable number of attributes with a possibility of having nested objects.
- *Extensible record stores*: They provide variable-width tables (Column Families) that can be partitioned vertically and horizontally across multiple nodes.

Here, we give a brief introduction about some of these projects. For the full list, we refer the reader to the NoSQL database website [34].

Cassandra [7] is presented as a highly scalable, eventually consistent, distributed, structured key-value store [167, 168]. It has been open sourced by Facebook in 2008. It is designed by Avinash Lakshman (one of the authors of Amazon's Dynamo) and Prashant Malik (Facebook Engineer). Cassandra brings together the distributed systems technologies from Dynamo and the data model from Google's BigTable. Like Dynamo, Cassandra is eventually consistent. Like BigTable, Cassandra provides a ColumnFamily-based data model richer than typical key/value systems. In Cassandra's data model, *column* is the lowest/smallest increment of data. It is a tuple (triplet) that contains a name, a value and a timestamp. A *column family* is a container for columns, analogous to the table in a relational system. It contains multiple columns, each of which has a name, value, and a timestamp, and are referenced by row keys. A *keyspace* is the first dimension of the Cassandra hash, and is the container for column families. Keyspaces are of roughly the same granularity as a schema or database (i.e. a logical collection of tables) in RDBMS. They can be seen as a namespace for ColumnFamilies and is typically allocated as one per application. *SuperColumns* represent columns that themselves have subcolumns (e.g. Maps). Like Dynamo, Cassandra provides a tunable consistency models which allows the ability to choose the consistency level that is suitable for a specific application. For example, it allows to choose how many acknowledgments are required to be receive from different replicas before considering a *WRITE* operation to be successful. Similarly, the application can choose how many successful response need to be received in the case of *READ* before return the result to the client. In particular, every *write* operation can choose one of the following consistency level:

(a) *ZERO*: It ensures nothing. The write operation will be executed asynchronously in the system background.
(b) *ANY*: It ensures that the write operation has been executed in at least one node.
(c) *ONE*: It ensures that the write operation has been committed to at least 1 replica before responding to the client.

(d) *QUORUM*: It ensures that the write has been executed on $(N/2 + 1)$ replicas before responding to the client where N is the total number of system replicas.
(e) *ALL*: It ensures that the write operation has been committed to all N replicas before responding to the client.

On the other hand, every *read* operation can choose on of the following available consistency levels:

(a) *ONE*: It will return the record of the first responding replica.
(b) *QUORUM*: It will query all replicas and return the record with the most recent timestamp once it has at least a majority of replicas $(N/2 + 1)$ reported.
(c) *ALL*: It will query all replicas and return the record with the most recent timestamp once all replicas have replied.

Therefore, any unresponsive replicas will fail the read operation. For read operations, in the *ONE* and *QUORUM* consistency levels, a consistency check is always done with the remaining replicas in the system background in order to fix any consistency issues.

HBase [10] is another project is based on the ideas of BigTable system. It uses the Hadoop distributed filesystem (HDFS) [26] as its data storage engine. The advantage of this approach is that HBase does not need to worry about data replication, data consistency and resiliency because HDFS already considers and deals with them. However, the downside is that it becomes constrained by the characteristics of HDFS, which is that it is not optimized for random read access. In the HBase architecture, data is stored in a farm of Region Servers. A *key-to-server* mapping is used to locate the corresponding server. The in-memory data storage is implemented using a distributed memory object caching system called *Memcache* [35] while the on-disk data storage is implemented as a HDFS file residing in the Hadoop data node server.

HyperTable [30] project is designed to achieve a high performance, scalable, distributed storage and processing system for structured and unstructured data. It is designed to manage the storage and processing of information on a large cluster of commodity servers, providing resilience to machine and component failures. Like HBase, Hypertable also runs over HDFS to leverage the automatic data replication and fault tolerance that it provides. In HyperTable, data is represented in the system as a multi-dimensional table of information. The HyperTable systems provides a low-level API and Hypertable Query Language (HQL) that provides the ability to create, modify, and query the underlying tables. The data in a table can be transformed and organized at high speed by performing computations in parallel, pushing them to where the data is physically stored.

CouchDB [8] is a document-oriented database that is written in Erlang can be queried and indexed in a MapReduce fashion using JavaScript. In CouchDB, documents are the primary unit of data. A CouchDB document is an object that consists of named fields. Field values may be strings, numbers, dates, or even ordered lists and associative maps. Hence, a CouchDB database is a flat collection of documents where each document is identified by a unique ID. CouchDB provides a RESTful HTTP API for reading and updating (add, edit, delete) database documents. The CouchDB document update model is lockless and optimistic. Document edits are made by client applications. If another client was editing the same document at the same time, the client gets an edit conflict error on save. To resolve the update conflict, the latest document version can be opened, the edits reapplied and the update retried again. Document updates are all or nothing, either succeeding entirely or failing completely. The database never contains partially saved or edited documents.

MongoDB [38] is another example of distributed schema-free document-oriented database which is created at *10gen*.[1] It is implemented in C++ but provides drivers for a number of programming languages including C, C++, Erlang. Haskell, Java, JavaScript, Perl, PHP, Python, Ruby, and Scala. It also provides a JavaScript command-line interface. MongoDB stores documents as *BSON* (Binary JSON) which are binary encoded JSON like objects. BSON supports nested object structures with embedded objects and arrays. At the heart of MongoDB is the concept of a *document* which is represented as an ordered set of keys with associated values. A *collection* is a group of documents. If a document is the MongoDB analog of a row in a relational database, then a collection can be thought of as the analog to a table. Collections are schema-free. This means that the documents within a single collection can have any number of different shapes. MongoDB groups collections into *databases*. A single instance of MongoDB can host several databases, each of which can be thought of as completely independent. It provides eventual consistency guarantees in a way that a process could read an old version of a document even if another process has already performed an update operation on it. In addition, it provides no transaction management so that if a process reads a document and writes a modified version back to the database, there is a possibility that another process may write a new version of the same document between the read and write operation of the first process. MongoDB supports indexing the documents on multiple fields. In addition, it provides a very rich API interface that supports different batch operations and aggregate functions.

Many other variant projects [34] have followed the NoSQL movement and support different types of data stores such as: key-value stores (e.g. Voldemort [52], Dynomite [15], document stores (e.g. Riak [41]) and graph stores (e.g. Neo4j [39], DEX [14].

3.4 Database-as-a-Service

Multi-tenancy, a technique which is pioneered by *salesforce.com* [43], is an optimization mechanism for hosted services in which multiple customers are consolidated onto the same operational system and thus the economy of scale

---

[1]http://www.10gen.com/.

principles help to effectively drive down the cost of computing infrastructure. In particular, multi-tenancy allows pooling of resources which improves utilization by eliminating the need to provision each tenant for their maximum load. Therefore, multi-tenancy is an attractive mechanism for both of the service providers who are able to serve more customers with a smaller set of machines, and also to customers of these services who do not need to pay the price of renting the full capacity of a server. Database-as-a-service (DaaS) is a new paradigm for data management in which a third party service provider hosts a database as a service [62, 144]. The service provides data management for its customers and thus alleviates the need for the service user to purchase expensive hardware and software, deal with software upgrades and hire professionals for administrative and maintenance tasks. Since using an external database service promises reliable data storage at a low cost, it represents a very attractive solution for companies especially that of startups. In this section, we give an overview of the-state-of-the-art of different options of DaaS from the key players Google, Amazon and Microsoft.

Google Datastore

Google has released the Google AppEngine datastore [20] which provides a scalable schemaless object data storage for web application. It performs queries over data objects, known as *entities*. An entity has one or more *properties* where one property can be a reference to another entity. Datastore entities are schemaless where two entities of the same kind are not obligated to have the same properties, or use the same value types for the same properties. Each entity also has a key that uniquely identifies the entity. The simplest key has a kind and a unique numeric ID provided by the datastore. An application can fetch an entity from the datastore by using its key or by performing a query that matches the entity's properties. A query can return zero or more entities and can return the results sorted by property values. A query does not allow the number of results returned by the datastore to be very large in order to conserve memory and run time.

With the AppEngine datastore, every attempt to create, update or delete an entity happens in a transaction. A transaction ensures that every change made to the entity is saved to the datastore. However, in the case of failure, none of the changes are made. This ensures consistency of data within an entity. The datastore uses optimistic concurrency to manage transactions. The datastore replicates all data to multiple storage locations, so if one storage location fails, the datastore can switch to another and still access the data. To ensure that the view of the data stays consistent as it is being updated, an application uses one location as its primary location and changes to the data on the primary are replicated to the other locations in parallel. An application switches to an alternate location only for large failures. For small failures in primary storage, such as a single machine becoming unavailable temporarily, the datastore waits for primary storage to become available again to complete an interrupted operation. This is necessary to give the application a

```
SELECT [* | __key__] FROM <kind>
[WHERE <condition> [AND <condition> ...]]
[ORDER BY <property> [ASC | DESC] [, <property> [ASC | DESC] ...]]
[LIMIT [<offset>,]<count>]
[OFFSET <offset>]

<condition> := <property> {< | <= | > | >= | = | != } <value>
<condition> := <property> IN <list>
<condition> := ANCESTOR IS <entity or key>
```

Fig. 3.5 Basic GQL syntax

reasonably consistent view of the data, since alternate locations may not yet have all of the changes made to the primary. In general, an application can choose between two read policies: (1) a read policy of *strong consistency* which always reads from the primary storage location. (2) a policy of *eventual consistency* [226] which will read from an alternate location when the primary location is unavailable.

The AppEngine datastore provides a Python interface which includes a rich data modeling API and a SQL-like query language called *GQL* [24]. Figure 3.5 depicts the basic syntax of GQL. A GQL query returns zero or more entities or Keys of the requested kind. In principle, a GQL query cannot perform a SQL-like "join" query. Every GQL query always begins with either *SELECT * FROM* or *SELECT (key) FROM* followed by the name of the kind. The optional *WHERE* clause filters the result set to those entities that meet one or more conditions. Each condition compares a property of the entity with a value using a comparison operator. GQL does not have an *OR* operator. However, it does have an *IN* operator which provides a limited form of *OR*. The optional *ORDER BY* clause indicates that results should be returned are sorted by the given properties in either ascending (ASC) or descending (DESC) order. An optional *LIMIT* clause causes the query to stop returning results after the first count entities. The *LIMIT* can also include an offset to skip the specified number of results in order to find the first result to be returned. An optional *OFFSET* clause can specify an offset if the no *LIMIT* clause is present. Chohan et al. [105] have presented *AppScale* as an open source extension to the Google AppEngine that facilitates distributed execution of its applications over virtualized cluster resources, including Infrastructure-as-a-Service (IaaS) cloud systems such as Amazon EC2 and Eucalyptus [16]. They have used AppScale to empirically evaluate and compare how well different NoSQL systems (e.g. Cassandra, HBase, Hypertable, MemcacheDB, MongoDB, Voldemort) map to the GAE Datastore API [89].

Google Cloud SQL [23] is another Google service that provide the capabilities and functionality of MySQL database servers which are hosted in Google's cloud. Although there is tight integration of the services with *Google App Engine*, it allows the software applications to easily move their data in and out of Google's cloud without any obstacles. In addition, it offers some automatic administrative tasks, such as scheduling backups, patching management, and replicating databases.

Amazon: S3/SimpleDB/Amazon RDS

Amazon Simple Storage Service (S3) is an online public storage web service offered by Amazon Web Services. Conceptually, S3 is an infinite store for objects of variable sizes. An object is simply a byte container which is identified by a URI. Clients can read and update S3 objects remotely using a simple web services (SOAP or REST-based) interface. For example, *get(uri)* returns an object and *put(uri, bytestream)* writes a new version of the object. In principle, S3 can be considered as an online backup solution or for archiving large objects which are not frequently updated.

Amazon has not published details on the implementation of S3. However, Brantner et al. [85] have presented initial efforts of building Web-based database applications on top of S3. They described various protocols for storing, reading and updating objects and indexes using S3. For example, the *record manager* component is designed to manages records where each record is composed of a key and payload data. Both key and payload are bytestreams of arbitrary length where the only constraint is that the size of the whole record must be smaller than the page size. Physically, each record is stored in exactly one page which in turn is stored as a single object in S3. Logically, each record is part of a *collection* (e.g., a table). The record manager provides functions to create new objects, read objects, update objects, and scan collections. The *page manager* component implements a buffer pool for S3 pages. It supports reading pages from S3, pinning the pages in the buffer pool, updating the pages in the buffer pool, and marking the pages as updated. All these functionalities are implemented in straightforward way just as in any standard database system. Furthermore, the page manager implements the commit and abort methods where it is assumed that the write set of a transaction (i.e. the set of updated and newly created pages) fits into the client's main memory or secondary storage (flash or disk). If an application commits, all the updates are propagated to S3 and all the affected pages are marked as unmodified in the client's buffer pool. Moreover, they implemented standard B-tree indexes on top of the page manager and basic redo log records. On the other hand, there are many database-specific issues that has not been addressed, yet, by this work. For example, DB-style strict consistency and transactions mechanisms are not provided. Furthermore, query processing techniques (e.g., join algorithms and query optimization techniques) and traditional database functionalities such as: bulkload a database, create indexes and drop a whole collection still need to be devised.

SimpleDB is another Amazon service which is designed for providing structured data storage in the cloud and backed by clusters of Amazon-managed database servers. It is a highly available and flexible non-relational data store that offloads the work of database administration. Storing data in SimpleDB does not require any pre-defined schema information. Developers simply store and query data items via web services requests and Amazon SimpleDB does the rest. There is no rule that forces every data item (data record) to have the same fields. However, the lack of schema means also that there are no data types as all data values are treated as variable length character data. Hence, the drawbacks of a schema-less data storage also include the lack of automatic integrity checking in the database (no foreign keys) and an increased burden on the application to handle formatting and type conversions. Following the AWS' pay-as-you-go pricing philosophy, SimpleDB has a pricing structure that includes charges for data storage, data transfer, and processor usage. There are no base fees and there are no minimums. Similar to most AWS services, SimpleDB provides a simple API interface which follows the rules and the principles for both of REST and SOAP protocols where the user sends a message with a request to carry out a specific operation. The SimpleDB server completes the operations, unless there is an error, and responds with a success code and response data. The response data is an HTTP response packet, which has headers, storing metadata, and some payload, which is in XML format.

The top level abstract element of data storage in SimpleDB is the *domain*. A domain is roughly analogous to a database table where the user can create and delete domains as needed. There are no design or configuration options to create a domain. The only parameter you can set is the domain name. All the data stored in a SimpleDB domain takes the form of key-value attribute pairs. Each attribute pair is associated with an item which plays the role of a table row. The attribute name is similar to a database column name. However different items (rows) can contain different attribute names which give you the freedom to store different attributes in some items without changing the layout of other items that do not have the same attributes. This flexibility allows the painless addition of new data fields in the most common situations of schema changing or schema evolution. In addition, it is possible for each attribute to have not just one value (multi-valued attributes) but an array of values. In this case, all the user needs to do is add another attribute to an item and use the same attribute name but with a different value. Each value is automatically indexed as it is added. However, there are no explicit indexes to maintain. Therefore, the user has no index maintenance work of any kind to do. On the other side, the user do not have any direct control over the created indices. SimpleDB provides a small group of API calls that enables the core functionality for building client applications such as: *CreateDomain*, *DeleteDomain*, *PutAttributes*, *DeleteAttributes* and *GetAttributes*. The SimpleDB API also provides a query language that is similar to the SQL *Select* statement. Hence, this query language makes SimpleDB Selects very familiar to the typical Database user which ensures a gentle learning curve. However, it should be noted that the language supports issuing queries only over the scope of a single domain (no joins, multi-domain or sub-select queries).

SimpleDB is implemented with complex replication and failover mechanisms behind the scenes. Therefore, it can provide a high availability guarantee with the stored data replicated to different locations automatically. Hence, a user does not need to do any extra effort or become an expert on high availability or the details of replication techniques to achieve the high availability goal. SimpleDB supports two options of for each user read request: eventual consistency or strong consistency. In general, using the option of a consistent read eliminates the consistency window for the request. The results of a consistent read are guaranteed to return the most up-to-date values. In most cases, a consistent read is no slower than an eventually consistent read. However, it is possible for consistent read requests to show higher latency and lower bandwidth on some occasions (e.g. high workloads). SimpleDB does not offer any guarantees about the eventual consistency window but it is frequently less than 1 s. There are quite a few limitations which a user needs to consider while using the simpleDB service such as: the maximum storage size per domain is 10 GB, the maximum attribute values per domain is 1 billion, the maximum attribute values per item is 256, the maximum length of item name, attribute name, or value is 1024 bytes, the maximum query execution time is 5 s, the max query results is 2500 and the maximum query response size is 1 MB.

Amazon Relational Database Service (RDS) is another Amazon service which gives access to the full capabilities of the familiar MySQL, Oracle and SQL Server relational database systems. Hence, the code, applications, and tools which are already designed on existing databases of these system can work seamlessly with Amazon RDS. Once the database instance is running, Amazon RDS can automate common administrative tasks such as performing backups or patching the database software. Amazon RDS can also provide data replication synchronization and automatic failover management services.

Microsoft SQL Azure

Microsoft has recently released the Microsoft SQL Azure Database system [44] which has been announced as a cloud-based relational database service that has been built on Microsoft SQL Server technologies [79]. It provides a highly available, scalable, multi-tenant database service hosted by Microsoft in the Cloud. So, applications can create, access and manipulate tables, views, indexes, referential constraints, roles, stored procedures, triggers, and functions. It can execute complex queries, joins across multiple tables, supports aggregation and full-text queries. It also supports Transact-SQL (T-SQL), native ODBC and ADO.NET data access.[2] In particular, the SQL Azure service can be seen as running an instance of SQL server in a cloud hosted server which is automatically managed by Microsoft instead of running on-premise managed server.

In SQL Azure, a logical database is called a *table group* which can be keyless or keyed. A keyless table group is an ordinary SQL server database where there are no restrictions on the choices of keys for the tables. On the other hand, if a table group is keyed, then all of its tables must have a common column called the *partitioning key* which does not need not to be a unique key for each relation. A *row group* is a set of all rows in a table group that have the same partition key value. SQL Azure requires that each transaction executes on one table group. If the table group is keyed, then the transaction can read and write rows of only one row group.

---

[2]http://msdn.microsoft.com/en-us/library/h43ks021(VS.71).aspx.

Based on these principles, there are two options for building transaction application that can scale out using SQL Azure. The first option is to store the data in multiple groups where each table group can fit comfortably on a single machine. In this scenario, the application takes the responsibility for scaling out by partitioning the data into separate table groups. The second option is to design the database as keyed table group so that the SQL Azure can perform the scale out process automatically.

In SQL Azure, the *consistency unit* of an object is the set of data that can be read and written by an ACID transaction. Therefore, the consistency unit of a keyed table group is the row group while the consistency unit of a keyless table group is the whole table group. Each replica of a consistency unit is always fully contained in a single instance of SQL server running one machine. Hence, using the two-phase commit protocol is never required. A query can execute on multiple partitions of a keyed table group with an isolation level of read-committed. Thus, data that the query read from different partitions may reflect the execution of different transactions. Transactionally consistent reads beyond a consistency unit are not supported.

At the physical level, a keyed table group is split into partitions based on ranges of its partitioning key. The ranges must cover all values of the partitioning key and must not overlap. This ensures that each row group resides in exactly one partition and hence that each row of a table has a well-defined home partition. Partitions are replicated for high availability. Therefore, a partition is considered to be the failover unit. Each replica is stored on one server. Since a row group is wholly contained in one replica of each partition that is scattered across servers such that no two copies reside in the same *failure domain*. To attain high availability on unreliable commodity hardware, the system replicates data. The transaction commitment protocol requires that only a quorum of the replicas be up. A Paxos-like consensus algorithm is used to maintain a set of replicas to deal with replica failures and recoveries. Dynamic quorums are used to improve availability in the face of multiple failures. In particular, for each partition, at each point in time one replica is designated to be the primary. A transaction executes using the primary replica of the partition that contains its row group and thus is non-distributed. The primary replica processes all query, update, and data definition language operations. The primary replica is also responsible for shipping the updates and data definition language operations to the secondary replicas.

Since some partitions may experience higher load than others, the simple technique of balancing the number of primary and secondary partitions per node might not balance the loads. The system can rebalance dynamically using the failover mechanism to tell a secondary on a lightly loaded server to become the primary by either demoting the former primary to secondary or moving the former primary to another server. A keyed table group can be partitioned dynamically. If a partition exceeds the maximum allowable partition size (either in bytes or the amount of operational load it receives), it is split into two partitions. In general, the size of each hosted SQL Azure database can not exceed the limit of 50 GB.

3.5   Virtualized Database Servers

NoSQL database as a service and relational database as a service offered by cloud providers both come with their own strengths. Firstly, the customers do not have to trouble themselves with administrative work, as the providers deal with software upgrades and maintenance tasks. Secondly, the cloud providers also implemented automatic replication failover and management. But there are obvious shortcomings as well. Firstly, customers may require extra migration efforts on modifying code and converting data. Secondly, customers have limited choices, if customers use PostgreSQL or DB2 as their database, there is no simple alternative for both solutions. And thirdly, customers have no full control on achieving the elasticity and scalability benefits.

Therefore, an approach like *virtualized database servers* is necessary sometimes. For this approach, customers simply port everything designed for a conventional data center into cloud, including database servers, and run in virtual machines. It is worth mentioning that there is no unique approach of deploying virtualized database servers. Therefore, no specific projects and examples will be discussed in this subsection. The virtualized database servers are considered as being good enough, as long as the deployment meets the application requirements.

With such a deployment, there would be minimum changes to existing application code. The customers have full control in configuring the required elasticity of allocated resources [96, 211]. And the customers can also build low cost solutions for geographic replication by taking advantage of cloud providers' multiple data centers across continents. However, achieving these goals requires the existence of control components [207] which are responsible for monitoring the system state and taking the corresponding actions, such as allocating more/less computing resources, according to the defined application requirements and strategies. Several approaches have been proposed for building control components which are based on the efficiency of utilization of the allocated resources [96, 211]. In Chap. 7, we present our proposed approach that focuses on building an SLA-based admission control component that provides a customer-centric view for achieving the requirements of their applications.

3.6   Web Scale Data Management: Trade-Offs

An important issue in designing large scale data management applications is to avoid the mistake of trying to be "everything for everyone". As with many types of computer systems, no one system can be best for all workloads and different systems make different tradeoffs in order to optimize for different applications. Therefore, the most challenging aspects in these application is to identify the most important features of the target application domain and to decide about the various design trade-offs which immediately lead to performance trade-offs. To tackle this problem,

Jim Gray came up with the heuristic rule of "20 queries" [151]. The main idea of this heuristic is that on each project, we need to identify the 20 most important questions the user wanted the data system to answer. He argued that five questions are not enough to see a broader pattern and a hundred questions would result in a shortage of focus.

In general, it is hard to maintain ACID guarantees in the face of data replication over large geographic distances. The CAP theorem [86, 138] shows that a shared-data system can only choose at most two out of three properties: *Consistency* (all records are the same in all replicas), *Availability* (a replica failure does not prevent the system from continuing to operate), and *tolerance to Partitions* (the system still functions when distributed replicas cannot talk to each other). When data is replicated over a wide area, this essentially leaves just consistency and availability for a system to choose between. Thus, the "C" (consistency) part of ACID is typically compromised to yield reasonable system availability [56]. Therefore, most of the cloud data management overcome the difficulties of distributed replication by relaxing the ACID guarantees of the system. In particular, they implement various forms of weaker consistency models (e.g. eventual consistency, timeline consistency, session consistency [219]) so that all replicas do not have to agree on the same value of a data item at every moment of time. Hence, NoSQL systems can be classified based on their support of the properties of the CAP theorem into three categories:

- *CA systems*: Consistent and highly available, but not partition-tolerant.
- *CP systems*: Consistent and partition-tolerant, but not highly available.
- *AP systems*: Highly available and partition-tolerant, but not consistent.

In principle, choosing the adequate NoSQL system (from the very wide available spectrum of choices) with design decisions that best fit with the requirements of a software application is not a trivial task and requires a careful consideration. Table 3.1 provides an overview of different design decision for sample NoSQL systems.

In practice, transactional data management applications (e.g. banking, stock trading, supply chain management) which rely on the ACID guarantees that databases provide, tend to be fairly write-intensive or require microsecond precision and are less obvious candidates for the cloud environment until the cost and latency of wide-area data transfer decreases. Cooper et al. [112] discussed the tradeoffs facing cloud data management systems as follows:

- *Read performance versus write performance*: Log-structured systems that only store update deltas can be very inefficient for reads if the data is modified over time. On the other hand, writing the complete record to the log on each update avoids the cost of reconstruction at read time but there is a correspondingly higher cost on update. Unless all data fits in memory, random I/O to the disk is needed to serve reads (e.g., as opposed to scans). However, for write operations, much higher throughput can be achieved by appending all updates to a sequential disk-based log.

Table 3.1 Design decisions of various web scale data management systems

System	Data model	Query interface	Consistency	CAP options	License
Dynamo	Key-value	API	Eventual	AP	Inter@AMZN
PNUTS	Key-value	API	Timeline	AP	Inter@YHOO
Bigtable	Column families	API	Strict	CP	Inter@GOOG
Cassandra	Column families	API	Tunable	AP	Apache
HBase	Column families	API	Strict	CP	Apache
Hypertable	Mul-dim. Tab	API/HQL	Eventual	AP	GNU
CouchDB	Document	API	Eventual	AP	Apache
SimpleDB	Key-value	API	Multiple	AP	Commercial
S3	Large obj.	API	Eventual	AP	Commercial
Table storage	Key-value	API/LINQ	Strict	AP/CP	Commercial
Blob storage	Large obj.	API	Strict	AP/CP	Commercial
Datastore	Column families	API/GQL	Strict	CP	Commercial
RDS	Relational	SQL	Strict	CA	Commercial
Azure SQL	Relational	SQL	Strict	CA	Commercial
Cloud SQL	Relational	SQL	Strict	CA	Commercial

- *Latency versus durability*: Writes may be synched to disk before the system returns success to the user or they may be stored in memory at write time and synched later. The advantages of the latter approach are that avoiding disk access greatly improves write latency, and potentially improves throughput The disadvantage is the greater risk of data loss if a server crashes and loses unsynched updates.
- *Synchronous versus asynchronous replication*: Synchronous replication ensures all copies are up to date but potentially incurs high latency on updates. Furthermore, availability may be impacted if synchronously replicated updates cannot complete while some replicas are offline. Asynchronous replication avoids high write latency but allows replicas to be stale. Furthermore, data loss may occur if an update is lost due to failure before it can be replicated.
- *Data partitioning*: Systems may be strictly row-based or allow for column storage. Row-based storage supports efficient access to an entire record and is ideal if we typically access a few records in their entirety. Column-based storage is more efficient for accessing a subset of the columns, particularly when multiple records are accessed.

Florescu and Kossmann [133] argued that in a cloud environment, the main metric that needs to be optimized is the cost as measured in dollars. Therefore, the big challenge of data management applications is no longer on how fast a database workload can be executed or whether a particular throughput can be achieved; instead, the challenge is how many machines are necessary to meet the performance requirements of a particular workload. This argument fits well with a rule of thumb calculation which has been proposed by Jim Gray regarding the opportunity costs of distributed computing in the Internet as opposed to local computations [139]. Gray reasons that except for highly processing-intensive applications outsourcing computing tasks into a distributed environment does not pay off because network traffic fees outnumber savings in processing power. In principle, calculating the tradeoff between basic computing services can be useful to get a general idea of the economies involved. This method can easily be applied to the pricing schemes of cloud computing providers (e.g Amazon, Google). Florescu and Kossmann [133] have also argued in the new large scale web applications, the requirement to provide 100 % read and write availability for all users has overshadowed the importance of the ACID paradigm as the gold standard for data consistency. In these applications, no user is ever allowed to be blocked. Hence, consistency has turned to be an optimization goal in modern data management systems in order to minimize the cost of resolving inconsistencies and not a constraint as in traditional database systems. Therefore, it is better to design a system that it deals with resolving inconsistencies rather than having a system that prevents inconsistencies under all circumstances.

Kossmann et al. [162] conducted an end-to-end experimental evaluation for the performance and cost of running enterprise web applications with OLTP workloads on alternative cloud services (e.g. RDS, SimpleDB, S3, Google AppEngine, Azure). The results of the experiments showed that the alternative services varied greatly both in cost and performance. Most services had significant scalability issues. They confirmed the observation that public clouds lack of support for uploading large data volumes. It was difficult for them to upload 1 TB or more of raw data through the APIs provided by the providers. With regard to cost, they concluded that Google seems to be more interested in small applications with light workloads whereas Azure is currently the most affordable service for medium to large services.

With the goal of facilitating performance comparisons of the trade-offs cloud data management systems, the Yahoo! Cloud Serving Benchmarks, YCSB [54, 112] and YCSB++ [53,192], have been presented as frameworks and core set of benchmarks for NoSQL systems. The benchmarking tools have been made available via open source in order to allow extensible development of additional cloud benchmark suites that represent different classes of applications and to facilitate the evaluation of different cloud data management systems.

3.7 Discussion and Conclusions

For more than a quarter of a century, the relational database management systems (RDBMS) have been the dominant model for database management. They provide an extremely attractive interface for managing and accessing data, and have proven to be wildly successful in many financial, business and Internet applications. However, with the new trends of Web scale data management, they started to suffer from some serious limitations [116]:

- *Database systems are difficult to scale.* Most database systems have hard limits beyond which they do not easily scale. Once users reach these scalability limits, time consuming and expensive manual partitioning, data migration, and load balancing are the only recourse.

- *Database systems are difficult to configure and maintain.* Administrative costs can easily account for a significant fraction of the total cost of ownership of a database system. Furthermore, it is extremely difficult for untrained professionals to get good performance out of most commercial systems
- *Diversification in available systems complicates its selection.* The rise of specialized database systems for specific markets (e.g. main memory systems for OLTP or column-stores for OLAP) complicates system selection, especially for customers whose workloads do not neatly fall into one category.
- *Peak provisioning leads to unnecessary costs.* Web scale workloads are often bursty in nature, and thus, provisioning for the peak often results in excess of resources during off-peak phases, and thus unnecessary costs.

Recently, the new wave of NoSQL systems have started to gain some mindshares as an alternative model for database management. In principle, some of the main advantages of NoSQL systems can be summarized as follows:

- *Elastic Scaling*: For years, database administrators have relied on the *scale up* approach rather than the *scale out* approach. However, with the current increase in the transaction rates and high availability requirements, the economic advantages of the scaling out approach on commodity hardware has become very attractive. RDBMS might not scale out easily on commodity clusters but NoSQL systems are initially designed with the ability to expand transparently in order to take advantage of the addition of any new nodes.
- *Less Administration*: Despite the many manageability improvements introduced by RDBMS vendors over the years, high-end RDBMS systems cannot be maintained without the assistance of expensive, highly trained DBAs. DBAs are intimately involved in the design, installation, and ongoing tuning of high-end RDBMS systems. On the contrary, NoSQL databases are generally designed from the ground up to require less management. For example, automatic repair and the simpler data model features should lead to lower administration and tuning requirements.
- *Better Economics*: While RDBMS tends to rely on expensive proprietary servers and storage systems, NoSQL databases typically use clusters of cheap commodity servers to manage the exploding data and transaction volumes. Therefore, the cost per gigabyte or transactions per second for NoSQL can be many times less than the cost for RDBMS which allows a NoSQL setup to store and process more data at a much lower price. Moreover, when an application uses data that is distributed across hundreds or even thousands of servers, simple economics points to the benefit of using no-cost server software as opposed to that of paying per-processor license fees. Once freed from license fees, an application can safely scale horizontally with complete avoidance of the capital expenses.
- *Flexible Data Models*: Even minor changes to the data model of a large production RDBMS have to be carefully managed and may necessitate downtime or reduced service levels. NoSQL databases have more relaxed (if any) data model restrictions. Therefore, application changes and database schema changes can be changed more softly.

These advantages have given NoSQL systems a lot of attractions. However, there are many obstacles that still need to be overcome before theses systems can appeal to mainstream enterprises such as[3]:

- *Programming Model*: NoSQL databases offer few facilities for ad-hoc query and analysis. Even a simple query requires significant programming expertise. Missing the support of declaratively expressing the important join operation has been always considered one of the main limitations of these systems.
- *Transaction Support*: Transaction management is one of the powerful features of RDBMS. The current limited support (if any) of the transaction notion from NoSQL database systems is considered as a big obstacle towards their acceptance in implementing mission critical systems.
- *Maturity*: RDBMS systems are well-know with their high stability and rich functionalities. In comparison, most NoSQL alternatives are in pre-production versions with many key features either being not stable enough or yet to be implemented. Therefore, enterprises are still approaching this new wave with extreme caution.
- *Support*: Enterprises look for the assurance that if a the system fails, they will be able to get timely and competent support. All RDBMS vendors go to great lengths to provide a high level of enterprise support. In contrast, most NoSQL systems are open source projects. Although there are few firms offering support for each NoSQL database, these companies often are small start-ups without the global reach, support resources, or credibility of the key market players such as Oracle, Microsoft or IBM.
- *Expertise*: There are millions of developers throughout the world, and in every business segment, who are familiar with RDBMS concepts and programming. In contrast, almost every NoSQL developer is in a learning mode. This situation will be addressed naturally over time. However, currently, it is far easier to find experienced RDBMS programmers or administrators than a NoSQL expert.

Currently, there is a big debate between the NoSQL and RDBMS campuses which is centered around the right choice for implementing online transaction processing systems. RDBMS proponents think that the NoSQL camp has not spent sufficient time to understand the theoretical foundation of the transaction processing model. For example, the eventual consistency model is still not well-defined and different implementations may differs significantly with each other. This means figuring out all these inconsistent behavior lands on the application developer's responsibilities and make their life very much harder. On the other side, the NoSQL camp argues that this is actually a benefit because it gives the domain-specific optimization opportunities back to the application developers who now is no longer constrained by a one-size-fits-all model. However, they admit that making such optimization decision requires a lot of experience and can be very error-prone and dangerous if the decisions are not made by experts.

---

[3]http://blogs.techrepublic.com.com/10things/?p=1772.

Fig. 3.6 Coexistence of
multiple data management
solution in one application

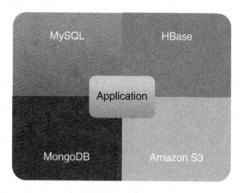

In principle, it is not expected that the new wave of NoSQL data management systems will provide a complete replacement of the relational data management systems. Moreover, there will be not be a single winner (one-size-fits-all) solution. However, it is more expected that different data management solutions will coexist in the same time for a single application (Fig. 3.6). For example, we can imagine an application which uses different datastores for different purposes as follows:

- MySQL for low-volume, high-value data like user profiles and billing information.
- A key value store (e.g. Hbase) for high-volume, low-value data like hit counts and logs.
- Amazon S3 for user-uploaded assets like photos, sound files and big binary files.
- MongoDB for storing the application documents (e.g. bills).

Finally, we believe that there is still huge required research and development efforts for improving the current state-of-the-art in order to tackle the current limitations in both of all campuses: NoSQL database systems, data management service providers and traditional relational database management systems.

Chapter 4
Performance Evaluation Framework
of Cloud Platforms

Amazon, Microsoft and Google are investing billions of dollars in building distributed data centers across different continents around the world providing cloud computing resources to their customers. In practice, a typical cloud platform includes a cloud application hosting server in addition to a cloud-hosted data storage service. Many cloud service provides also offer additional services such as customizable load balancing and monitoring tools. In this chapter, we focus on the following three cloud platforms:

- Amazon offers a collection of services, called *Amazon Web Services*, which includes Amazon Elastic Compute Cloud (EC2) as cloud hosting server, offering infrastructure as a service, Amazon SimpleDB and Simple Storage Service (S3) as cloud databases.
- *Microsoft Azure* is recognized as a combination of infrastructure as a service and platform as a service. It features *web role* and *worker role* for web hosting tasks and computing tasks, respectively. It also offers a variety of database options including Windows Azure Table Storage and Windows Azure Blob Storage as the NoSQL database options, and Azure SQL Database as the relational database option.
- *Google App Engine* supports a platform as a service model, supporting programming languages including Python and Java, and Google App Engine Datastore as a Bigtable-based [99], non-relational and highly shardable cloud database.

There have been a number of research efforts that specifically evaluate the Amazon cloud platform [130, 152]. However, there has been little in-depth evaluation research conducted on other cloud platforms, such as Google App Engine and Microsoft Windows Azure. More importantly, these work lack a more generic evaluation method that enables a fair comparison between various cloud platforms.

L. Zhao et al., *Cloud Data Management*, DOI 10.1007/978-3-319-04765-2_4,
© Springer International Publishing Switzerland 2014

In this chapter, we present the CARE framework (Cloud Architecture Runtime Evaluation) [241] that has been developed as an attempt to address the following research questions:

- What are the performance characteristics of different cloud platforms, including cloud hosting servers and cloud databases?
- What availability and reliability characteristics do cloud platforms typically exhibit? What sort of faults and errors may be encountered when services are running on different cloud platforms under high request volume or high stress situations?
- What are some of the reasons behind the faults and errors? What are the architecture internal insights that may be deduced from these observations?
- What are the software engineering challenges that developers and architects could face when using cloud platforms as their production environment for service delivery?

An empirical experiment has been carried out by applying the CARE framework against three different cloud platforms. The result facilitates an in-depth analysis of the major runtime performance differences under various simulated conditions, providing useful information for decision makers on the adoption of different cloud computing technologies.

This chapter presents the CARE evaluation framework in Sect. 4.1, followed by discussions on the empirical experiment set up and its execution in Sect. 4.2. Section 4.3 presents the experimental results of all test sets and error analysis captured during the tests. Section 4.4 discusses the application experience of CARE and evaluates the CARE approach.

4.1   The CARE Framework

The CARE framework is a performance evaluation approach specifically tailored for evaluating across a range of cloud platform technologies. The CARE framework exhibits the following design principles and features:

- Common and consistent test interfaces across all test targets by employing web services and RESTful APIs. This is to ensure that, as much as possible, commonality across the tests against different platforms is maintained, hence resulting in a fairer comparison.
- Minimal business logic code is placed in the test harness, in order to minimize variations in results caused by business logic code. This is to ensure that performance results can be better attributed to the performance characteristics of the underlying cloud platform as opposed to the test application itself.
- Use of canonical test operations, such as read, write, update, delete. The principle enables simulating a wide range of cloud application workloads using composites of these canonical operations. This approach provides a precise way of describing the application profile.

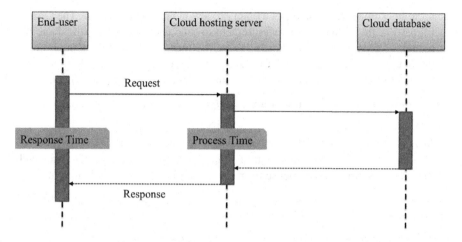

Fig. 4.1 Time measurement terminologies

- Configurable end-user simulation component for producing stepped request volume simulations for evaluating the platform under varying load conditions.
- Reusable test components including test harness, result compilation, and error logging.
- Consistent measurement terminology and metric that can be used across all test case scenarios and against all test cloud platforms.

Measurement Terminology

CARE employs a set of measurement terminology that is used across all tests to ensure consistency in the performance instrumentation, analysis and comparison of the results. It considers major variables of interest in the evaluation of cloud platforms, including response time based on those observed by the end-user side, and from the cloud host server side.

Figure 4.1 illustrates the time measurement terminologies in a typical end-user request and round-trip response. From an end-user's perspective, a cloud hosting server and a cloud database provides the following three time-relevant terminologies:

- *Response time* is the total round-trip time, including time taken at the networking layer, as seen by the end-user, starting from sending the request, through to receiving the corresponding response.
- *Processing time* is the amount of time spent on processing the request on the server side.
- *Database processing time* is the amount of time a cloud database takes to process a database request. However, it is practically impossible to measure

accurately, due to the absence of a timer process in the cloud database. The CARE framework thus equates this measurement to time taken to process the database request as seen by the cloud hosting server by measuring the processing time of the database API as the database processing time as the latency between the hosting servers and cloud databases within the same cloud platform is negligible.

Additional terminologies used refer to different response types that are based on the request:

- *Incomplete request* is a type of request where an end-user fails to send or receive.
- *Completed request* refers to a request where an end-user successfully sends and receives a confirmation response from the cloud platform at completion time.

Subsequently, depending on the response, the completed request can be further classified as:

- *Failed request* that contains an error message in the response.
- *Successful request* which completes the transaction without an error.

Test Scenarios

The CARE framework provides three key test scenarios to differentiate the candidate cloud platforms. While there are potentially other more sophisticated test scenarios, the three test scenarios provided by CARE cover most of the usage scenarios of typical cloud applications. Hence, the CARE framework provides a set of test scenarios that strikes a good balance between simplicity and coverage.

- *End-user-cloud host* represents the scenario that an end-user accesses a web service application hosted on the cloud platform from a client side application. The response time would be the end-user's primary concern in terms of the cloud application performance.
- *Cloud host-cloud database* represents the scenario that an end-user operates on a form or an article hosted in the cloud database through the cloud hosting server. The time taken to send the request from the end-user to the cloud host server is excluded as the focus is on the impact of different data sizes on the database processing time. It is especially interesting to be able to measure the database processing time of concurrent request that have been simultaneously generated by thousands of end-users. The database contention due to concurrent requests will be a key-determining factor in the overall scalability of the cloud platform in this type of scenario. Besides identifying different performance characteristics across cloud databases, a local database (LocalDB) is also provided by the CARE framework in a cloud hosting server as a reference point for comparison to other cloud databases.
- *End-user-cloud database* illustrates a large file transfer scenario. It is conceivable that data-intensive computing would be increasingly pervasive in the cloud where a large variety of new media content, such as video, music, medical

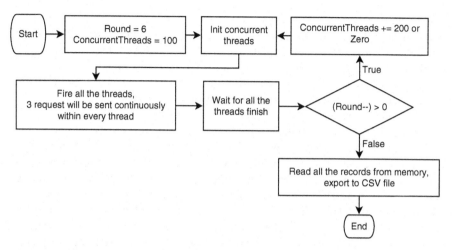

Fig. 4.2 The flow chart of evaluation strategies

images, and etc, would be stored and retrieved from the cloud. Understanding the characteristics of cloud and associated network behavior in handling *big data* is an important contribution towards improving the ability to better utilize cloud computing to handle such data.

Load Test Strategies

The CARE framework supports two types of load test strategies: high stress test strategy and low stress test strategy. The different load test strategies are applied across the various test scenarios listed in Sect. 4.1, in order to provide a more comprehensive evaluation and comparison.

The low stress test strategy sends multiple requests from the end-user side in a sequential manner. This is appropriate for simulating systems where there is a single or small number of end-users. It also provides a reference point for comparison to the high stress test strategy and also for obtaining base network latency benchmarks.

The high stress test strategy provides simulated concurrent requests to cloud platforms in order to obtain key insights on the cloud architecture, particularly for observing performance behavior under load.

Figure 4.2 illustrates the workflow of the high stress test strategy. The configurable parameter called *repeating rounds* is set to 6 by default. This represents the warm-up period, where there is typically a large performance variation due to certain phenomena such as cloud connection time. The performance results arising from the warm-up time stage are discarded by the performance results compilation framework, in order to produce more repeatable and stable testing results. Another configurable parameter *concurrent threads* is set to start at 100 by default. It is then incremented by another configurable parameter *increment* after every round of testing, the CARE framework currently sets the default value to 200 for the high stress test strategy, and 0 for the low stress test strategy. For example, for the high stress test strategy, after the initial 6 rounds, the number of concurrent threads fired by one end-user would go from 100 to 300, 500, 700, 900 and 1,100 in successive rounds. Therefore, a maximum of 3,300 concurrent threads can be achieved since 3 end-users are applied in the evaluation.

For the high stress test strategy, a number of continuous requests are sent within every thread to maintain its stress on the cloud platform over a period of time. If only a single request is sent to the cloud in each thread, our observation is that the expected concurrent stress cannot always be reached, and due to network latency and variability, the arrival time and order of packets at the cloud platform can vary widely. Hence in the CARE framework, another configurable parameter *continuous request* is provided with a default value of 3, striking a balance of providing a more sustained and even workload to the cloud and enabling the test to be conducted across different concurrent clients.

Lastly, as cloud computing is essentially a large-scale shared system, where the typical cloud end-user would be using a publicly shared network in order to access cloud services, it must be that there can be variations in network capacity, bandwidth, and latency issues, that fluctuates over time. The CARE framework thus provides a scheduler that support scheduled *cron*[1] jobs to be automatically and repeatedly activated to retrieved testing samples across different times over a 24 h period.

The flow chart of the low stress test strategy for requests is essentially a simplified version of the high stress strategy shown in Fig. 4.2, with the difference being that the multi-threaded functions are deactivated.

Building a Test Set with CARE

By using the CARE framework, it is possible to combine the various test scenarios with the various load test strategies to produce a comprehensive test set.

While the test set can be designed and created using the CARE framework depending on the precise test requirement, the CARE framework also comes with a reusable test set that aims to provide the test coverage of a large number of commonly found cloud application types. Table 4.1 illustrates a view of all test sets.

Firstly, there are five Contract-First Web Service based test methods, namely high stress round-trip, low stress database read and write, and high stress database read and write. There are also three RESTful Web Service based methods, low stress large file read, write and delete, respectively. The four key methods in the test set are listed in Table 4.1.

---

[1]http://linux.die.net/man/8/cron.

Table 4.1 Building a test set

Test set method	Test scenario	Load test
High stress round-trip	End-user-cloud host	High stress test strategy
Low stress database read and write	Cloud host-cloud database	Low stress test strategy
High stress database read and write	Cloud host-cloud database	High stress test strategy
Low stress large file read, write, and delete	End-user-cloud database	Low stress test strategy

- *High stress round-trip*: The end-users concurrently send message requests to cloud hosting servers. For each request received, the servers immediately echo back to the end-users with the received messages. The response time is recorded in this test. This is the base test that provides a good benchmark for a total round trip cloud application usage experience as the response time as experienced by the average end-user will be affected by the various variable network conditions. This is a useful test to indicate the likely end-user experience in an end-to-end system testing scenario.
- *Low stress database read and write* uses the cloud host-cloud database scenario. It starts with the low stress test strategy, which provides an initial reference result set for subsequent high stress load tests. This test is performed with varying data sizes, representing different cloud application data types. The data types provided by the CARE framework are: a single character of 1 byte, a message of 100 bytes, an article of 1 KB, and a small file of 1 MB. These data types are sent along with the read or write requests, one after another to the cloud databases via the cloud hosting servers. The database processing time will be recorded and then returned to the end-user within the response. In terms of request size the CARE framework follows the conventional cloud application design principle of storing data that are no larger than 1 kB in structured data oriented storage, namely Amazon SimpleDB and Microsoft Windows Azure Table Storage. Data that are larger than 1 KB will be put into binary data oriented databases, including Amazon S3 and Microsoft Windows Azure Blob Storage. In addition, Google App Engine Datastore supports both structured data and binary data in the same cloud database.
- *High stress database read and write* are based on the high stress test strategy. It simulates multiple read/write actions concurrently. The number of concurrent requests range is configurable, as described in Sect. 4.1. Due to some common cloud platform quota limitations, for example Google App Engine by default limits incoming bandwidth to a maximum of 56 MB/min, this test uses a default test data size of 1 kB. This test data size can be configured to use alternative test data sizes if the target testing cloud platform does not have those quota limitations. Lastly, a cron job is scheduled to perform the stress database test repeatedly over different time periods across the 24 h period.

- *Low stress large file read, write, and delete* are tests designed to evaluate large data transfer in the end-user-cloud database scenario. The throughput measure is as observed by the end-user. Once again, this test aims to characterize the total end-to-end large data handling capability by the cloud platform, taking into consideration the various network variations. The CARE framework provides some default test data: ranging from 1 MB, 5 MB, 10 MB, and through to 15 MB. A RESTful Web Service based end-user is implemented for a set of target cloud databases, including Amazon S3 and Microsoft Windows Azure Blob Storage. Note that the CARE framework does not provide a test for the Google App Engine, as Google App Engine Datastore does not support an interface for direct external connection for large file access.

4.2   Application of CARE to Cloud Platform Evaluation

Providing a common reusable test framework across a number of different clouds is a very challenging research problem. This is primarily due to the large variations in architecture, service delivery mode, and functionality provided across various cloud platforms, including Amazon Web Services, Google App Engine, and Microsoft Windows Azure. Firstly, the service models of cloud hosting servers are different: Amazon EC2 uses the infrastructure as a service model; Google App Engine uses the platform as a service model; while Microsoft Windows Azure combines both the infrastructure as a service and platform as a service models. Different service models have different levels of system privileges and different system architectures. Moreover, the connections among cloud hosting servers, cloud databases and client applications tend to utilize different protocols, frameworks, design patterns and programming languages which all add to the complexities to the task of providing a common reusable evaluation method and framework.

Therefore, we proposed a unified and reusable evaluation interface based on Contract-First Web Services and RESTful Web Services, for the purpose of keeping as much commonality as possible. As illustrated in Fig. 4.3, for the Contract-First Web Services: a WSDL file is firstly built; then, the cloud hosting servers implement the functions defined in this WSDL file; lastly, a unified client interface is created from the WSDL file which allows communication via the same protocol, despite of existing variants. While for RESTful Web Services, direct access to cloud databases is made without passing the cloud hosting servers. The CARE framework currently provides the reusable common client components, and the cloud server components for Microsoft Windows Azure, Google App Engine and Amazon EC2.

The evaluation interface maximizes reusability of client application on the end-user side. The Contract-First Web Service based client application is able to talk to different cloud hosting servers via the same WSDL whereas a RESTful Web Service based client application can talk to cloud databases directly without passing the cloud hosting servers via the standard HTTP protocol.

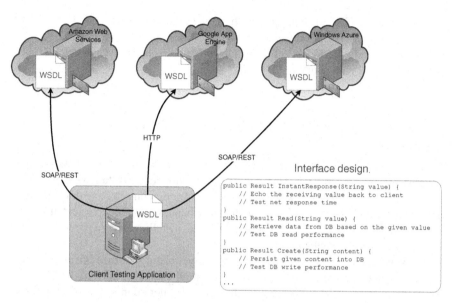

Fig. 4.3 Contract-First Web Service based client application

The evaluation interface hides variations on the cloud side. In practice, the underline design of the three cloud platforms are different from each other. The Contract-First Web Services hide heterogeneous implementation of each cloud platform: Tomcat 6.0, Apache CXF, and a local PostgreSQL database are used on a small Ubuntu-based instance in Amazon EC2; Windows Communication Foundation (WCF) and C# codes are used on Microsoft Windows Azure; while Python-based ZSI and Zope Interface frameworks are used in Google App Engine. However, it is noted that potential performance difference is inevitable due to different programming languages. Thus, the CARE framework cloud server components follow the design principle of always using the native/primary supported language of the cloud platform in order to build the most optimal and efficient test components for each cloud platform.

4.3 Experiment Results and Exception Analysis

In this section, quantitative results of four test set methods will be examined. Moreover, exceptions and errors captured during the evaluation will be analyzed by considering the results as an average over all test results. Some environmental information for the conducted tests are noted here:

- The client environment executing the CARE evaluation strategy runs on 3 Debian machines with Linux kernel 2.6.21.6-ati. Each evaluation machine is a standard

Dell Optiplex GX620, equipped with Intel Pentium D CPU 3.00 GHz, 2 GB memory, and 10/100/1000 Base-T Ethernet.

• Both Amazon EC2 and Microsoft Windows Azure instances use the default type, small instance with single core.

Qualitative Experience of Development Utilities

In Amazon EC2, an administration role will be granted to developers when a virtual machine instance is created. This allows the developers to install whatever they want in the instance. In other words, there is no restriction on selecting development environments for Amazon EC2. But on the other hand, being able to select different work needs to be done, such as uploading and installing the required runtime environments for the application.

The key highlights of the Microsoft Windows Azure platform are its heavily equipped frameworks and environments. Almost all existing Microsoft web development frameworks and runtime environments are supported in Microsoft Windows Azure. As a result of this, developers can simply focus on the business logic implementation with C# or PHP. But the key downside is that they have to stick with Microsoft development environments, Microsoft Visual Studio.

In contrast to Microsoft Windows Azure which offers fully functioned frameworks, and Amazon EC2 which provides highly configurable environment, Google App Engine re-implements programming languages to suit the different development approaches. Google has currently enabled Python and JVM-supported languages on its cloud platform where developers are free to choose frameworks based on Python and JVM-supported languages to improve their productivity. But, in practice, there are some limitations on the Google App Engine which restrict the range of choices, such as no multiple threads, no local I/O access, and 30 s timeout a request handler. Additionally, Google also offers other Google APIs to integrate Google App Engine with other Google services.

Quantitative Results of Test Sets

High Stress Round-Trip

Figures 4.4–4.6 indicate the cumulative distribution function of response time under varying amount of concurrent stress requests, which range from 300, 900, 1,500, 2,100, 2,700, up to 3,300 requests respectively.

The observation of three cumulative distribution functions confirms that the larger the requests, the longer the response time will be. But the incremental step of response time varies from one group of requests to another, depending on the cloud hosting servers. For 80 % of cumulative distribution functions, the response

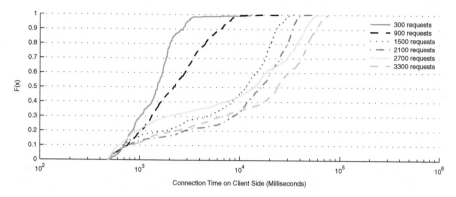

Fig. 4.4 The cumulative distribution function of high stress round-trip between the end-user and the Amazon EC2 cloud hosting servers

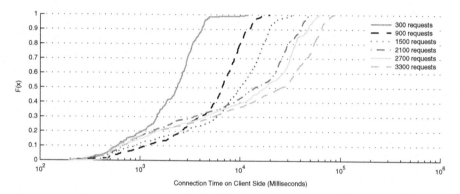

Fig. 4.5 The cumulative distribution function of high stress round-trip between the end-user and the Microsoft Windows Azure cloud hosting servers

time of Amazon EC2 in Fig. 4.4 and Microsoft Windows Azure in Fig. 4.5 are dramatically increased at 1,500 requests and 900 requests respectively. For Google App Engine in Fig. 4.6, although the response time shows an increasing trend, there is no significant leap between neighboring groups of requests.

The reason for these observations could be explained from the scalability aspect. If response time increases steadily and linearly under stress in Google App Engine, there is certainly some good scalability capability as its cloud hosting server is thread based, allowing more threads to be created for additional requests. Nevertheless, the cloud hosting servers of Amazon EC2 and Microsoft Windows Azure are instance based. The computing resources for one instance are preconfigured and more resources for additional requests cannot be obtained unless extra instances are deployed.

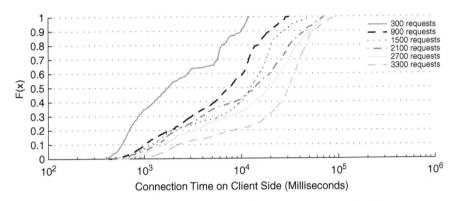

Fig. 4.6 The cumulative distribution function of high stress round-trip between the end-user and the Google App Engine cloud hosting servers

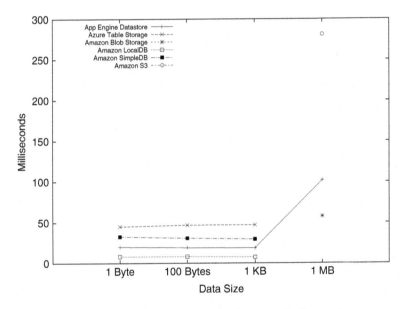

Fig. 4.7 The average read time in cloud databases with low stress database read test set

Low Stress Database Read and Write

In Fig. 4.7, the average database processing time of reading 1 byte, 100 bytes, and 1 kB are within 50 ms, while the database processing time of writing small size data in Fig. 4.8 varies from 10 ms to 120 ms. From this, it is obvious that for each cloud database, the reading performance is faster than the writing performance for the same amount of data. The two figures also state that the local database in Amazon EC2 instance shows its strength for message sizes that ranges from 1 byte to 1 kB.

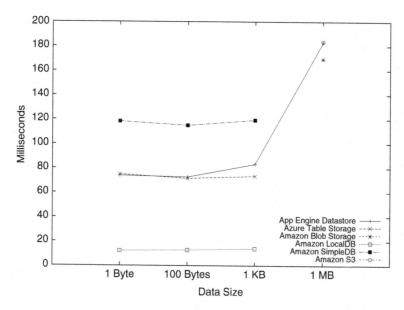

Fig. 4.8 The average write time in cloud databases with low stress database write test set

As the evaluation environment is low stress, and as such, the cloud host is not under load, so it is consistent that the local database without any optimizations can handle requests effectively. The latency from the cloud hosting server to the local database is also smaller, since they are in the same Amazon EC2 instance.

When the size of request reaches 1 MB, Amazon S3, shown as orange dots in figures, almost has the same write performance as Google App Engine Datastore, but the former is almost three times slower than the latter in reading. Microsoft Windows Azure Blob Storage, shown as green triangles in figures, takes less time than the others in both reading and writing.

The cumulative distribution functions of read and write throughput in cloud databases demonstrated similar behavior as in Figs. 4.9 and 4.10. Moreover, for the 1 MB database reading and writing test, the cumulative distribution functions also show that approximately 80 % of requests are processed at 10 MB/s.

High Stress Database Read and Write

In this test, the number of concurrent requests in the evaluation varies from 300 to 3,300 with step increments of 300. The collection of database processing time of each cloud database under 2,100 concurrent requests are shown in Fig. 4.11. From 2,100 concurrent requests onwards, cloud host servers started to produce errors, these are listed in detail in Tables 4.3 and 4.4 in Sect. 4.3. Instead of being the best performer as in low stress database read and write, the local database

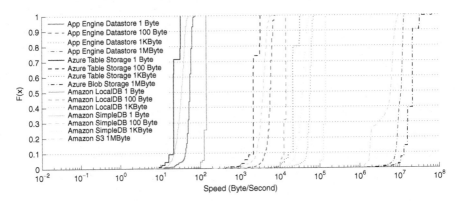

Fig. 4.9 The cumulative distribution function of read throughput in cloud databases with low stress database read test set

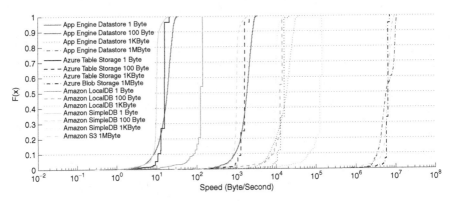

Fig. 4.10 The cumulative distribution function of write throughput in cloud databases with low stress database write test set

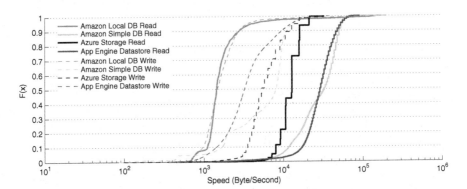

Fig. 4.11 The cumulative distribution function of read and write throughput in cloud databases with high stress database read and write test sets

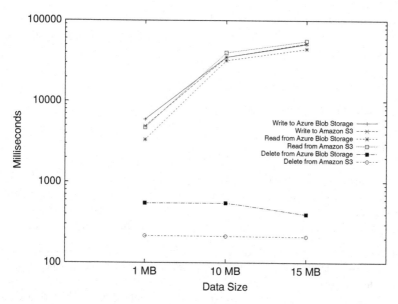

Fig. 4.12 The database processing time of read, write, and delete in cloud databases with low stress large file read, write, and delete test sets

in Amazon EC2 now performs the worst among all platforms. It implies the poor capability of handling concurrent requests within the same instance as the compute capability. Moreover, Google App Engine Datastore, Amazon SimpleDB and Microsoft Windows Azure Storage all continue to show faster speeds in read operations than write operations.

Low Stress Large File Read, Write, and Delete

Figure 4.12 shows the average database processing time of reading, writing and deleting binary files in the cloud databases directly. It can be seen that reading, shown in the left figure, is faster than writing, shown in the middle figure, in general. Both database processing time of read and write for Amazon S3 and Microsoft Windows Azure Blob Storage are linearly increasing with increasing proportion of data size. It is likely the limitation of the local network environment will come before getting insights of the cloud databases. This is why the CARE framework provides a range of scenarios, for example, end-user-cloud database, as well as cloud host-cloud database, so that the performance characteristics can be evaluated with and without the network variations and effects in place.

The average database processing time of the delete operation, shown in the right figure, is interesting as the observation shows a constant result regardless of data sizes. It is confirmed that neither Amazon S3 nor Microsoft Windows Azure Blob

Storage will delete data entries on the fly. Both of them mark the entity and reply with successful request message at the first instant where the actual delete operation will be completed afterwards.

Exception Analysis and Error Details

Overall Error Details

All error messages and exceptions were logged and captured by the CARE framework. This is a useful feature for carrying out offline analysis. The observations show that all errors occurred during the high stress database read and write tests. The CARE framework also logs the errors/exceptions according to various categories:

- *Database error* happens during the period of processing in cloud databases.
- *Server error* occurs within cloud hosting servers, for instance, not being able to allocate resources.
- *Connection error* is encountered if a request does not reach cloud hosting servers due to network connection problems, such as package loss and proxy being unavailable.

In general, a response with connection error is classified as an incomplete request; and a request to server error or database error is classified as a failed request. The error details of each category are listed in Table 4.2.

Average Errors Over Different Time Periods

The CARE framework is also able to produce unavailability information based on error and exceptions logs over a long period of time. Tables 4.3 and 4.4 show different average error rates of high stress database read and write methods over different time periods. As shown in the table, both read and write connection error rates of the local database in Amazon EC2 and Google App Engine Database vary in a range from 15 % to 20%. This figure is highly variable over the 24-hour period especially as it is subjected to network conditions, as well as the health status of the cloud server. Amazon SimpleDB achieves the lowest error rates for both reading and writing operations with an error average of less than 10%, with average reading error rate that approaches 0%. On the contrary, Microsoft Windows Azure Table Storage has the highest reading error rate of more than 30%.

In spite of read and write connection error rates, average successful read request rates are high at almost 99.99% of completed request. Although Google Datastore and Amazon SimpleDB responded with write database error for 31.67 and 111.17 times respectively, the successful write request rates are generally high, with the worst one logging at more than 99.67% of completed request.

Table 4.2 Total error detail analysis

Category	Error messages	Reasons	Locations
Database error	datastore_errors: Timeout	Multiple action perform at the same entry, one will be processed others will fail due to contention	Google Datastore
		Request takes too much time to process	Google Datastore
	datastore_errors: TransactionFailedError	An error occurred for the API request datastore_v3.RunQuery()	Google Datastore
	apiproxy_errors: Error	Too much contention on datastore entities	Google Datastore
	Amazon SimpleDB is currently unavailable	Too many concurrent requests	Amazon simpleDB
Server error	Unable to read data from the transport connection	WCF failed to open connection	Microsoft Windows Azure
	500 Server Error	HTTP 500 ERROR : Internal Error	Google App Engine
	Zero sized reply		Amazon EC2
Connection error	Read timed out	HTTP time out	Microsoft Windows Azure/ Amazon EC2
	Access denied	HTTP 401 ERROR	Microsoft Windows Azure/ Google App Engine/ Amazon EC2
	Unknown host exception		Microsoft Windows Azure
	Network Error (tcp_error)	Local proxy connection error	Microsoft Windows Azure/ Google App Engine

Among all cloud hosting servers, Google App Engine exhibits the most number of server errors where most errors were 500 Server Error messages. The largest group of server errors happened after May 20 23:30:00 PST 2009. Meanwhile, some significant latency started appearing in the Google App Engine's overall system status dashboard around one or half an hour earlier than the given time. It is likely that the significant latency of the overall Google App Engine system could be a cause of the server errors in the experiment. However, there is no direct evidence to prove such a causality.

Average Connection Error Rates Under Different Loads

In high stress database read and write tests, as expected, the trend of the average connection error rates raises as the number of concurrent requests increases. Google Datastore via Google App Engine and Amazon SimpleDB via Amazon EC2 have a

Table 4.3 Average error (rates) of high stress database read over different time periods

Cloud databases	Database error (%)	Server error (%)	Connection error error (%)	Successful request (%)
Amazon simpleDB	0.00 (0.000)	0.00 (0.000)	41.00 (0.127)	32,359.00 (99.873)
Amazon localDB	0.00 (0.000)	16.40 (0.051)	6368.40 (19.656)	26,015.20 (80.294)
Microsoft windows azure table storage	0.00 (0.000)	0.00 (0.000)	11,593.80 (35.783)	20,806.20 (64.217)
Google datastore	2.25 (0.007)	4.75 (0.015)	5462.75 (16.860)	26,930.25 (83.118)

Table 4.4 Average error (rates) of high stress database write over different time periods

Cloud databases	Database error (%)	Server error (%)	Connection error (%)	Successful request (%)
Amazon simpleDB	111.17 (0.343)	9.50 (0.029)	2470.83 (7.626)	29,808.50 (92.002)
Amazon localDB	0.00 (0.000)	25.20 (0.075)	5262.60 (16.243)	27,112.20 (83.680)
Microsoft windows azure table storage	0.00 (0.000)	0.17 (0.001)	4810.33 (14.847)	27,589.50 (85.153)
Google datastore	31.67 (0.098)	3037.37 (9.374)	4787.50 (14.776)	24,543.66 (75.752)

smaller percentage trend in reading than writing, while Microsoft Windows Azure Table Storage and the local database in Amazon EC2 on the contrary, display higher rates in read operations than write operations.

Amazon SimpleDB via Amazon EC2 maintains the lowest error rates in both reading and writing, almost approaching 0% in read tests. While the local database via Amazon EC2, which shares the same instance with the web application of Amazon SimpleDB via Amazon EC2, started receiving a high percentage of connection errors from 1,500 concurrent requests. The reason of this phenomenon could be explained by that the local database causes additional resource contention by virtually being inside the same instance as the host server instance. This leads to a less scalable architecture, as a trade-off to smaller latency from host server to cloud database.

For Microsoft Windows Azure, the connection error percentage begins to leap, from less than 1% at 1,500 requests, to more than 50% and 30% in reading and writing separately at 3,300 concurrent requests. This indicates that a limit in terms of what this Azure server instance can handle has been hit.

For Google App Engine, a large number of connection errors under high load has been observed. Most connection errors from Google App Engine contain the access denied message, which is a standard HTTP 401 error message. Through cross checking the server side, there is no record of HTTP 401 at all in the Google App Engine. This means that these requests are blocked before getting into the web application. The assumption can be made that the access is restricted due to a firewall in Google App Engine. When thousands of requests go into Google App Engine concurrently from the same IP, the firewall may be triggered. Upon some analysis of how App Engine manages incoming requests by using a HTTP traffic monitor, it is reasonable to conclude that this may be a security feature around to prevent denial of service attacks. There seems no way to get around of it, except reducing the number of requests.

4.4 Discussion

An empirical experiment was carried out to examine the effectiveness of CARE when applied to testing different cloud platforms. Results indicate CARE is a feasible approach by directly comparing three major cloud platforms, including cloud hosting servers and cloud databases. Analysis revealed the importance of acknowledging different service models, and that the scalability of cloud hosting servers is achieved in different ways. Horizontal scalability is available to some extent in Google App Engine, but is always restricted by the quota limitation. On the contrary, Amazon EC2 and Microsoft Windows Azure can only scale through manual work in which developers can specify rules and conditions for when instances should be added. This leads the classic trading off issue of complexity against scalability. Vertical scalability is not possible in Google App Engine since every process has to be finished within 30 s, and that it is beyond the control over the type of machines used for our application in the Google cloud. Where on the other hand, Amazon EC2 and Microsoft Windows Azure allow you to choose and deploy instances with varying sizes of memory and CPUs.

The unpredictable unavailability of cloud is of a greater issue, particularly for enterprise organizations with mission critical application requirements. Whilst bursts of unavailability are noticed, during the tests which are caused by a range of environmental factors, including variable network conditions. It is also observed that the cloud providers sometimes experience challenges in maintaining uninterrupted service availability. Despite sophisticated replication strategies, there is still a potential risk of data center breakdown even in the cloud, which may in turn affect the performance and availability of hosted applications. It is also noticed that at the time of writing, most cloud vendors provide an SLA availability of 99.9%, which is still some way away from the typical enterprise requirement of 99.999%.

The network condition makes a significant impact on the total performance and end-user experience for cloud computing. The performance of the end-to-end cloud experience highly relies on the network condition. If an end-user accesses cloud services through a poor network environment, it is not possible to take full advantage of the cloud platforms.

Chapter 5
Database Replication of NoSQL Database-as-a-Service

NoSQL database as a service is part of the database as a service offering to complement traditional database systems often by removing the requirement ACID transactions as one common feature. NoSQL database as a service has been supported by many service providers that offer various consistency options, from eventual consistency to single-entity ACID. For the service provider, weaker consistency is related to a longer replication delay, and therefore should allow better availability and lower read latency.

This chapter investigates the replication delay of NoSQL databases by observing the consistency and performance characteristics of various offerings from the customers' perspective. In this chapter, we present a detailed measurements over several NoSQL databases, that show how frequently, and in what circumstances, different inconsistency situations are observed, and what impact the customers sees on performance characteristics from choosing to operate with weak consistency mechanisms. In addition, we describe the development of the overall methodology of experiments for measuring consistency from the customer's view. The chapter first presents an architecture for benchmarking various NoSQL databases in Sect. 5.1. Then, Sect. 5.2 reports on the experiments that investigate how often a read sees a stale value. For several platforms, data is always, or nearly always, up-to-date. For one platform, specifically Amazon SimpleDB, stale data is frequently observed. Thus, in Sect. 5.3, the performance and cost trade-offs of different consistency options are explored. Section 5.4 discusses some limitations of generalizing results and gives some conclusions.

5.1 Architecture of Benchmark Application

Figure 5.1 illustrates the architecture of the benchmark applications in this study. There are three roles composed: the NoSQL database, the *writer*, and the *reader*. A writer repeatedly writes 14 bytes of string data into a particular data element where the value written is the current time, so that it is easy to check which write

L. Zhao et al., *Cloud Data Management*, DOI 10.1007/978-3-319-04765-2_5,

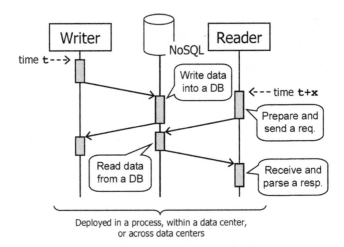

Fig. 5.1 The architecture of NoSQL database as a service benchmark applications

is observed in a read. In most of the experiments that are reported, writing happens once every 3 s. A reader role repeatedly reads the contents from the data element and also notes the time at which the read occurs; in most experiments reading happens 50 times every second. Comparing read values reveals the probability of reading stale values over time. Assume a writer invokes a write operation at time t and a reader invokes a read operation at time $t + x$. "A period of time" to make replicas consistent is obtained by finding x when no stale value is observed.

In some experiments, the writer and reader roles are deployed as a single thread for the writer role, and single or multiple threads for the reader role, while in other experiments, a single thread takes both roles. For one experiment measurement, the writing and reading operations are run for 5 min, doing 100 writes and 15.000 reads. The measurement is repeated once every hour, for at least 1 week, in October and November 2010. It must be noted that each measurement includes not only the processing time on NoSQL databases but also that of applications and network latency. In all measurement studies, it is confirmed that benchmark applications and networks are not performance bottlenecks.

In a post-processing data analysis phase, each read is determined to be either fresh or stale, depending on whether the value observed has a timestamp from the closest preceding write operation, based on the times of occurrence; also each read is placed in a bucket based on how much clock-time has elapsed since the most recent write operation. By examining all the reads within a bucket, from a single measurement run, or indeed aggregating over many runs, the probability of observing the freshest value by a read is calculated. Repeating the experiment through a week ensures that we will notice any daily or weekly variation in behavior.

5.2 Staleness of Data on Different Cloud Platforms

Amazon SimpleDB

Amazon SimpleDB is a distributed key-value store offered by Amazon. Each key has an associated collection of attributes, each with a value. For these experiments, a data element is taken to be a particular attribute kept for a particular key, which identifies, in SimpleDB terms, an *item*. SimpleDB supports a write operation call via *PutAttributes* and two types of read operations, distinguished by a parameter in the call to *GetAttributes*: *eventual consistent read* and *consistent read*. The consistent read is supposed to ensure that the value returned always comes from the most recently completed write operation, while an eventually consistent read does not give this guarantee. This study investigates how these differences appear to the customers who consume data.

Amazon SimpleDB is currently operated in several independent geographic regions and each of them offers a distinct URL as its access point. For example, https://sdb.us-west-1.amazonaws.com is the URL of SimpleDB operated in *us-west* region. It is used as the testbed in all experiments. The benchmark application for Amazon SimpleDB is implemented in Java and runs in Amazon EC2. It accesses SimpleDB through its REST interface. The writer writes timestamps, each of which is 14 bytes of string data, in a key-value pair. The reader reads a value from the same key-value pair using *eventual consistent read* or *consistent read* option. The study of Amazon SimpleDB comprises of both parts based on the access patterns. The access patterns determine the location options of EC2 instances that the writer and the reader could reside, including options of being in the same region or in different regions.

Access Patterns

In the first pattern, the writer and reader run in the same single thread on an *m1.small* instance provided by Amazon EC2 with Ubuntu 9.10. The instance is deployed in the same region of SimpleDB, in the hope of minimizing the network latency. Although, it is not guaranteed that data items from SimpleDB will be in the same physical data center as the thread in EC2, using the same geographic region is the best mechanism to the customer to reduce network latency. For this access pattern, two consistency options, *read-your-write* and *monotonic read* are examined.

While in the second pattern, the writer and the reader are deliberately separated to multiple threads, with the following configurations:

1. A writer and a reader run in different threads but in the same process. In this case, read and write requests originate from the same IP address.

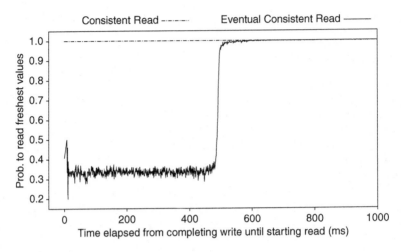

Fig. 5.2 Probability of reading freshest value

2. A writer and a reader run in different processes but in the same instance that is also in the same geographic domain as the data storage in *us-west* region. In this case, read and write requests still have the same IP address.
3. A writer and a reader run on different instances but both are still in the same region. In this case, requests originate from different IP addresses but from the same geographical region.
4. A writer and a reader run on different instances and different regions, one in *us-west* region and one in *eu-west* region. In this case, requests originate from different IP addresses in different regions.

The measurement is executed once every hour for 11 days from October 21, 2010. In total 26,500 writes and 3,975,000 reads were performed for accessing from a single thread. Since only one thread is used in the first study, the average throughput of reading and writing are 39.52 per second and 0.26 per second, respectively, where each measurement runs at least for 5 min. The same set of measurements was performed with eventual consistent read and with consistent read.

In the study of accessing from multiple threads and processes, each experiment was run for 11 days as well. In all four cases the probability of reading updated values shows a similar distribution as in Fig. 5.2. Therefore, it is concluded that customers of Amazon SimpleDB see the same data consistency model regardless of where and how clients are placed. Hence, this section will focus on reporting observations of accessing from single thread with regards to two consistency options, read-your-write consistency and monotonic read consistency respectively.

Table 5.1 Probability of reading freshest value

Time elapsed from starting write until starting read	Eventual consistent read	Consistent read
[0, 450)	33.40% (168,908/505,821)	100.00% (482,717/482,717)
[500, 1000)	99.78% (1192/541,062)	100.00% (509,426/509,426)

Read-Your-Write Consistency

Figure 5.2 shows the probability of reading the fresh value plotted against the time interval that elapsed from the time when the write begins, to the time when the read is submitted. Each data point in the graph is an aggregation over all the measurements for a particular bucket containing all time intervals that conform to millisecond granularity. With eventual consistent read the probability of reading the freshest data stays about 33% from 0 ms to 450 ms. It surges sharply between 450 ms and 500 ms, and finally reaches 98% at 507 ms. A spike and a valley in the first 10 ms are perhaps random fluctuations due to a small number of data points. While with consistent read, the probability is 100% from about 0 ms onwards. To summarize further, Table 5.1 places all buckets whose time is in a broad interval together and shows actual numbers as well as percentages.

A type of relevant consistency is read-your-writes, which says that when the most recent write is from the same thread as the reader, then the value seen should be fresh. As stale eventual consistent reads are possible with Amazon SimpleDB within a single thread, so it is concluded that eventual consistent reads do not satisfy read-your-writes; however, consistent reads do achieve such level of consistency.

Moreover, the variability of the time is also examined when freshness is possible or highly likely, among different measurement runs. For eventual consistent reads, Fig. 5.3 shows the first time when a bucket has the freshness probability of over 99%, and the last time when the probability is less than 100%. Each data point is obtained from a 5 min measurement run, so there are 258 data points in each time series. The median of the time to exceed 99% is 516.17 ms and coefficient of variance is 0.0258. There does not seem to be any regular daily or weekly variation, rather the outliers seem randomly placed. Out of the 258 measurement runs, second and twenty-first runs show a non-zero probability of stale read after 4,000 ms and 1,000 ms respectively. Those outliers are considered to be generated by network jitter and other similar effects.

Monotonic Read Consistency

Monotonic read is an important consistency option [226]. It is defined as a condition where subsequent operations see data that is at least as fresh as what was seen before. This property can be examined across multiple data elements or for a single element as is considered here. The consistent read meets monotonic as it should

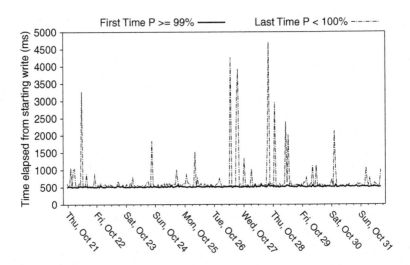

Fig. 5.3 Time to see freshness with eventual consistent read

Table 5.2 Successive eventual consistent reads

First read/Second read	Stale	Fresh
Stale	39.94% (189, 926)	21.08% (100, 1949)
Fresh	23.36% (111, 118)	15.63% (74, 337)

be, since each read should always see the most recent value. However, eventual consistent read is not monotonic and indeed the freshness of a successive operation seems essentially independent of what was seen before. Thus, eventual consistent read also does not meet stronger consistency options such as causal consistency.

Table 5.2 shows the probability of observing fresh or stale values in each pair of successive eventual consistent reads performed during the range from 0 ms to 450 ms after the time of a write. The table also shows the actual number of observations out of 475,575 of two subsequent reads performed in this measurement study. The monotonic read condition is violated, that is the first read returns a fresh value but the second read returns a stale value, in 23.36% of the pairs. This is reasonably close to what one would expect of independent operations, since the probability of seeing a fresh value in the first read is about 33% and the probability of seeing a stale value in the second read is about 67%. The Pearson correlation between the outcomes of two successive reads is 0.0281, which is very low, and it is concluded that eventual consistent reads are independent from each other.

Amazon S3

A similar measurement study was conducted on Amazon Simple Storage Service (S3) for 11 days. In S3, storage consists of objects within buckets, so our writer updates an object in a bucket with the current timestamp as its new value, and each reader reads the object. In this experiment, measurements for the same five configurations as SimpleDB's case are conduced, including a writer and a reader run in a single thread, different threads, different processes, different instances, and different regions. Amazon S3 supports two types of write operations, namely standard and reduced redundancy. A standard write operation stores an object so that its probability of durability is at least 99.999,999,999%, while a reduced redundancy write aims to provide at least 99.99% probability of durability. The same set of measurements was performed with both standard write and reduced redundancy write.

Documentation states that Amazon S3 buckets provide eventual consistency for overwrite *PUTS* operations. However, no stale data was ever observed in this study regardless of write redundancy options. It seems that staleness and inconsistency might be visible to a customer of Amazon S3 only in executions in the event of a failure in the particular nodes of the platform where the data is stored, during the time of their access; this is a very low probability event.

Microsoft Windows Azure Table Storage and Blob Storage

The experiment was also conducted on Microsoft Windows Azure Table Storage and Blob Storages for 8 days. Since it is not possible to start more than one process on a single instance, specifically for a *web role* in this experiment, measurements for four configurations are conducted: a write and a reader run in a single thread, different threads, different instances or different regions. On Azure Table Storage a writer updates a property of a table and a reader reads the same property. On Azure Blob Storage a write updates a blob and a reader reads it.

The measurement study observed no stale data at all. It is known that all types of Microsoft Windows Azure Storages support strong data consistency [165] and this experiment confirms it.

Google App Engine Datastore

Similar to Amazon SimpleDB, Google App Engine Datastore keeps key-accessed entities with properties and it offers two options for reading: *strong consistent read* and eventual consistent read. However, the observed behavior for eventual consistent read in the Datastore is completely different from that of Amazon SimpleDB.

It is known that the eventual consistent read of Datastore reads from a secondary replica only when a primary replica is unavailable. Therefore, it is expected that customers see consistent data in most reads, regardless of the consistency option they choose.

The benchmark application for Google App Engine Datastore is coded in Java and deployed in Google App Engine. Applications deployed in App Engine are not allowed to create threads; a thread automatically starts upon an HTTP request and it can run for no more than 30 s. Therefore, each measurement on App Engine runs for 27 s and measurements are executed every 10 min for 12 days. The same set of measurements was performed with strong consistent read and eventual consistent read. App Engine also offers no option to control the geographical location of applications. Therefore, only two configurations are examined: a writer and a reader are run in the same application, and a writer and a reader are run in different applications. Each measurement consists of 9.4 writes and 2787.9 reads on average, and in total 3,727,798 reads and 12,791 writes are recorded on average for each configuration.

With strong consistent read no stale value was observed. With eventual consistent read and both roles in the same application, no stale value was observed. However 11 out of 3,311,081 readings, approximately $3.3 \times 10^{-4}\%$, observed stale values when a writer and an eventual consistent reader are run in different applications. It is hard to conclude for certain whether stale values might sometimes be observed when a writer and a reader are run in the same application. However, it suggests the possibility that Google App Engine offers read-your-writes level of eventual consistency. In any case, it is also clear that consistency errors are very rare.

5.3   Trade-Off Analysis of Amazon SimpleDB

In the hope of assisting the customer to make a well-informed decision about consistency options for reading data, the trade-off analysis could be made by considering consistency levels against response time and throughput, monetary cost, and implementation ideas, respectively. The benchmark architecture described in Sect. 5.1 is reused for the analysis. The measurement ran between 1 and 25 instances in *us-west* region to read and write one attribute, which is a 14 bytes string data, from an item in Amazon SimpleDB. Each instance runs 100 threads, acting as emulated end-users, each of which executes one read or write request every second in a synchronous manner. Thus, if all requests' response time is below 1.000 ms, the throughput of SimpleDB can be reported as 100% of the potential load. Three different read/write ratios were studied, including 99/1, 75/25, and 50/50 cases. Each measurement runs for 5 min with a set number of virtual machines, once every hour for 1 day.

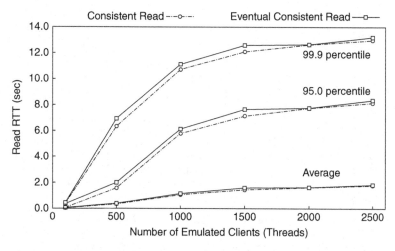

Fig. 5.4 The average, 95 percentile, and 99.9 percentile response time of reads at various levels of load

Response Time and Throughput

As advised in Amazon SimpleDB FAQs,[1] the benefits of eventual consistent read can be summarized as minimizing response time and maximizing throughput. To verify this advice, the difference in response time, throughput, and availability of the two consistency options is investigated, as the load is increased. Figure 5.4 shows the average, 95 percentile, and 99.9 percentile response time of eventual consistent reads and consistent reads at various levels of load. The result is obtained from the case of 99% read ratio and all failed requests are excluded. The result shows no visible difference in average response time. However, consistent read slightly outperforms eventual consistent read in 95 percentile and 99.9 percentile response time.

Figures 5.5 and 5.6 show the average response time of reads and writes at various read/write ratios, plotted against the number of emulated end-users. A conclusion could be drawn that changing the level of replication intensity has a negligible impact on the read and write response times. Intuitively, it would be surprised that eventual consistent read does not outperform the consistent read as expected, but it is still reasonable if the possible implementation ideas are taken into consideration. Figure 5.7 shows the absolute throughput, the average number of processed requests per second. Whiskers are plotted surrounding each average with the corresponding minimum and maximum throughput. Similar to the response time, consistent read results slightly outperforms that of eventual consistent read, though the difference is not significant. Figure 5.8 shows the throughput as a percentage of what is possible

---

[1] http://aws.amazon.com/simpledb/faqs/.

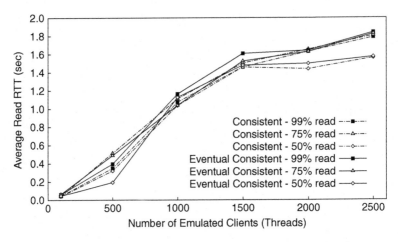

Fig. 5.5 Response time of reads at various read/write ratios on Amazon SimpleDB

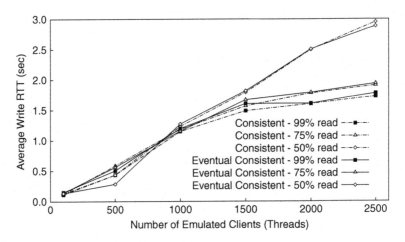

Fig. 5.6 Response time of writes at various read/write ratios on Amazon SimpleDB

with this number of end-users. As the response time increased, each end-user sent less than one request every second and, therefore, the throughput percentage decreased.

It must be noted that Amazon SimpleDB often returns exceptions with status code 503, representing "Service is currently unavailable", under heavy load. Figure 5.9 shows the average failure rates of eventual consistent reads and consistent reads, with each data point being marked with whiskers to highlight the corresponding maximum and minimum failure rates. Clearly the failure rate increased as the load increased, but again the observation is that eventual consistent read does less well than consistent read, although the difference is not significant.

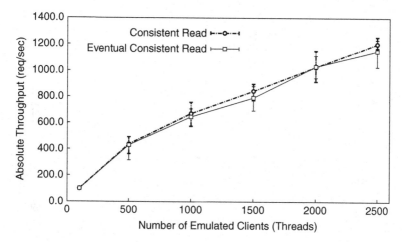

Fig. 5.7 Processed requests of Amazon SimpleDB

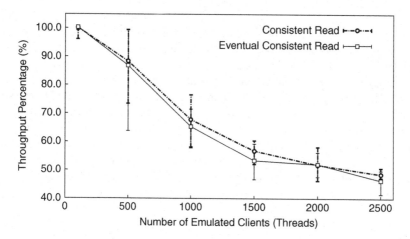

Fig. 5.8 Throughput percentage of Amazon SimpleDB

Monetary Cost

A new perspective on which customers are usually concerned in the context of cloud computing is the trade-off against monetary cost. In *us-west* region, Amazon SimpleDB charges $0.154 per SimpleDB machine hour, which is the amount of cost for using SimpleDB server capacity to complete requests, and therefore can vary depending on factors such as operation types and the amount of data to access. The monetary costs of two read consistency options for the runs described above are compared based on reported SimpleDB machine hour usage. Because the read operations of all runs constantly read 14 bytes string data from SimpleDB, the cost of read is constant, at $1.436 per one million requests, regardless of the consistency

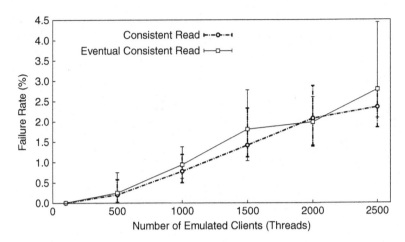

Fig. 5.9 Request failure rate of Amazon SimpleDB

options or workload. Also, the cost of write operations is constant at \$3.387 per one million requests as well, because the write operations of all runs always update SimpleDB with 14 bytes string data.

Although there is no published details about the implementation of Amazon SimpleDB, based on experiments, a few implementation ideas of SimpleDB can still be extracted. It seems feasible that Amazon SimpleDB maintains each item stored in three replicas, one primary and two secondaries. It is suspected that an eventually consistent read chooses one replica at random, and returns the value found there, while a consistent read will return the value from the primary. This aligns with previous experiment results showing the same latency and computational effort for the two kinds of read.

5.4   Discussion

This chapter reports on the performance and consistency of various cloud-based NoSQL storage platforms, as observed during some experiments. However, it is hard to say whether results can be extrapolated to predict expected experience for customers when using one of the platforms as all the usual caveats of benchmarks measurements still apply. For example, the workload may not be representative of the customers' needs, the size of the writes in the experiments is too small, and the number of data elements is small. Similarly, the metrics quoted may not be what matters to the customer as well, for example, the customer may be more or less skilled in operating the system; the experiments were not run for sufficiently long periods and the figures might reflect chance occurrences rather than system fundamentals.

Additionally, there are other particular issues when measuring cloud computing platforms. The cloud service provider moves on quickly and might change any aspect of hardware or software without providing sufficient advance notice to the customers. For example, even if the algorithm used by a platform currently provides read-your-writes, the cloud service provider could shift to a different implementation that does not provide the current guarantee. As another example, a cloud service provider that currently places all replicas within a single data center might implement geographical distribution, with replicas stored across data centers for better reliability. Such a change could happen without awareness of the customers, but it might lead to a situation where eventual consistent reads have observably better performance than consistent reads. Similarly, the background load on the cloud computing platforms might have a large impact, on latency or availability or consistency, but the customer cannot control or even measure what that load is at any time [208]. For all these reasons, our current observations that eventual consistent reads are no better for the customer, might not hold true in the future.

Also taking the observations reported in this chapter as an example, The reported results are mainly obtained during October and November in 2011. Before that a similar experiments were conducted in May 2011 as well. By doing the comparison, most aspects were similar between the two sets of experiments, in particular the 500 ms latency till Amazon SimpleDB reached 99% chance for a fresh response to a read, the high chance of fresh data in eventual consistent reads in Amazon S3, Microsoft Windows Azure Blob Storage, and Google App Engine Datastore, and the lack of performance difference between SimpleDB for reads with different consistency. Other aspects had changed, for example in the earlier measurements there was less variation in the response time seen by reads on SimpleDB.

In order to achieve high availability and low latency, many NoSQL storage platforms drop the guarantee of strong consistency, by avoiding two-phase commit or synchronous access to a quorum of sites. Therefore, it is commonly said that developers should work around this by designing applications that can work with eventual consistency or similar weaker models. This chapter also examined the experience of the customer of NoSQL storage, in regard to weak consistency and possible performance trade-offs to justify its use, specifically by focusing on Amazon SimpleDB. This information should help a developer who is seeking to understand the new NoSQL storage platforms, and who needs to make sensible choices about choosing the right storage platform.

This chapter found that platforms differed widely in how much weak consistency is seen by customers. On some platforms, the customer is not able to observe any inconsistency or staleness in the data, over several million reads through a week. It seems that inconsistency is presumably possible, but are very rare. It might only happen if there is a failure of the NoSQL storage platforms. Therefore, the risk of inconsistency seems less important when compared to other sources of data corruption, such as bad data entry, operator error, customers repeating input, fraud by insiders, and etc. Any system design needs to have recourse to manual processes to fix the mistakes and errors from these other sources, and the same processes should be able to cover rare inconsistency-induced difficulties. On these platforms, it might be an option for the developer to sensibly treat eventual consistent reads as if they are consistent, accepting the rare errors as being unavoidable and thus its impact needs to be carefully managed.

On Amazon SimpleDB, the customer who requests eventual consistent reads experiences frequent stale reads. Also, this choice does not provide other desirable options like read-your-writes and monotonic reads. Thus the developer who uses eventual consistent reads must take great care in application design, to code around the potential dangers. However, in regard to no incentive in reducing latency, observed availability, and monetary cost, there is, in fact, no compensating benefit for the developer from choosing eventual consistent reads instead of using consistent reads. There may be benefits to the service provider when eventual consistent reads are done, but at present these gains have not been passed on to the customer. Thus on this platform in its current implementation, there is no significant monetary and performance benefits for a developer to code with eventual consistent reads.

Chapter 6
Replicating Virtualized Database Servers

In general, virtualization technology is increasingly being used to improve the manageability of software systems and lower their total cost of ownership. Resource virtualization technologies add a flexible and programmable layer of software between applications and the resources used by these applications. One among several approaches for deploying data-intensive applications in cloud platforms, called the *virtualized database servers* approach, takes advantage of virtualization technologies by taking an existing application designed for a conventional data center, and then porting it to run on virtual machines in the public cloud. Such migration process usually requires minimal changes in the architecture or the code of the deployed application. In this approach, database servers, like any other software components, are migrated to run in virtual machines. One of the main advantages of this approach is that the application can have full control in dynamically allocating and configuring the physical resources of the database tier as needed. Hence, software applications can fully utilize the elasticity feature of the cloud environment to achieve their defined and customized scalability or cost reduction goals. In addition, this approach enables the software applications to build their geographically distributed database clusters. Without the cloud, building such in-house cluster would require self-owned infrastructure which represent an option that can be only afforded by big enterprises.

A common feature to the different cloud offerings of the NoSQL database as a service and the relational database as a service is the creation and management of multiple replicas of the stored data while a replication architecture is running behind-the-scenes to enable automatic failover management and ensure high availability of the service. In the previous chapter, experimental investigation of customer-based observations of the consistency, data staleness and performance properties of various cloud NoSQL databases have been carried out. In this chapter, virtualized database servers are the main target for exploration. The aim is to set a first yard stone in evaluating the performance characteristics of virtualized database

L. Zhao et al., *Cloud Data Management*, DOI 10.1007/978-3-319-04765-2__6,
© Springer International Publishing Switzerland 2014

servers in cloud environment. In particular, this chapter focuses on addressing the following questions with regards to the *master-slave* database replication strategy on Amazon EC2:

- How well does the master-slave replication strategy scale with an increasing workload and an increasing number of virtualized database replica servers in cloud? In principle, we try to understand what factors act as limits on achievable scale.
- What is the average replication delay or window of data staleness that could exist with an increasing number of virtualized database replica servers and different configurations to the geographical locations of the slave databases?

The remainder of this chapter is structured as follows. In Sect. 6.1, a few design decisions that are related to the benchmark application are explained, including customizing Cloudstone implementing fine-grained time/date function in MySQL, and applying clock synchronization in cloud. Meanwhile, Sect. 6.2 details the implementation of the experimental framework and the experimental environment. While the results of our experiments are presented in Sect. 6.3. Finally, the conclusion of the experiments are discussed Sect. 6.4.

6.1   Design of Benchmark Application

Figure 6.1 shows the overall architecture of relational database as a service benchmark application. In general, it is a three-layer implementation. The first layer is a customized Cloudstone benchmark [1] which controls the read/write ratio and the workload. The second layer includes a master database that receives write operations from the benchmark and is responsible for propagating *writesets* to slaves. The third layer is a group of slaves which are responsible for processing read operations and updating writesets.

The design of the benchmark tool is relational-database-focused and replication-precision-driven [242]. Therefore, there are several issues need to be addressed during the design of the benchmark application. Such as enforcing Cloudstone to benchmark database tier only, enabling the ability of benchmarking replication delay, tweaking time/date function in MySQL for precious resolution to calculate a replication delay, and enforcing clock synchronizations. All the detailed design decisions are discussed as following.

Customized Cloudstone

The Cloudstone benchmark has been designed as a performance measurement tool for Web 2.0 applications. The benchmark mimics a Web 2.0 social events calendar that allows users to perform individual operations such as browsing, searching,

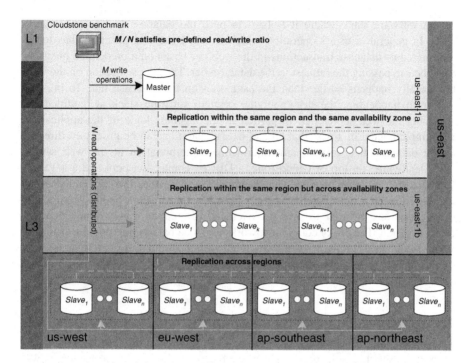

Fig. 6.1 The architecture of relational database as a service benchmark application

and creating events, as well as, social operations such as joining and tagging events [210]. Unlike Web 1.0 applications, Web 2.0 applications impose many different behavioral demands on the database. One of the differences is on the write pattern. As contents of Web 2.0 applications depend on user contributions via blogs, photos, videos and tags. More write transactions are expected to be processed. Another difference is on the tolerance with data consistency. In general, Web 2.0 applications are more acceptable to data staleness. For example, it might not be a mission-critical goal for a social network application like Facebook to immediately have a user's new status available to his friends. However, a consistency window of some seconds or even some minutes would be still acceptable. Therefore, it is believed that the design and workload characteristics of the Cloudstone benchmark is more suitable to the purpose of the study rather than other benchmarks such as TPC-W [49] or RUBiS [42] which are more representative of Web 1.0-like applications.

The original software stack of Cloudstone consists of three components: web application, database, and load generator. Throughout the benchmark, the load generator generates load against the web application which in turn makes use of the database. The benchmark has been designed for benchmarking the performance of each tier for Web 2.0 applications. However, the original design of the benchmark limits the purpose of the experiments by mainly focusing on the database tier of the software stack where it is hard to push the database to its performance limit. In general, a user's operation which is sent by a load generator has to be interpreted as database transactions in the web tier based on a predefined business logic before passing the request to the database tier. Thus the saturation on the web tier usually happens earlier than the saturation on the database tier. To prevent this from happening, the design of the original software stack is modified by removing the web server tier. In particular, the business logic of the application is re-implemented in a way that an end-user's operation can be processed directly at the database tier without any intermediate interpretation at the web server tier. Meanwhile, on top of Cloudstone, a DBCP[1] connection pool and a MySQL Connector/J[2] are implemented. The pool component enables the application users to reuse the connections that have been released by other users who have completed their operations in order to save the overhead of creating a new connection for each operation. The proxy component works as a load balancer among the available virtualized database replica servers where all write operations are sent to the master while all read operations are distributed among slaves.

MySQL Replication with a Fine-Grained Time/Date Function

Multiple MySQL replication are deployed to compose the database tier. Two components are implemented to monitor replication delay in MySQL, including a *Heartbeats* database and a time/date function for each virtualized database replica server. The Heartbeats database, synchronized in the form of an SQL statement across replica servers, maintains a *heartbeat* table which records an *id* and a *timestamp* in each row. A heartbeat plug-in for Cloudstone is implemented to periodically insert a new row with a global id and a local timestamp to the master during the experiment. Once the insert query is replicated to slaves, every slave re-executes the query by committing the global id and its own local timestamp. The replication delay from the master to slaves is then calculated as the difference of two timestamps between the master and each slave. In practice, there are two challenges with respect to achieving a fine-grained measurement of replication delay: the resolution of the time/date function and the clock synchronization between the master and slaves. The time/date function offered by MySQL has a resolution of a second which represents an unacceptable solution because accurate measuring of the replication delay requires a higher precision. Thus, a user defined time/date function with a microsecond resolution is implemented based on a proposed solution to MySQL Bug #8523[3]. The clock synchronizations between the master and slaves

---

[1] http://commons.apache.org/dbcp/

[2] http://www.mysql.com/products/connector/

[3] http://bugs.mysql.com/bug.php?id=8523

are maintained by Network Time Protocol (NTP)[4] on Amazon EC2. The system clock is set to synchronize with multiple time servers every second to have a better resolution. More details in dealing with the clock synchronization issue in the cloud will be discussed in Sect. 6.1.

With the customized Cloudstone[5] and the heartbeat plug-in, it is possible to achieve the goal of measuring the end-to-end database throughput and the replication delay. In particular, two configurations of the read/write ratios, 50/50 and 80/20 are defined. More over, three configurations of the geographical locations based on *availability zones* and *regions* are also defined and listed as follows where availability zones are defined as distinct locations within a region and zones are separated into geographic areas or countries:

- *Same zone*: all slaves are deployed in the same availability zone of a region of the master database.
- *Different zones*: all slaves are in the same region as the master database, but in different availability zones.
- *Different regions*: all slaves are geographically distributed in a different region from where the master database is located.

The workload and the number of virtualized database replica servers start with a small number and gradually increase at a fixed step. Both numbers stop increasing if there are no throughput gained.

Clock Synchronization in Cloud

The clock synchronization issue refers to the fact that internal clocks of physical machines may differ due to the initial clock setting and subsequent clock drift. It results in time differences between two machines even though both machines perform the read operation at the same time. This issue could also happen to instances in the cloud environment, if two instances are deployed in distinct physical machines where the clock is not shared. As a matter of fact, it has been observed by [199] that all instances launched by a single Amazon EC2 account never run in the same physical node. Hence, all running instances that belong to a single account will exhibit the clock synchronization issue.

The replication delay in experiments is measured based on committed local timestamps on two or more virtualized database replica servers. Thus, the clock synchronization issue also exists in the replication delay. As the study is more interested in the changes of replication delay, rather than that of accuracy, an average relative replication delay is adopted to eliminate the time differences introduced by the clock synchronization issue. The average relative replication

---

[4]http://www.ntp.org/

[5]http://code.google.com/p/clouddb-replication/

delay is represented as the difference between two average replication delays on the same slave. One average replication delay represents the average of delays without running workloads while another represents the average of delays under a number of concurrent users. Both average is sampled with the top 5% and the bottom 5% data removed as outliers, because of network fluctuation. As both average delays come with stable time differences with NTP protocol enabled every second, the time difference can then be eliminated subtracting the difference. In experiments, the NTP is set to synchronize with multiple time servers every second for a more stable time difference.

6.2   Implementation of Benchmark Application

As the Fig. 6.1 illustrated, the replication experiments are conducted in Amazon EC2. The experiment setup is a three-layer implementation. The Cloudstone benchmark in the first layer controls the read/write ratio and the workload by separately adjusting the number of read and write operations and the number of concurrent users. As a large number of concurrent users emulated by the benchmark could be very resource-consuming, the benchmark is deployed in a large instance to avoid any overload on the application tier. The master database in the second layer receives the write operations from the benchmark and is responsible for propagating the writesets to the slaves. The master database runs in a small instance so that saturation is expected to be observed early. Both the master database server and the application benchmark are deployed in location of *us-east-1a*. The slaves in the third layer are responsible for processing read operations and updating writesets. The number of slaves in a group varies from one to the number where throughput limitation is hit. Several options for the deployment locations of the slaves have been used, namely, the same zone as the master in *us-east-1a*, different zones in *us-east-1b* and four possible different regions, ranging among *us-west*, *eu-west*, *ap-southeast* and *ap-northeast*. All slaves run in small instances for the same reason of provisioning the master instance.

Several sets of experiments have been implemented in order to investigate the end-to-end throughput and the replication delay. Each of these sets is designed to target a specific configuration regarding the geographical locations of the slave databases and the read/write ratio. Multiple runs are conducted by compounding different workloads and numbers of slaves. The benchmark is able to push the database system to a limit where no more throughput can be obtained by increasing the workload and the number of virtualized database replica servers. Every run lasts 35 m, including 10 m for ramp-up, 20 m for steady stage and 5 m for ramp-down. Moreover, for each run, both the master and slaves should start with a preloaded, fully-synchronized database.

6.3 Trade-Off Analysis of Virtualized Database Servers

End-to-End Throughput

Figure 6.2 to 6.7 show the throughput trends for up to 4 and 11 slaves with mixed configurations of three locations and two read/write ratios. Both experiment results indicate that MySQL with asynchronous master-slave replication is limited to scale due to the saturation that happened to the master database.

In particular, the throughput trends react to saturation movement and transition in virtualized database replica servers in regard to an increasing workload and an increasing number of replica servers. In general, the observed saturation point (the point right after the observed maximum throughput of a number of slaves), appearing in slaves at the beginning, moves along with an increasing workload when more slaves are synchronized to the master. But eventually, the saturation will transit from slaves to the master where the scalability limit is achieved. Taking the Fig. 6.5 of throughput trends with configurations of same zone and 50/50 ratio as an example, the saturation point of 1 slave is initially observed under 100 workloads due to the full utilization of the slave's CPU. When a 2nd slave is attached, the saturation point shifts to 175 workloads where both slaves reach their maximum CPU utilization while the master's CPU usage rate is also approaching its limit. Thus, ever since the 3rd slave is added, 175 workloads remain as the saturation point, but with the master being saturated instead of the slaves. Once the master

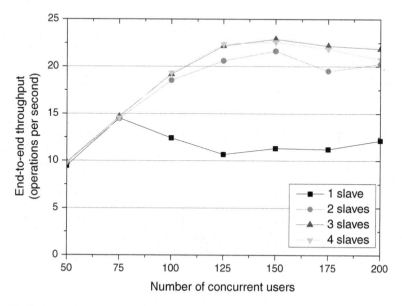

Fig. 6.2 End-to-end throughput with 50/50 read/write ratio and 300 initial data size in the same zone

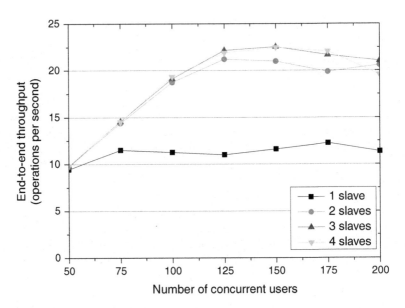

Fig. 6.3 End-to-end throughput with 50/50 read/write ratio and 300 initial data size in different zones

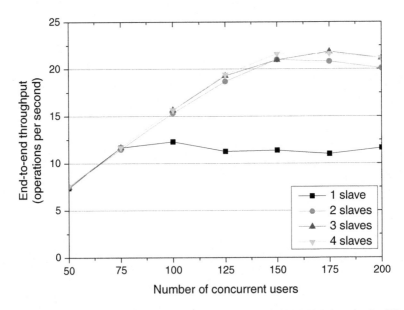

Fig. 6.4 End-to-end throughput with 50/50 read/write ratio and 300 initial data size in different regions

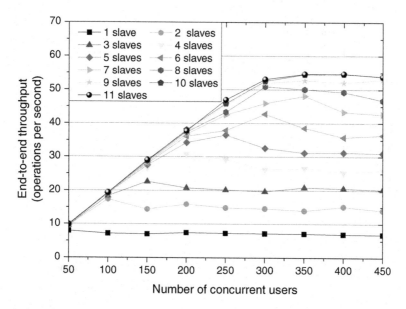

Fig. 6.5 End-to-end throughput with 80/20 read/write ratio and 600 initial data size in the same zone

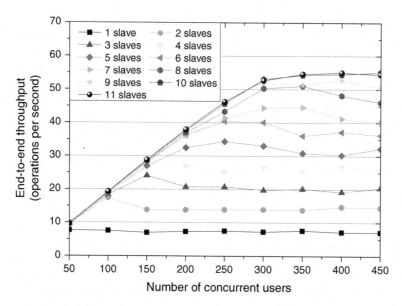

Fig. 6.6 End-to-end throughput with 80/20 read/write ratio and 600 initial data size in different zones

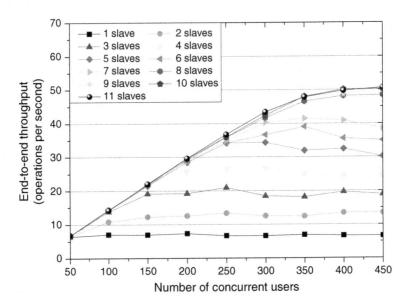

Fig. 6.7 End-to-end throughput with 80/20 read/write ratio and 600 initial data size in different regions

is in the saturation status, adding more slaves does not help with improving the scalability because the overloaded master fails to offer extra capacity for improving write throughput to maintain the read/write ratio that corresponds to the increment of the read throughput. Hence, the read throughput is constrained by the benchmark, for the purpose of maintaining the predefined read/write ratio at 50/50. The slaves are over provisioned in the case of 3 and 4 slaves, as the suppressed read throughput prevents slaves from being fully utilized. The similar saturation transition also happens to 3 slaves at 50/50 ratio in different zones and different regions in Figs. 6.3 and 6.4 respectively, 10 slaves at 80/20 ratio in the same zone and different zones in Figs. 6.5 and 6.6 respectively, and also 9 slaves at 80/20 ratio in different regions in 6.7.

The configuration of the geographic locations is a factor that affects the end-to-end throughput, in the context of locations of users. In the case of our experiments, since all users emulated by Cloudstone send read operations from *us-east-1a*, distances between the users and the slaves increase by following in the order of same zone, different zones and different regions. Normally, a long distance incurs a slow round-trip time, which results in a small throughput for the same workload. Therefore, it is expected that a decrease of maximum throughput can be observed when configurations of locations follow the order of same zone, different zones and different regions. Moreover, the throughput degradation is also related to read percentages, the higher percentage the larger degradation. It explains why degradation of maximum throughput is more significant with the configuration of

80/20 read/write ratio as shown in Figs. 6.5–6.7. Hence, it is a good strategy to distribute replicated slaves to places that are close to users to improve end-to-end throughput.

The performance variation of instances is another factor that needs to be considered when deploying a database in the cloud. For throughput trends of 1 slave at 50/50 read/write ratio with configurations of different zones and different regions, respectively, if the configuration of locations is the only factor, it is expected that the maximum throughput in different zones in Fig. 6.3 would be larger than the one in different regions in Fig. 6.4. However, the main reason of throughput difference here is caused by the performance variation of instances rather than the configuration of the locations. The 1st slave from the same zone runs on top of a physical machine with an Intel Xeon E5430 2.66 GHz CPU. While another 1st slave from different zones is deployed in a physical machine powered by an Intel Xeon E5507 2.27 GHz CPU. Because of the performance differences between physical CPUs, the slave from the same zone performs better than the one from different zones. Previous research indicated that the coefficient of variation of CPU of small instances is 21% [208]. Therefore, it is a good strategy to validate the instance performance before deploying applications into the cloud, as poor-performing instances are launched randomly and can largely affect application performance.

Replication Delay

Figure 6.8–6.13 show the trends of the average relative replication delay for up to 4 and 11 slaves with mixed configurations of three locations and two read/write ratios. The results of both figures imply that the impact of the configurations of the geographical locations on replication delay is less important than that from the workload characteristics. The trends of the average relative replication delay respond to an increasing workload and an increasing number of virtualized database replica servers. For most cases, with the number of virtualized database replica servers being kept constant, the average relative replication delay surges along with an increasing workload. Because an increasing workload leads to more read and write operations sent to the slaves and the master database, respectively, the increasing read operations result in a higher resource demand on every slave, while the increasing write operations on the master database leads to, indirectly, increasing resource demand on slaves as more writesets are propagated to be committed on slaves. The two increasing demands push resource contention higher, resulting in the delay of committing writesets which subsequently increasing replication delay. Similarly, the average relative replication delay decreases along with an increasing number of replica servers as adding a new slave leads to a reduction in the resource contention and hence decreasing the replication delay. The configuration of the geographic location of the slaves play a less significant role in affecting replication delay, in comparison to the change of the workload characteristics. We measured the 1/2 round-trip time between the master in *us-west-1a* and the slave that uses

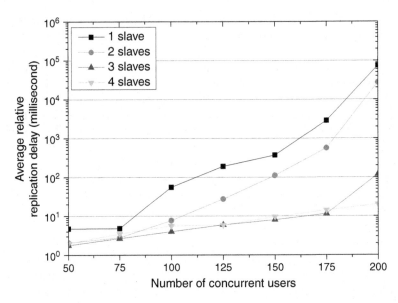

Fig. 6.8 Average relative replication delay with 50/50 read/write ratio and 300 initial data size in the same zone

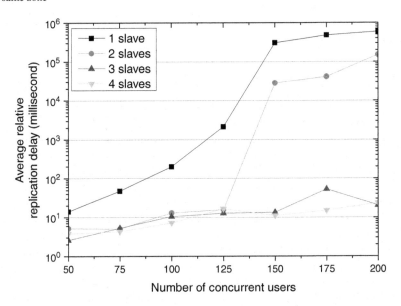

Fig. 6.9 Average relative replication delay with 50/50 read/write ratio and 300 initial data size in different zones

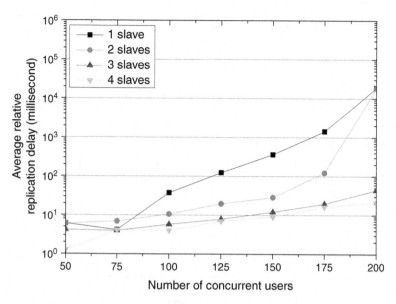

Fig. 6.10 Average relative replication delay with 50/50 read/write ratio and 300 initial data size in different regions

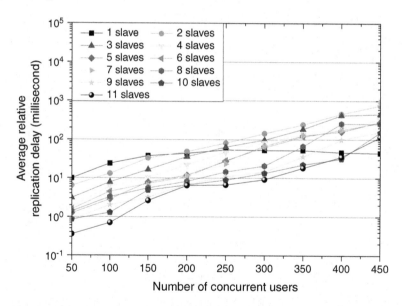

Fig. 6.11 Average relative replication delay with 80/20 read/write ratio and 600 initial data size in the same zone

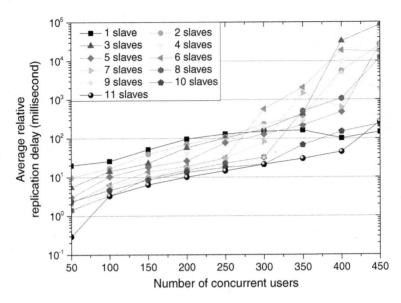

Fig. 6.12 Average relative replication delay with 80/20 read/write ratio and 600 initial data size in different zones

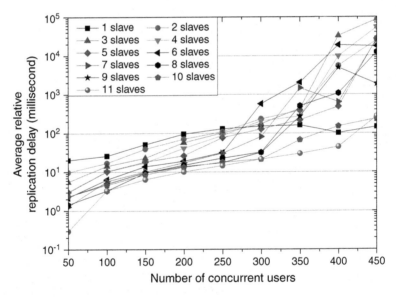

Fig. 6.13 Average relative replication delay with 80/20 read/write ratio and 600 initial data size in different regions

different configurations of geographic locations by running *ping*[6] command every second for a 20-minute period. The results suggest an average of 16, 21, and 173 ms for the 1/2 round-trip time for the same zone in Figs. 6.8 and 6.11, different zones in Figs. 6.9 and 6.12, and different regions in Figs. 6.10 and 6.13, respectively. However, the trends of the average relative replication delay can usually go up to two to four orders of magnitude as shown from Figs. 6.8–6.10, or one to three orders of magnitude as shown in Figs. 6.11–6.13. Therefore, it could be suggested that the geographic replication would be applicable in the cloud as long as workload characteristics can be well managed, such as having a smart load balancer which is able to balance the operations based on the estimated processing time.

6.4 Discussion

In practice, there are different approaches for deploying data-intensive applications in cloud platforms. In this chapter, the study is focused on the *virtualized database servers* approach where the resources of the database tiers are migrated to virtual machines in the public cloud. The behavior of the master-slave database replication strategy on Amazon EC2 has been experimentally evaluated using the Cloudstone benchmark and MySQL databases. The experiments involved two configurations of different workload read/write ratios, namely 50/50 and 80/20, and different configuration of the geographical locations of the virtualized database replica servers.

The results of the study show that the performance variation of the dynamically allocated virtual machines is an inevitable issue that needs to be considered when deploying database in the cloud. Clearly, it affects the end-to-end throughput. Additionally, different configurations of geographic locations can also noticeably affect the end-to-end throughput. For most cases, as the number of workload increases, the replication delay increases. However, as the number of slaves increases, the replication delay is found decreases. The effect of the configurations of geographic location is not as significant as increasing workloads in affecting the replication delay.

---

[6]http://linux.die.net/man/8/ping

Chapter 7
SLA-Driven Database Replication on Virtualized Database Servers

One of the main advantages of the cloud computing paradigm is that it simplifies the time-consuming processes of hardware provisioning, hardware purchasing and software deployment. Currently, the increasing numbers of cloud-hosted applications are generating and consuming increasing volumes of data at an unprecedented scale. Cloud-hosted database systems, such as virtualized database servers, powering these applications form a critical component in the software stack of these applications. Service level agreements (SLAs) represent the contract which captures the agreed upon guarantees between a service provider and its customers. The specifications of existing SLA for cloud services are not designed to flexibly handle even relatively straightforward performance and technical requirements of customer applications.

In this chapter, the problem of adaptive customer-centric management for replicated virtualized database servers in single or multiple data centers is tackled. A novel adaptive approach for SLA-based management of virtualized database servers from the customer perspective is presented. The framework is database platform-agnostic, supports virtualized database servers, and requires zero source code changes of the cloud-hosted software applications. It facilitates dynamic provisioning of the database tier in software stacks based on application-defined policies for satisfying their own SLA performance requirements, avoiding the cost of any SLA violation and controlling the monetary cost of the allocated computing resources. In this framework, the SLA of the customer applications are declaratively defined in terms of goals which are subjected to a number of constraints that are specific to the application requirements. The framework continuously monitors the application-defined SLA and automatically triggers the execution of necessary corrective actions, such as scaling out the database tier, when required. Therefore, the framework is able to keep several virtualized database replica servers in different data centers to support the different availability, scalability and performance improvement goals. The experimental results demonstrate the effectiveness of the SLA-based framework in providing the customer applications with the required flexibility for achieving their SLA requirements.

L. Zhao et al., *Cloud Data Management*, DOI 10.1007/978-3-319-04765-2_7,
© Springer International Publishing Switzerland 2014

The remainder of this chapter is structured as follows. Section 7.2 introduces the architecture of the adaptive framework. Details of the experiment implementation of the different components of the framework are discussed on Sect. 7.3. Then, the results of the experimental evaluation for the performance of the approach are presented in Sect. 7.4, followed by discussions and conclusions in Sect. 7.7.

7.1 SLA Management for Virtualized Database Servers

Cloud-based data management poses several challenges which go beyond traditional database technologies. In principle, outsourcing the operation of database applications to a cloud provider who, on the one hand, takes responsibility for providing the infrastructure and maintaining the system but, on the other hand, this cloud provider need to pool resources and operate them in a cost-efficient and dynamic way promise cost savings and elasticity in usage. In practice, most customers of cloud services will be willing to move their on premise setup to a cloud-hosted environment only if they can guarantee that their data are kept securely and privately as well as non-functional properties such as availability or performance are can be maintained.

An SLA is a contract between a service provider and its customers. SLAs capture the agreed upon guarantees between a service provider and its customer. They define the characteristics of the provided service including service level objectives (SLOs), such as maximum response times, minimum throughput rates, and data freshness, and define penalties if these objectives are not met by the service provider. In general, SLA management is a common general problem for the different types of software systems which are hosted in cloud environments for different reasons such as the unpredictable and bursty workloads from various users in addition to the performance variability in the underlying cloud resources. In particular, there are three typical parties in the cloud. To keep a consistent terminology through out the rest of this chapter, these parties are defined as follows:

- *Cloud service providers*: They offer the client provisioned and metered computing resources, such as CPU, storage, memory, and network, for rent within flexible time durations. In particular, they include: infrastructure as a service providers and platform as a service providers. The platform as a service providers can be further broken into several subcategories of which database as a service provider is one of them.
- *Cloud customers*: They represent the cloud-hosted software applications that utilize the services of cloud service providers and are financially responsible for their resource consumptions. Most of software as a service providers can be categorized into this party.
- *End-users*: They represent the legitimate users for the services or applications that are offered by cloud customers.

While cloud service providers charge cloud customers for renting computing resources to deploy their applications, cloud customers may or may not charge their

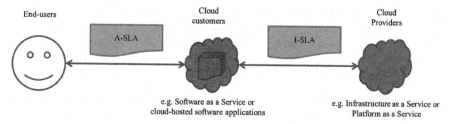

Fig. 7.1 SLA parties in cloud environments

end-users for processing their workloads, depending on the customers' business model. In both cases, the cloud customers need to guarantee their users' SLA. Otherwise, penalties are applied, in the form of lost revenue or reputation. For example, Amazon found that every 100 ms of latency costs them 1 % in sales and Google found that an extra 500 ms in search page generation time dropped traffic by 20 %.[1] In addition, large scale Web applications, such as eBay and Facebook, need to provide high assurances in terms of SLA metrics such as response times and service availability to their end-users. Without such assurances, service providers of these applications stand to lose their end-user base, and hence their revenues.

In practice, resource management and SLA guarantee falls into two layers: the cloud service providers and the cloud customers. In particular, the cloud service provider is responsible for the efficient utilization of the physical resources and guarantee their availability for their customers. The cloud customers are responsible for the efficient utilization of their allocated resources in order to satisfy the SLA of their end-users and achieve their business goals. Therefore, there are two types of service level agreements (SLAs):

- *Cloud infrastructure SLA (I-SLA)*: These SLA are offered by cloud providers to cloud customers to assure the quality levels of their cloud computing resources, including server performance, network speed, resources availability, and storage capacity.
- *Cloud application SLA (A-SLA)*: These guarantees relate to the levels of quality for the software applications which are deployed on a cloud infrastructure. In particular, cloud customers often offer such guarantees to their application's end users in order to assure the quality of services that are offered such as the application's response time and data freshness.

Figure 7.1 illustrates the relationship between I-SLA and A-SLA in the software stack of cloud-hosted applications. In practice, traditional cloud monitoring technologies, such as Amazon CloudWatch, focus on low-level computing resources. However, translating the SLAs of applications' transactions to the thresholds of utilization for low-level computing resources is a very challenging task and is

---

[1]http://glinden.blogspot.com/2006/11/marissa-mayer-at-web-20.html.

usually done in an ad-hoc manner due to the complexity and dynamism inherent in the interaction between the different tiers and components of the system. In particular, meeting SLAs which are agreed with end-users by cloud customers' applications using the traditional techniques for resource provisioning is a very challenging task due to many reasons such as:

- *Highly dynamic workload*: An application service can be used by large numbers of end-users and highly variable load spikes in demand can occur depending on the day and the time of year, and the popularity of the application. In addition, the characteristic of workload could vary significantly from one application type to another and possible fluctuations on the workload characteristics which could be of several orders of magnitude on the same business day may occur [83]. Therefore, predicting the workload behavior and consequently devising an accurate plan to manage of the computing resource requirements are very challenging tasks.
- *Performance variability of cloud resources*: Several studies have reported that the variation of the performance of cloud computing resources is high [112,172,208]. As a result, currently, cloud service providers do not provide adequate SLAs for their service offerings. Particularly, most providers guarantee only the availability, rather than the performance, of their services [68, 124].
- *Uncertain behavior*: One complexity that arises with the virtualization technology is that it becomes harder to provide performance guarantees and to reason about a particular application's performance because the performance of an application hosted on a virtual machine becomes a function of applications running in other virtual machines hosted on the same physical machine. In addition, it may be challenging to harness the full performance of the underlying hardware, given the additional layers of indirection in virtualized resource management [199].

Several approaches have been proposed for dynamic provisioning of computing resources based on their effective utilization [115, 190, 232]. These approaches are mainly geared towards the perspective of cloud providers. Wood et al. [232] have presented an approach for dynamic provisioning of virtual machines. It defines a unique metric based on the data consumption of the three physical computing resources, including CPU, network, and memory to make the provisioning decision. Padala et al. [190] carried out black-box profiling of the applications and built an approximated model which relates performance attributes such as the response time to the fraction of processor allocated to the virtual machine on which the application is running. *Dolly* [96] is a virtual machine cloning technique to spawn database replicas and provisioning shared-nothing replicated databases in the cloud. The technique proposes database provisioning cost models to adapt the provisioning policy to the low-level cloud resources according to application requirements. Rogers et al. [200] proposed two approaches for managing the resource provisioning challenge for cloud databases. The black-box provisioning uses end-to-end performance results of sample query executions, whereas white-box provisioning uses a finer grained approach that relies on the DBMS optimizer to predict the physical resource consumption, such as disk I/O, memory, and CPU, for each query. Floratou et al. [131] have studied the performance and associated costs in the relational database as a service environments. The results show that given a range of pricing models and the flexibility of the allocation of resources in cloud-based environments, it is hard for a user to figure out their actual monthly cost upfront. Soror et al. [211] introduced a virtualization design advisor that uses information about the database workloads to provide offline recommendations of workload-specific virtual machines configurations.

In practice, it is a very challenging goal to delegate the management of the SLA requirements of the customer applications to the cloud service provider due to the wide heterogeneity in the workload characteristics, details and granularity of SLA requirements, and cost management objectives of the very large number of customer applications that can be simultaneously running in a cloud environment. Therefore, it becomes a significant issue for the cloud customers to be able to monitor and adjust the deployment of their systems if they intend to offer viable SLAs to their customers. Failing to achieve these goals will jeopardize the sustainable growth of cloud computing in the future and may result in valuable applications being moved away from the cloud. In the following sections, we present our customer-centric approach for managing the SLA requirements of virtualized database servers.

7.2 Architecture of SLA Management Framework

Figure 7.2 shows an overview of the framework architecture which consists of three main modules: the *monitor module*, the *control module* and the *action module*. In this architecture, the monitor module is responsible for continuously tracking the replication delay of each virtualized database replica server and feeding the control module with the collected information. The control module is responsible for continuously checking the replication delay of each replica server against its associated application-defined SLA of data freshness and triggers the action module to scale out the database tier with a new virtualized database replica server when it detects any SLA-violation in any current replica server.

The key design principles of the framework architecture are to be application-independent and to require no code modification on the customer software applications that the framework will support. In order to achieve these goals, the framework relies on a database proxying mechanism which forwards database requests to the underlying databases and returns the results to the client transparently using an intermediate piece of software, the proxy, without the need of having any database drivers installed [203]. In particular, a database proxy software is a simple program that sits between the client application and the database server that can monitor, analyze or transform their communications. Such flexibility allows for a wide variety of uses such as load balancing, query analysis and query filtering. The implementation details for each of the three main modules of the framework architecture will be discussed in the remaining part of the section.

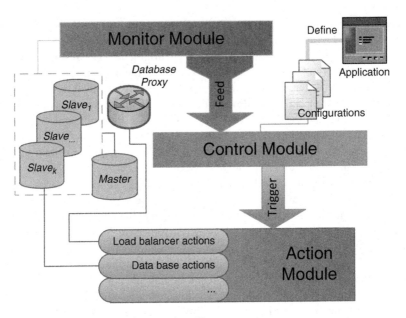

Fig. 7.2 The SLA management framework architecture

As mentioned before, the design of the framework follows two main principles, function-extensible and application-independent. Any new objectives, such as throughput, can be easily added with pairs of implementations in both monitor and control modules. Actions, such as starting a new virtualized database replica server, for new objectives can be reused from a list of available actions in the action module, or can be added when no satisfied actions is found. It is worth bearing in mind that all objectives are added with no code modification to existing application that is managed by the framework. However, some tools, databases, or plug-ins need to be enabled at the system level to enable the objectives to be monitored properly, for example, recording all queries to be bypassed in the load balancer.

In general, there exist many forms of SLAs with different metrics. In this chapter, we focus on the following two main consumer-centric SLA metrics:

- *Data freshness*: which represents the tolerated window of data staleness for each database replica. In other words, it represents the time between a committed update operation on the master database and the time when the operation is propagated and committed to the database replica.
- *Transaction response time*: which represents the time between a transaction is presented to the database system and the time when the transaction execution is completed.

Monitor Module

The monitor module is responsible for tracking the replication delay between the virtualized database master server and each virtualized database replica server. The replication delay for each replica server is computed by measuring the time difference of two associated local timestamps committed on the master and the replica server. Therefore, a *Heartbeats* database is created in the master and each synchronized slave database server. Each Heartbeats database maintains a *heartbeat* table with two fields: an *id* and a *timestamp*. A database request to insert a new record with a global id and a local timestamp is periodically sent to the master. Once the insert record request is replicated to the slaves, every slave re-executes the request by committing the same global id and its own local timestamp. The update frequency of a record in the master is configurable, named as *heartbeat interval* in millisecond unit. The default configuration of the heartbeat interval is set to be 1 s in the experiments. While records are updated in the master database and propagated over all slaves periodically, the monitor module maintains a pool of threads that are run frequently to read up-to-date records from the master and slaves. The read frequency is also a configurable parameter in millisecond unit, known as *monitor interval*. In order to reduce the burden of repetitive read requests on the virtualized database replica servers, all records are only fetched once, and all local timestamps extracted from records are kept locally in the monitor module for further calculation.

The replication delay calculation between the master and a slave is initiated by the corresponding thread of the slave every time after fetching the records. In the general case of assuming that there are n and k local timestamps in total in the master array, $timestamps_m$, and the slave array, $timestamps_s$, the slave's i^{th} replication delay $delay[i]$ is computed as follows:

$$delay[i] = timestamps_s[i] - timestamps_m[i] \qquad (7.1)$$

where $i \leq k = n$ and the master and the slave databases are fully synchronized. In the case of $k < n$ where there is partial synchronization between the master and the slave databases which composes of both a consistent part and an inconsistent part, the computation of the $delay[i]$ of the slave can be broken into two parts: The delay of the consistent part with $i \leq k$ is computed using Eq. 7.1.

The delay of the inconsistent part with $k < i \leq n$ is computed as follows:

$$delay[i] = timestamps_s[k] - timestamps_m[k]$$
$$+ timestamps_m[i] - timestamps_m[k] \qquad (7.2)$$

In the case of $n < k$ where indeterminacy could happen due to the missing of $k + 1^{th}$ local timestamp and beyond (this situation could happen when a recent fetch of the slave occurs later than the fetch of the master), the $delay[i]$ of the slave uses Eq. 7.1 for $i \leq n$ and the $delay[i]$ of the slave for $n < i \leq k$ will be neglected as there is no appropriate local timestamps of the master that can be used for calculating the replication delay. The neglected calculations will be carried out later after the array of the master is updated.

Control Module

The control module maintains the configuration information about:

- The configurations of the load balancer, including proxy address and proxy script.
- The configurations of the monitor module, such as heartbeat interval and monitor interval.
- The access information of each virtualized database replica server, namely host address, port number, user name, and password.
- The location information of each virtualized database replica server, such as *us-east*, *us-west*, *eu-west*.
- And in addition to the application-defined SLA, the tolerated replication delay of each virtualized database replica server for this study.

In practice, the SLA of the replication delay for each virtualized database replica server, $delay_{sla}$, is defined as an integer value in the unit of millisecond which represents two main components:

$$delay_{sla} = delay_{rtt} + delay_{tolerance} \tag{7.3}$$

where the round-trip time component of the SLA replication delay, $delay_{rtt}$, is the average round-trip time from the virtualized database master server to the virtualized database replica server. In particular, it represents the minimum delay cost for replicating data from the master to the associated slave. The tolerance component of the replication delay, $delay_{tolerance}$, is defined by a constant value which represents the tolerance limit of the period of the time for the replica server to be inconsistent. This tolerance component can vary from one replica server to another depending on many factors such as the application requirements, the geographic location of the replica server, and the workload characteristics and the load balancing strategy of each application.

One of the main responsibilities of the control module is to trigger the action module for adding a new virtualized database replica server, when necessary, in order to avoid any violation in the application-defined SLA of data freshness for the active replicas. In framework implementation, an intuitive strategy is followed to trigger the action module for adding a new replica server when it detects a number of continuous up-to-date monitored replication delays of a replica server which exceeds its application-defined threshold, T, of SLA violation of data freshness. In other words, for a running replica server, if the latest T monitored replication delays are violating its SLA of data freshness, the control module will trigger the action module to activate the geographically closest replica server according to the location of the violating replica server. It is worthy to note that the strategy of the control module in making the decisions regarding the addition a new replica server in order to avoid any violence of the application-defined SLA can play an important role in determining the overall performance of the framework. However, it is not the main focus of this chapter to investigate different strategies for making these decisions. This aspect will be left for future work.

In the last chapter, it has been noted that the effect of the configurations of geographic location of the virtualized database replica server is not as significant as the effect of the overloading workloads in increasing the staleness window of the replica servers. Therefore, the control module can decide to stop an active replica server when it detects a decreasing workload that can be served by less number of replica servers without violating the application-defined SLAs in order to reduce the monetary cost of the running application.

Action Module

The action module is responsible for adding a new virtualized database replica server when it is triggered by the action module. In general, adding a new replica server involves extracting database content from an existing replica server and copying that content to a new replica server. In practice, the time of executing these operations mainly depends on the database size. To provision virtualized database replica servers in a timely fashion, it is necessary to periodically snapshot the database state in order to minimize the database extraction and copying time to that of only the snapshot synchronization time. There is a trade-off between the time to snapshot the database, the size of the transactional log and the amount of update transactions in the workload. This trade-off can be further optimized by applying recently proposed live database migration techniques [96, 128].

In order to keep the experiments focused on the main concerns of the framework, a set of hot backups, which are originally not used for serving the application requests but kept synchronized, are used and then can be made active and used by the load balancer for serving the application requests when the action module is triggered for adding a new virtualized database replica server. The study of the cost and effect of the live database migration activities will also be left as future work.

7.3 Implementation of SLA Management Framework

Figure 7.3 illustrates the setup of experiments for the SLA management framework in the Amazon EC2 platform. Besides the SLA management framework, the experiment setup also adopts the customized Cloudstone benchmark, MySQL replication with a fine-grained time/date function, and MySQL Proxy,[2] as necessary, components.

---

[2]https://launchpad.net/mysql-proxy.

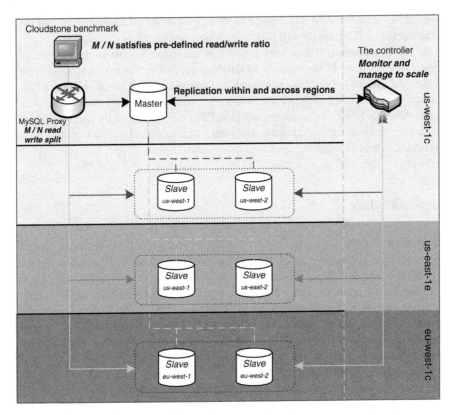

Fig. 7.3 The implementation of the SLA management framework in the setup of experiments

The experiment setup is a multiple-layer implementation. The first layer represents the Cloudstone benchmark which generates an increasing workload of database requests with a fixed read/write ratio. The benchmark is deployed in a large instance to avoid any overload on the application tier. The second layer hosts the MySQL Proxy and the SLA management framework. MySQL Proxy with read and write split enabled resides in the middle between the benchmark and the virtualized database replica servers, and acts as a load balancer to forward read and write operations to the master and slaves correspondingly. The third layer represents the database tier that consists of all the replica servers where the master database receives the write operations from the load balancer after which it becomes responsible for propagating the *writesets* to all the virtualized database slave servers. The master database runs in a small instance so that an increasing replication delay is expected to be observed along with an increasing workload. The master database is closely located to the benchmark, the load balancer and the SLA management framework. They are all deployed in the location of *us-west*. The slave servers are responsible for serving the read operations and updating the writesets. They are deployed in three regions, namely: *us-west*, *us-east* and *eu-west*. All slaves run in small instances for the same reason of provisioning the master instance.

Two sets of experiments are implemented in order to evaluate the effectiveness of the SLA management framework in terms of its effectiveness on maximizing the end-to-end system throughput and minimizing the replication delay for the underlying virtualized database servers. In the first set of experiments, the value of the tolerance component, $delay_{tolerance}$, of the SLA replication delay is fixed at 1,000 ms, and the monitor interval, $intvl_{mon}$, is varied among the following set of values, 60, 120, 240, and 480 s. In the second set of experiments, in contrast to the first test, the monitor interval, $intvl_{mon}$, is fixed at 120 s, and the SLA of replication delay is adjusted by varying the tolerance component of the replication delay, $delay_{tolerance}$, among the values of 500, 1,000, 2,000, and 4,000 ms. In the experiment environment, the round-trip component for the virtualized database replica servers is determined with *ping* command running every second for a 10 min period. The average round-trip time of three geographical regions is 30, 130, and 200 ms from the master to slaves in *us-west*, *us-east*, and *eu-west* respectively.

Every experiment runs for a period of 3,000 s with a starting workload of 220 concurrent users and database requests with read/write ratio at 80/20. The workload gradually increases in steps of 20 concurrent users every 600 s so that each experiment ends with a workload of 300 concurrent users. Each experiment deploys 6 virtualized database replica servers in 3 regions where each region hosts two replica servers: the first replica server is an active replica which is used from the start of the experiment for serving the database requests of the application while the second one is a hot backup which is not used for serving the application requests at the beginning of the experiment but can be added by the action module, as necessary, when triggered by the control module. Finally, in addition to the two sets of experiments, two experiments without the adaptive SLA management framework are conducted as baselines for measuring the end-to-end throughputs and replication delays of 3 and 6 slaves, representing the minimum and the maximum number of running replica servers, respectively. For all experiments, the value of the heartbeat interval, $intvl_{heart}$, is set to 1 s and the value of the threshold, T, for the maximum possible continuous SLA violations for any replica server is calculated using the following formula $T = \frac{intvl_{mon}}{intvl_{heart}}$.

7.4 Evaluation of SLA Management Framework

End-to-End Throughput

Table 7.1 presents the end-to-end throughput results for the set of experiment with different configuration parameters. The baseline experiments represent both the minimum and the maximum end-to-end throughput results with 22.33 and 38.96 operations per second respectively. The end-to-end throughput delivered by the

Table 7.1 The effect of the adaptive SLA management framework on the end-to-end system throughput

Experiment parameters	The monitor interval, $intvl_{mon}$, in seconds	The tolerance of replication delay, $delay_{tolerance}$, in milliseconds	Number of running replica servers	Running time of all replica servers in seconds	End-to-end throughput in operations per seconds	Figure
Baselines with fixed number of replica servers	N/A	N/A	3	9,000	22.33	Fig. 7.4
	N/A	N/A	6	18,000	38.96	Fig. 7.5
Varying the monitor interval, $intvl_{mon}$	60	1,000	3 → 6	15,837	38.43	Fig. 7.6
	120	1,000	3 → 6	15,498	36.45	Fig. 7.7
	240	1,000	3 → 6	13,935	34.12	Fig. 7.8
	480	1,000	3 → 6	12,294	31.40	Fig. 7.9
Varying the tolerance of replication delay, $delay_{tolerance}$	120	500	3 → 6	15,253	37.44	Fig. 7.10
	120	1,000	3 → 6	15,498	36.45	Fig. 7.7
	120	2,000	3 → 6	13,928	36.33	Fig. 7.11
	120	4,000	3 → 6	14,437	34.68	Fig. 7.12

adaptive SLA management framework for the different experiments fall between the two baselines based on the variance on the monitor interval, $intvl_{mon}$, and the tolerance of replication delay, $delay_{tolerance}$. However, it is worth noting that the end-to-end throughput can be still affected by a lot of performance variations in the cloud environment such as hardware performance variation, network variation and warm up time of the virtualized database servers. Similarly, The two baseline experiments also represent the minimum and the maximum running time of all virutalized database replica servers with 9,000 and 18,000 s respectively. Therefore, the total running time of the replica servers for the different experiments fall within the range of 9,000 and 18,000 s. Each experiment starts with 3 active replicas which are gradually increased during the experiments based on the configurations of the monitor interval and the SLA of replication delay parameters until it finally ends with 6 replica servers.

In general, the relationship between the running time of all slaves and end-to-end throughput is not straightforward. Intuitively, a longer monitor interval or a longer tolerance of replication delay usually postpones the addition of new virtualized database replica servers and consequently reduces the end-to-end throughput. The results show that the tolerance of the replication delay parameter, $delay_{tolerance}$ is more sensitive than the monitor interval parameter, $intvl_{mon}$. For example, setting the values of the tolerance of the replication delay to 4,000 and 1,000 result in longer running times of the replica servers than when the values are set to 2,000 and 500. On the other hand, the increase of running time of all replica servers clearly follows a linear trend along with the increase of the end-to-end throughput. However, a general conclusion can not be made as the trend is likely affected by the workload characteristics.

Replication Delay

Figures 7.4–7.12 illustrate the effect of the adaptive SLA management framework on the performance of the replication delay for the virtualized database replica servers. Figures 7.4 and 7.5 show the replication delay of the two baseline cases that will be used for comparison purposes. They represent the experiments of running with a fixed number of virtualized database replica servers, 3 and 6 respectively, from the start until the end of the experiments. Figure 7.4 shows that the replication delay tends to follow different patterns for different replica servers. The two trends of virtualized database servers in *us-west-1* and *eu-west-1* surge significantly at 260 and 280 users respectively. At the same time, the trend of virtualized database server in *us-east-1* tends to be stable through out the entire running time of the experiment. The main reason behind that is the performance variation between the virtualized database servers for replicas, as both virtualized database servers in *us-west-1* and *eu-west-1* are powered by Intel(R) Xeon(R) E5507 @ 2.27 GHz CPU, whereas the server in *us-east-1* is deployed with a higher performance CPU, Intel(R) Xeon(R) E5645 @ 2.40 GHz CPU. Due to the performance differences between the physical

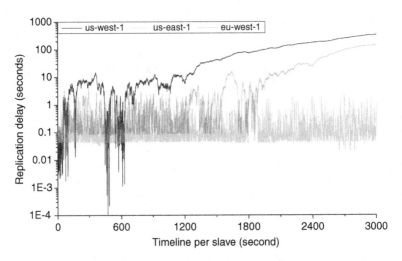

Fig. 7.4 The performance of the replication delay for fixed 3 replica servers with the framework disabled

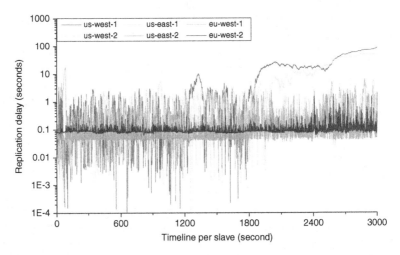

Fig. 7.5 The performance of the replication delay for fixed 6 replica servers with the framework disabled

CPUs specifications, the virtualized database server in *us-east-1* is able to handle the amount of operations that saturated the servers in *us-west-1* and *eu-west-1*. Moreover, with an identical CPU for *us-west-1* and *eu-west-1*, the former seems to surge at an earlier point than the latter. This is basically because of the difference in the geographical location of the two virtualized database servers. As illustrated in Fig. 7.3, the MySQL Proxy location is closer to the virtualized database server in *us-west-1* than the server in *eu-west-1*. Therefore, the forwarded database operations by the MySQL Proxy take less time to reach the server in *us-west-1* than to the server

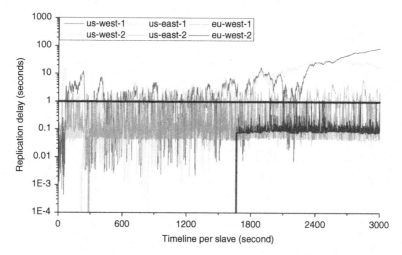

Fig. 7.6 The performance of the replication delay for up to 6 replica servers with the framework enabled, $delay_{tolerance} = 1,000$ ms, and $intvl_{mon} = 60$ s

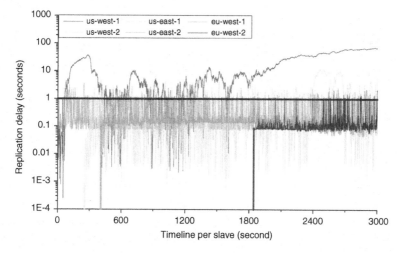

Fig. 7.7 The performance of the replication delay for up to 6 replica servers with the framework enabled, $delay_{tolerance} = 1,000$ ms, and $intvl_{mon} = 120$ s

in *eu-west-1* which leads to more congestion on the *us-west-1* side. Similarly, in Fig. 7.5, the replication delay tends to surge in both virtualized database servers in *us-west-1* and *us-west-2* for the same reason of the difference in the geographic location of the underlying virtualized database server.

Figures 7.7, and 7.10–7.12 show the results of the replication delay for the experiments using different values for the monitor interval, $intvl_{mon}$, and the tolerance of replication delay, $delay_{tolerance}$, parameters. For example, Fig. 7.7 shows that the virtualized database replica servers in *us-west-2*, *us-east-2*,

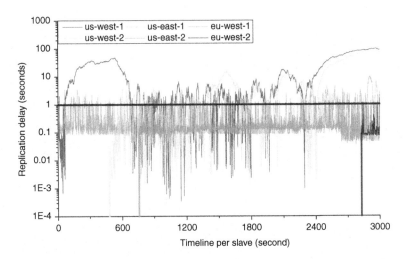

Fig. 7.8 The performance of the replication delay for up to 6 replica servers with the framework enabled, $delay_{tolerance} = 1,000$ ms, and $intvl_{mon} = 240$ s

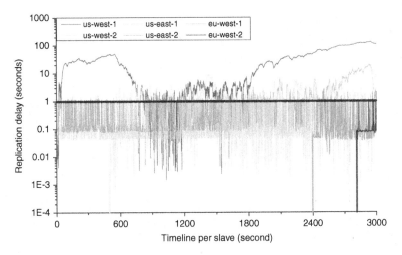

Fig. 7.9 The performance of the replication delay for up to 6 replica servers with the framework enabled, $delay_{tolerance} = 1,000$ ms, and $intvl_{mon} = 480$ s

and *eu-west-2* are added in sequence at the 255th, 407th, and 1,843th seconds, where the drop lines are emphasized. The addition of the three replica servers are caused by the SLA-violation of the virtualized database replica server in *us-west-1* at different periods. In particular, there are four SLA-violation periods for the replica server in *us-west-1* where the period must exceed the monitor interval, and all calculated replication delays in the period must exceed the SLA of replication delay. These four periods are: from 67 to 415 in total of 349 s, from 670 to 841 for

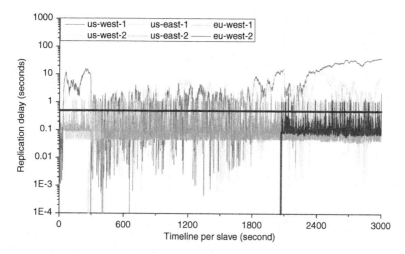

Fig. 7.10 The performance of the replication delay for up to 6 replica servers with the framework enabled, $delay_{tolerance} = 500\,\text{ms}$, and $intvl_{mon} = 120\,\text{s}$

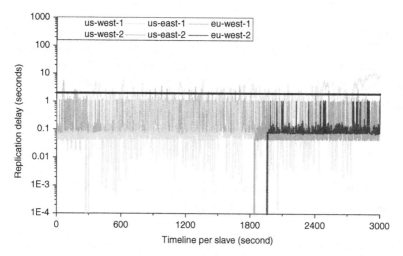

Fig. 7.11 The performance of the replication delay for up to 6 replica servers with the framework enabled, $delay_{tolerance} = 2{,}000\,\text{ms}$, and $intvl_{mon} = 120\,\text{s}$

a total of 172 s, from 1,373 to 1,579 for a total of 207 s, and from 1,615 to 3,000 for a total of 1,386 s. The adding of new replica servers is only triggered on the 1st and the 4th periods based on the time point analysis. The 2nd and the 3rd periods do not trigger the addition of any new replica servers as the number of detected SLA violations does not exceed the defined threshold, T.

Figures 7.6–7.9 show the effect of varying the monitor interval, $intvl_{mon}$ on the replication delay of the different virtualized database replica servers. The results show that virtualized database replica server in *us-west-2* is always the first location

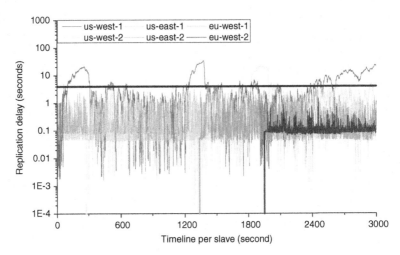

Fig. 7.12 The performance of the replication delay for up to 6 replica servers with the framework enabled, $delay_{tolerance} = 4,000$ ms, and $intvl_{mon} = 120$ s

that add a new replica server because it is the closest location to the virtualized database server in *us-west-1* which hosts the replica server that is first to violate its defined SLA data freshness. The results also show that as the monitor interval increases, the triggering points for adding new replica servers are usually delayed. On the contrary, the results of Figs. 7.7, and 7.10–7.12 show that increasing the value of the tolerance of the replication delay parameter, $delay_{tolerance}$, does not necessarily cause a delay in the triggering point for adding new replica servers.

7.5   Provisioning the Database Tier Based on SLA of Transaction Response Times

Another consumer-centric SLA metric that we consider in our framework is the total execution times of database transactions (response time). In practice, this metric has a great impact on the user experience and thus satisfaction of the underlying services. In other words, individual users are generally more concerned about when their transaction will complete rather than how many transactions the system will be able to execute in a second (system throughput) [133]. To illustrate, assuming a transaction (T) with an associated SLA for its execution time (S) is presented to the system at time 0, if the system is able to finish the execution of the transaction at time ($t \leq S$) then the service provider has achieved his target otherwise if ($t > S$) then the transaction response cannot be delivered within the defined SLA and hence a penalty p is incurred. In practice, the SLA requirements can vary between the different types of application transactions (for example, a login application request may have an SLA of 100 ms execution time, a search request may have an SLA of 600 ms while a request of submitting an order information would have 1,500 ms). Obviously, the variations in the SLA of different applications transactions is due to their different natures and their differences in the consumption behaviour of system resources (e.g. disk I/O, CPU time). In practice, each application transaction can send one or more operations to the underlying database system. Therefore, in our framework, consumer applications can define each transaction as pattern(s) of SQL commands where the transaction execution time is computed as the total execution time of these individual operations in the described pattern. Thus, the monitoring module is responsible for correlating the received database operations based on their sender in order to detect the transaction patterns [203]. Our framework also enables the consumer application to declaratively define application-specific *action rules* to adaptively scale out or scale in according to the monitored status of the response times of application transactions. For example, an application can define to scale out the underlying database tier if the average percentage of SLA violation for transactions T_1 and T_2 exceeds 10 % (of the total number of T_1 and T_2 transactions) for a continuous period of more than 8 min. Similarly, the application can define to scale in the database tier if the average percentage of SLA violation for transactions T_1 and T_2 is less than 2 % for a continuous period that is more than 8 min and the average number of concurrent users per database replica is less than 25.

We conducted our experiments with 4 different rules for achieving elasticity and dynamic provisioning for the database tier in the cloud. Two rules are defined based on the average CPU utilization of allocated virtual machines for the database server as follows: Scale out the database tier (add one more replica) when the average CPU utilization of the virtual machines exceeds of 75 % for (**R1**) and 85 % for (**R2**) over a continuous period of 5 min. Two other rules are defined based on the percentage of the SLA satisfaction of the workload transactions (the SLA values of the different transactions are defined as specified in the Cloudstone benchmark) as follows: Scale out the database tier when the percentage of SLA satisfaction is less than 97 % for (**R3**) and 90 % for (**R4**) over a continuous period of 5 min. Our evaluation metrics are the overall percentage of SLA satisfaction and the number of provisioned database replicas during the experimental time.

Figure 7.13 illustrates the results of running our experiments over a period of 1 h for the 80/20 workload (Fig. 7.13a) and the 50/50 workload (Fig. 7.13b). In these figures, the *X-axis* represents the elapsed time of the experiment while the *Y-axis* represents the SLA satisfaction of the application workload according to the different elasticity rules. In general, we see that, even for this relatively small deployment, the incorporation of SLA-based rules can show improved overall SLA satisfaction of different workloads of the application. The results show that the SLA-based rules (**R3** and **R4**) are, by design, more sensitive for achieving the SLA satisfaction and thus they react earlier than the resource-based rules. The resource-based rules (**R1** and **R2**) can accept a longer period SLA violations before taking any necessary action (CPU utilization reaches the defined limit). The benefits of SLA-based rules become clear with the workload increase (increasing the number of users during the experiment time). The gap between the resource-based rules

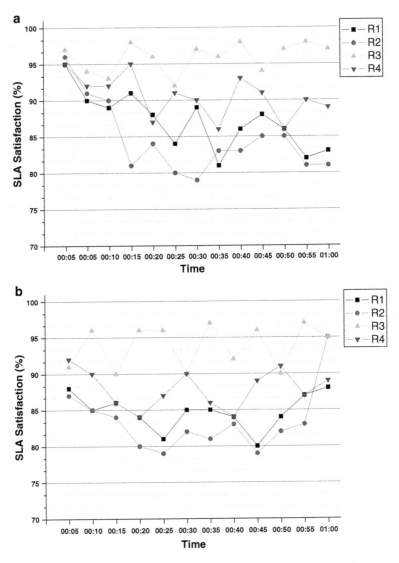

Fig. 7.13 Comparison of SLA-based vs resource-based database provisioning rules. (**a**) Workload: 80/20 (r/w). (**b**) Workload: 50/50 (r/w)

and SLA-based rules is smaller for the workload with the higher write ratio (50/50) due to the higher contention of CPU resources for the write operations and thus the conditions of the resource-based rules can be satisfied earlier.

Table 7.2 shows the total number of provisioned database replicas using the different elasticity rules for the two different workloads. Clearly, while the SLA-based rules achieves better SLA satisfaction, they may also provision more database

Table 7.2 Number of
provisioned database replicas

Workload / Rule	R1	R2	R3	R4
80/20	4	3	5	5
50/50	5	4	7	6

replicas. This trade-off shows that there is no clear winner between the two
approaches and we can not favour one approach over the other. However, the
declarative SLA-based approach empowers the cloud consumer with a more
convenient and flexible mechanism for controlling and achieving their policies in
dynamic environments such as the Cloud.

7.6   Related work

Several approaches have been proposed for dynamic provisioning of computing
resources based on their effective utilization [115, 190, 232]. These approaches
are mainly geared towards the perspective of cloud providers. Wood et. al. [232]
have presented an approach for dynamic provisioning of virtual machines. They
define a unique metric based on the data consumption of the three physical
computing resources: CPU, network and memory to make the provisioning decision.
Padala et.al. [190] carried out black box profiling of the applications and built
an approximated model which relates performance attributes such as the response
time to the fraction of processor allocated to the virtual machine on which the
application is running. Dolly [96] is a virtual machine cloning technique to
spawn database replicas and provisioning shared-nothing replicated databases in
the cloud. The technique proposes database provisioning cost models to adapt the
provisioning policy to the low-level cloud resources according to the application
requirements. Rogers et al. [200] proposed two approaches for managing the
resource provisioning challenge for cloud databases. The Black-box provisioning
uses end-to-end performance results of sample query executions, whereas white-
box provisioning uses a finer grained approach that relies on the DBMS optimizer
to predict the physical resource (e.g., I/O, memory, CPU) consumption for each
query. Floratou et al. [131] have studied the performance and cost in the relational
database as a service environments. The results show that given a range of
pricing models and the flexibility of the allocation of resources in cloud-based
environments, it is hard for a user to figure out their actual monthly cost upfront.
Soror et al. [211] introduced a virtualization design advisor that uses information
about the database workloads to provide offline recommendations of workload-
specific virtual machines configurations. To the best of our knowledge, our approach
is the first to tackle the problem of dynamic provisioning the cloud resources of the
database tier based on consumer-centric and application-defined SLA metrics.

7.7 Discussion

In this chapter, we presented the design and implementation details[3] of an end-to-end framework that facilitates adaptive and dynamic provisioning of the database tier of the software applications based on consumer-centric policies for satisfying their own SLA performance requirements, avoiding the cost of any SLA violation and controlling the monetary cost of the allocated computing resources. The framework provides the consumer applications with declarative and flexible mechanisms for defining their specific requirements for fine-grained SLA metrics at the application level. The framework is database platform-agnostic, uses virtualization-based database replication mechanisms and requires zero source code changes of the cloud-hosted software applications.

---

[3]http://cdbslaautoadmin.sourceforge.net/.

Chapter 8
QoS-Aware Service Compositions in Cloud Computing

Services in cloud computing can be categorized into application services and utility computing services [68]. Almost all the software/applications that are available through the Internet are application services, e.g., flight booking services, hotel booking services. Utility computing services are software or virtualized hardware that support application services, e.g., virtual machines, CPU services, and storage services. Service compositions in cloud computing therefore include compositions of application services and utility computing services. Compositions in the application level are similar to the Web service compositions in Service-Oriented Computing (SOC). Compositions in the utility level are similar to the task matching and scheduling in grid computing. A composite application service fulfills several tasks (i.e. *abstract services*). Each task is implemented by several substitute application services (i.e. *concrete services*). The choice among these substitute services is based on their non-functional properties, which are also referred to as Quality of Service (QoS). QoS values of these substitute application services are further dependent on the choices of utility computing services. In a word, once a concrete application service is selected for each abstract service, the following decisions have to be made: *matching*, i.e. assigning concrete application services to utility computing services, and *scheduling*, i.e. ordering execution sequence of application services.

Several approaches and systems are proposed to solve Web service composition problems in SOC. Most of them [201, 238] only consider the compositions in the application level. Composition approaches in cloud computing need to consider compositions both in the application level and utility computing level. Besides, most existing composition approaches in SOC [201,238] use integer programming to find the global optimized solution. Although this is useful for small-scale compositions, it incurs a significant performance penalty if applied to large-scale composition problems such as compositions in cloud computing [202]. Contrasts to these existing approaches, Genetic Algorithms (GAs) are heuristic approaches to iteratively find near-optimal solutions in large search spaces. There is ample evidence regarding the applicability of GAs for large-scale optimization problems [202,229]. Whereas, no GA based approach is available to compose services in cloud computing.

L. Zhao et al., *Cloud Data Management*, DOI 10.1007/978-3-319-04765-2_8,
© Springer International Publishing Switzerland 2014

In this chapter, a genetic-algorithm-based service composition approach is proposed for cloud computing. In particular, a coherent way to calculate the QoS values of services in cloud computing is presented. At last, comparisons between the proposed approach and other approaches show the effectiveness and efficiency of the proposed approach. The rest of the chapter is structured as follows: Section 8.1 illustrates the background and preliminaries of service composition in cloud computing. Section 8.2 elaborates the details of the proposed approach. Section 8.3 evaluates the approach and shows the experiment results. Section 8.4 presents the related work to the proposed approach. Section 8.5 concludes this chapter and highlights some future work.

8.1   Preliminaries

This section presents preliminary knowledge about cloud computing, service compositions in cloud computing. Genetic algorithms are also introduced at the end of this section. Services in a cloud, refers to both the applications delivered as services over the Internet and the hardware and system software in the data centers that provide those services [68]. Cloud computing provides easy access to *Application Services* (i.e. SaaS) and *Utility Computing Services* (UCS) (Fig. 8.1).

- Application Services are the most visible services to the end users. Examples of application services include: Salesforce's CRM applications, Google Apps etc. Application services that contain other component application services are *Composite Application Services*. *Simple Application Services* do not contain

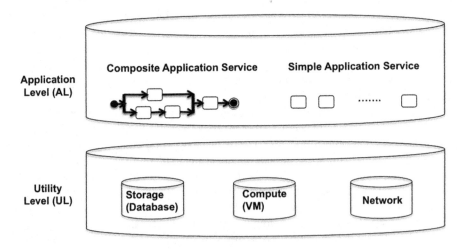

Fig. 8.1 Cloud system

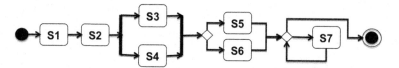

Fig. 8.2 Control flows

other component application services. *Application Users* can be end users or other application services. *Application Providers* are providers of application services.

• Utility Computing Services. Some vendors use terms such as PaaS (Platform as a Service) or IaaS (Infrastructure as a Service) to describe their products. In this chapter, PaaS and IaaS are considered together as UCSs. PaaS are platforms that are used to develop, test, deploy and monitor application services. For example, Google has Google App Engine works as the platform to develop, deploy and maintain Google Apps. Microsoft Azure and Force.com are also examples of PaaS. IaaS services provide fundamental computing resources, which can be used to construct new platform services or application services. UCSs can be categorized into computation services, i.e., *Virtual Machines* (VMs); storage services, i.e., *Databases*; and network services. *UCS Users* are these application providers or other utility computing services etc. *UCS Vendors* are these companies or organizations that make their computing resources available to the public.

Service Compositions in Cloud Computing

A composite service is specified as a collection of abstract application services according to a combination of control-flow and data-flow. Control-flow graphs are represented using UML activity diagrams. Each node in the graph is an abstract application service. There are four control-flow patterns. For example, Fig. 8.2 shows a composite service consists of four patterns of control-flows. S_1 and S_2 run in a sequence pattern. S_3 runs in parallel with S_4 (parallel pattern). After that, either S_5 or S_6 is selected to run (conditional pattern). Finally, S_7 cycles for a certain times (loop pattern).

There are several data-flow graphs for the same control-flow graph, if the control-flow graph contains conditional patterns. Figure 8.3 shows the two data-flow graphs corresponding to the control-flow shown in Fig. 8.2. Directed acyclic graphs (DAGs) are used to represent data-flow graphs. The start node of an edge is denoted as *source service*, the node where the edge ends is denoted as *destination service*. Source services must be executed before the destination services. The destination service can only be executed after all its source services are finished. Node S_b represents

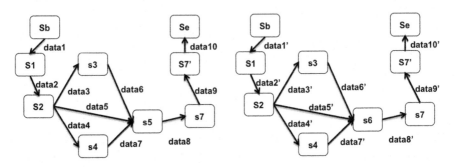

Fig. 8.3 Data flow graphs

the start point of the composite service. S_e represents the end point. The data items transferred between these abstract application services form a set $D = \{data_i, 1 \leq i \leq d\}$.

A set of k_n concrete application services $\{s_{n1}, s_{n2}, \ldots, s_{nk_n}\}$ is available to execute the abstract service S_n. A concrete application service can be executed on several virtual machines, databases and network services. After mapping each abstract service to a concrete application service, VM UCSs and Database UCSs need to be selected for each application service. Network UCSs need to be selected for each data transfer in the data-flow graph. Assume each VM can only execute one application service at a time. A late application service can only execute on the VM after the former application services finish their executions. To sum up, any solution to a composition problem in cloud computing includes: (1) Map the abstract application services to concrete application services and corresponding UCSs (VM, database and network services). (2) Schedule the execution order of the application services. This execution order is a topological sort [114] of the data-flow graph, i.e. a total ordering of the nodes in the DAG that obeys the precedence constraints.

QoS Model

QoS attributes contains (1) ascending QoS attributes, i.e. a higher value is better; (2) descending QoS attributes, i.e. a smaller value is better; (3) equal QoS attributes, i.e. no ordering but only equality, e.g. security protocol should be X.509. Four QoS attributes are considered in this work: response time, price, availability and reputation. Among them, time and price belong to the descending attributes while availability and reputation belong to the ascending attributes. Vector $\mathbf{Q} = Q^1, Q^2, Q^3, Q^4$ denotes all the available QoS attributes. $Q^i, 1 \leq i \leq 4$ represents time, price, availability and reputation.

QoS values of an application service consist of three parts: execution, network and storage QoSs. Existing QoS models in SOC [238] only consider the execution QoSs. *Execution QoS* refers to the QoS value for executing an application service in

QoS Attributes	Time Q^1	Price Q^2	Availability Q^3	Reputation Q^4
Aggregation Function	$\sum\limits_{i=1}^{m} Q_i^1$	$\sum\limits_{i=1}^{m} Q_i^2$	$\prod\limits_{i=1}^{m} Q_i^3$	$\prod\limits_{i=1}^{m} Q_i^4$

Fig. 8.4 Aggregation functions for each QoS attribute

a specified VM. Same application service has different execution QoS in different VMs. *Network QoS* refers to the QoS for transferring data from one application service to another using a specified network UCS. Data transfers are determined by the source services and the destination services. Each data will be transferred as soon as the source service produces them. Hence, network QoS values are only calculated at the destination services. *Storage QoS* refers to the QoS for storing certain amount of data for a certain time using specified database service. Assume no data will be stored during the execution of an application service. Therefore, the only data needs to be stored are the input data. For example, a destination service has two input data. One input data arrives early, the other arrives later. The earlier arrived data need to be stored when waiting the second input data to arrive. The QoS value for a service therefore equals to the sum of execution QoS, network QoS and storage QoS. Figure 8.4 shows the aggregation functions for calculating the overall QoS for composite services. m is the number of component services in the composite service. QoS values are normalized using Simple Additive Weighting (SAW), which is also used in [238]. The best QoS values are normalized to 0, the worst QoS values are normalized to 1. Thus, higher normalized values indicate worse quality.

QoS constraints (denoted as QC) for composite services have two types: *Global Constraints* and *Local Constraints*. Global Constraints are the QoS constraints for the overall composite service, while Local Constraints apply to component services within the composition. A global constraint (GC) for a given QoS attribute Q^l is denoted as GC^l. Local constraints are denoted as LC^l. Constraints on different QoS attributes are transformed into inequality constraints [107]. QC^1 (time) and QC^2 (price) can be transformed by subtract the threshold to the constraints, e.g. $QC^1 \leq 1\ minute$ is transformed to $QC^1 \Leftarrow QC^1 - 1 \leq 0$; $QC^2 \leq 5\ USdollars$ is transformed to $QC^2 \Leftarrow QC^2 - 5 \leq 0$. QC^3 (availability) and QC^4 (reputation) can be transformed by subtracting the QoS value from the threshold, e.g. $QC^3 \geq 0.9$ is transformed to $QC^3 \Leftarrow 0.9 - QC^3 \leq 0$. Constraints on equal QoS attributes can be transformed using this function: $QC \Leftarrow |QC| - \epsilon \leq 0$, where ϵ is the tolerance allowed range (a very small value).

Genetic Algorithms

Genetic Algorithms (GAs) are heuristic approaches to iteratively find near-optimal solutions in large search spaces. Any possible solution to the optimization problem is encoded as a *Chromosome* (normally a string). A set of chromosomes is referred to as a *Population*. The first step of a GA is to derive an initial population. A random set of chromosomes is often used as the initial population. This initial population is the first generation from which the evolution starts. The second step is *selection*. Each chromosome is eliminated or duplicated (one or more times) based on its relative quality. The population size is typically kept constant. The next step is *Crossover*. Some pairs of chromosomes are selected from the current population and some of their corresponding components are exchanged to form two valid chromosome. After crossover, each chromosome in the population may be *mutated* with some probability. The mutation process transforms a chromosome into another valid one. The new population is then *evaluated*. Each chromosome is associated with a *fitness value*, which is a value obtained from the objective function (details will be discussed in Sect. 8.2). The objective of the evaluation is to find a chromosome that has the optimal fitness value. If the stopping criterion is not met, the new population goes through another cycle (iteration) of selection, crossover, mutation, and evaluation. These cycles continue until the stopping criterion is met.

8.2   QoS-Aware Service Composition in Cloud Computing

Assume there are m VM UCSs ($vm_1, vm_2, \ldots, vm_m$), p database UCSs ($db_1, db_2, \ldots, db_p$) and q network UCSs ($net_1, net_2, \ldots, net_q$) in different cloud systems. Each composition solution (chromosome) consists of two parts, the matching string (ms) and the scheduling string (ss). ms is a vector of length n, such that $ms(i) = s_j vm_x db_y net_z$, where $1 \leq i \leq n$, $1 \leq j \leq k_n$, $1 \leq x \leq m$, $1 \leq y \leq p$ and $1 \leq z \leq q$. A matching string means that abstract service S_i is assigned to concrete service s_{ij} which is lodged on virtual machine vm_x and has database service db_y, network service net_z. The scheduling string is a topological sort of the data-flow graph. $ss(k) = i$, where $1 \leq i, k \leq n$; i.e. service S_i is the kth running service in the scheduling string. Thus, a chromosome represents the mapping from each abstract service to concrete service and UCSs, together with the execution order of the application services. Figure 8.5 shows a solution to the composite problem that has the control-flow shown in Fig. 8.2, and the data-flow shown in Fig. 8.3 (left

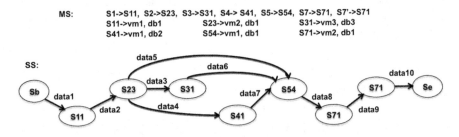

Fig. 8.5 Composition solution

DAG). In this solution, *ms* represents the mapping string, e.g., abstract service S_1 is mapped to application service S_{11}, S_{11} is further deployed on virtual machine vm_1 and database db_1. The network service for a transferred data is determined when the source service and the destination service are mapped to the corresponding virtual machine and database services. *ss* represents the scheduling string of the solution, e.g., the execution order of this solution in Fig. 8.5 is $S_{11}, S_{23}, S_{31}, S_{41}, S_{54}, S_{71}, S_{71}$.

Genetic Algorithm Based Approach

In the first step, a predefined number of chromosomes are generated to form the initial generation. The chromosomes in a generation are first ordered by their fitness values (explained later) from the best to worst. These having the same fitness value are ranked arbitrarily among themselves. Then a rank-based roulette wheel selection schema is used to implement the selection step [213]. There is a higher probability that one or more copies of the better solution will be included in the next generation, since a better solution has a larger sector angle than that of a worse solution. In this way, the chromosomes formed the next generation are determined. Notice that the population size of each generation is always P.

The crossover operator for a matching string randomly chooses some pairs of the matching strings. For each pair, it randomly generates a cut-off point to divide both matching strings into two parts. Then the bottom parts are exchanged. The crossover operator for a scheduling string randomly chooses some pairs of the scheduling strings. For each pair, it randomly generates a cut-off point, which divides the scheduling strings into top and bottom parts. The abstract application services in each bottom part are reordered. The new ordering of the services in one bottom part is the relative positions of these services in the other original scheduling string in the pair. This guarantees that the newly generated scheduling strings are valid schedules. Figure 8.6a demonstrates the crossover operator for a scheduling string.

The mutation operator for a matching string randomly selects an abstract service and randomly replaces the corresponding concrete service and other utility computing services. The mutation operator for a scheduling string randomly chooses some scheduling strings. It then randomly selects a target service. The *valid range* of this target service is the set of the positions in the scheduling string at which the target service can be placed without violating any data dependency constraints. The valid range is after all source services of the target service and before any destination service of the target service. The mutation operator can move this target service randomly to another position in the scheduling string within its valid range. Figure 8.6b demonstrates the mutation operator for a scheduling string. s_v is between s_b and s_c before the mutation, it is between s_a and s_b after the mutation operator.

After crossover and mutation operators, GA will evaluate the chromosomes using *fitness function*. The fitness function needs to maximize some QoS attributes (i.e. ascending attributes), minimize some other attributes (i.e. descending attributes) and satisfy other QoS attributes (i.e. equal QoS attributes). In addition, the fitness

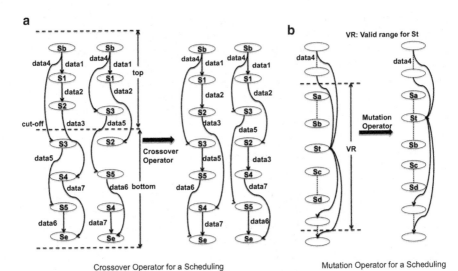

Crossover Operator for a Scheduling   Mutation Operator for a Scheduling

Fig. 8.6 Crossover and mutation operators

function must penalize solutions that do not meet the QoS constraints and drive
the evolution towards satisfaction. The distance from constraint satisfaction for a
solution c is defined as:

$$D(c) = \Sigma_{i=1}^{l} QC^{i}(c) \times e_i \times weight^i, e_i = \begin{cases} 0 & QC^{i}(c) \leq 0 \\ 1 & QC^{i}(c) > 0 \end{cases} \quad (8.1)$$

where $weight^i$ indicates the weight of the QoS constraint. Notice that this distance
function for constraints include both local and global constraints specified. The
fitness function for a chromosome c is then defined as follows:

$$F(c) = \Sigma_{i=1}^{4} w^i * Q^i(c) + weight_p * D(c) \quad (8.2)$$

w^i are the weights for each QoS attribute. $weight_p$ is the *penalty factor*. Several
features are highlighted when calculating the fitness function based on the match
string and the scheduling string:

1. Services are executed exactly in the order specified by the scheduling string. For
   example, Fig. 8.7a shows a scheduling string for a composition. Assume there
   are two different match strings for this ss. (a) ms_1: Let S_1 and S_2 be assigned to
   the same VM vm_1, and S_3 be assigned to another VM vm_2. In this chromosome,
   because S_1 is to be executed before S_2, $data_1$ is available before $data_2$. Thus,
   $data_1$ will be transferred to S_3 before $data_2$. And $data_1$ will be stored in S_3's
   database service till $data_2$ has been transferred to S_3. (b) ms_2: Let the three
   services S_1, S_2, and S_3 be assigned to three different VMs vm_1, vm_2 and vm_3.

Fig. 8.7 Example of scheduling string. (**a**) Example 1. (**b**) Example 2 for data forwarding

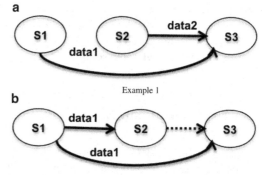

Example 1

Example 2 for Data Forwarding

S_2 starts to execute just after S_1 starts, S_1 and S_2 can be considered to start their execution at the same time. If $data_2$ is available (S_2 executes faster) before $data_1$, $data_2$ will be stored in S_2's database service till $data_1$ has been transferred to S_3.

2. Another important feature is *data forwarding* [229]. For an input data, the source service can be chosen among the services that produce or consume this input data. All the consumers of this input data can be forwarders. For example, Fig. 8.7b shows a scheduling string. S_2 and S_3 both have the input data from S_1. S_2 may forward $data_1$ from S_1 to S_3, i.e. shown as the dashed line in Fig. 8.7b. This kind of data forwarding is not allowed in our work. Data must be only transferred from the original data producer to its consumers.

Stop criterions for the proposed approach are: (1) Iterate until the constraints are met (i.e. $D(c) = 0$). (2) If this does not happen within $MAXGEN$ generations, then iterate until the best fitness value remains unchanged for a given number ($MAXGEN$) of generations. (3) If neither (1) nor (2) happens within $MAXGEN$ generations, then no solution will be returned.

Handling Multiple Data Flow Graphs

Assume the composite service (e.g. shown in Fig. 8.2) has multiple data-flow graphs (shown in Fig. 8.3). For each data-flow graph, an optimal composition solution can be generated using the proposed GA-based approach. Since each of the optimal solution only covers a subset of the composite service, further actions are needed to aggregate these partial composition solutions into an overall solution. Assume the composite service has f data-flow graphs (i.e. $dfg_1, dfg_2, \ldots, dfg_f$). The approach adopts the following strategies to aggregate multiple solutions into an overall solution:

- Given an abstract service S_i, if S_i only belongs to one data-flow graph (e.g. dfg_j), then the proposed approach selects dfg_j's solution *chromosome$_j$* to execute abstract service S_i.

- Given an abstract service S_i, if S_i belongs to more than one data-flow graphs, then there are many solutions can be used to execute S_i. The proposed approach will select the most frequently used solution (from execution history), or ask end users to select a preferable solution.

8.3   Experiment and Evaluation

Our experiments consist of two parts. First, comparisons are conducted between the proposed approach and other approaches in small-scale scenarios. Second, comparisons are conducted in large-scale scenarios. All the experiments are conducted on computers with Intel Core 2 Duo 6400 CPU (2.13 GHz and 2GB RAM).

Creation of Experimental Scenarios

Randomly generated scenarios are used for the experiments. Each scenario contains a control-flow graph and a data-flow graph. QoS values of different concrete services, virtual machines, database services and network services for each abstract service are generated randomly with uniform probability. A scenario generation system is designed to generate the scenarios for experiments. The system first determines a root pattern (i.e. sequence, conditional, parallel, loop patterns) with uniform probability for the control-flow. Within this root, the system chooses with equal probability to either place an abstract services into it or to choose another composition pattern as substructure. This procedure ends until the generation system has spent the predefined number (n) of abstract services. All the conditional patterns have 2 possible options, either of them has the probability of 0.5. Each loop pattern will run for twice. There are k candidate concrete services to implement each abstract service. The number of data transferred between each abstract services in the flow graph is d. Each concrete service can be lodged in m virtual machines, p database services and q network services. These variables are predefined and used as input (denoted as $\{n, k, d, m, p, q\}$) to the generation system. Small-scale scenarios have the input $\{5, 2, 6, 3, 3, 3\}$. Large-scale scenarios have 100 abstract services. Each abstract service can be executed by 30 concrete services. 120 data items are transferred between services and each concrete service is suitable to run in 20 different VMs, 20 different database services and 20 network services. The four QoS attributes and the four QoS constraints have same weight equals 1. The execution QoS, network QoS and storage QoS were randomly generated with uniform distribution from the following intervals: $Q^1(Time) \in [100, 2, 000]$, $Q^2(Price) \in [200, 1, 000]$, $Q^3(Availability) \in [0.9750, 0.9999]$ and $Q^4(Reputation) \in [1, 100]$.

Every approach runs 50 times for each scenario. All the results shown below are the average values from these experiments. Each experiment for the GA-based approach starts from a different initial population each time. The probability of crossover $p_{cross} = 0.4$ is the same for the matching string and scheduling string. The probability of mutation $p_{mut} = 0.1$ is also the same for the matching string and scheduling string. The approach uses rank-based roulette wheel schema for selection. The angle ratio of the sectors on the roulette wheel for two adjacently ranked chromosomes, i.e. R, was chosen to be $1 + 1/P$, where P is the population size. By using this simple formula, the angle ratio between the slots of the best and median chromosomes for $P = 50$ (and also for $P = 200$ for large-scale scenarios) is very closely to the optimal empirical ratio value of 1.5 in [231]. $MAXFIT$ equals to 150. $MAXGEN$ equals to 1, 000. *Exhaustive search approach* would traverse all the possible solutions to the composition problem and find the optimized solution that has the smallest fitness value. Although this approach would always find the most optimal composition solution, the execution time is extremely high. *Random selection approach* is also a GA-based approach. This approach would randomly select chromosomes to form a new generation. Comparisons with these approaches show the effectiveness and efficiency of the proposed approach. Integer Programming (IP) approaches have been proposed to solve QoS-aware service composition in SOC. The IP approach is implemented using LPSolve [77], which is an open source integer programming system. Comparisons with IP approach show the scalability of the proposed approach.

Experiments Results

Small-scale experiments are conducted on 10 different test datasets. We only show two of them in Fig. 8.9 to make the graph much easier to read. Figure 8.8 shows the results between the proposed approach and the exhaustive search approach. Proposed GA-based approach would always find near-optimal solution compared to exhaustive search algorithms. Figure 8.9 shows the comparisons between the proposed approach and the random selection solution. As shown in this figure, proposed approach will always reach an optimized fitness value while random selection seldom converges. To sum up, the proposed GA based approach will always reach an optimal fitness value and the converged point is very close to the actual optimal point. Figure 8.10 shows the efficiency of the proposed approach. These experiments are conducted on small-scale scenarios. Each test dataset has the same configuration, except for the number of concrete services for each abstract service. As shown in Fig. 8.10, the execution time increases quickly at the beginning, but keeps stable when the number of concrete services for each abstract service is larger than 200.

As shown in Fig. 8.11a, IP approach performs as good as the GA based approach at the beginning. Notice that, when the number of the abstract services becomes more than 40, IP approaches would cost exponential growing time to solve the

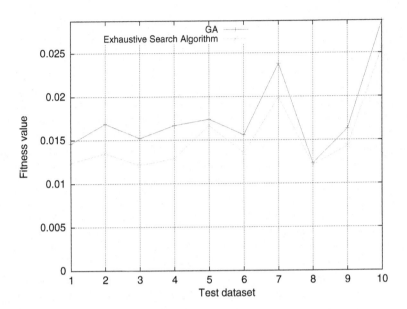

Fig. 8.8 Fitness vs Dataset

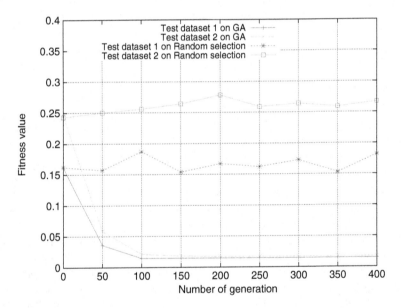

Fig. 8.9 GA vs Random selection

composition problems. Figure 8.11b shows the fitness value's trend corresponding
to the increment of the number of the abstract services. Both IP approach and GA
based approach behave well when the number of abstract services is relatively small.

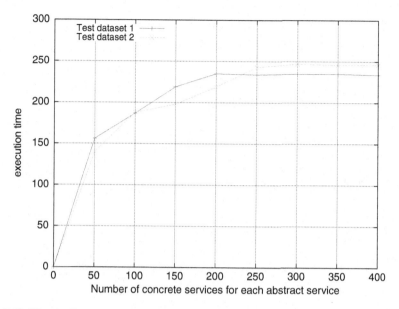

Fig. 8.10 Time vs Concrete services

When the number of abstract services increases, the optimal fitness value obtained from GA based approach also increases. This is because population size and other related variables stay the same when the number of the abstract services varies. Hence, GA based approach are more scalable and efficient than IP approaches.

8.4   Related Work

Most composition approaches in SOC use linear programming methods. [238] presents two approaches: one focuses on local optimization, the other on global optimization. They use integer programming to solve the global optimization problem. The limit of this approach is that all QoS attributes need to be linearized as integer programming is a linear programming approach. [66] proposes an improved approach based on [238], using Mixed Linear Programming (MILP) approach. They also introduce several concepts such as loop peeling and negotiation mechanisms to address situation where no feasible solution can be found. [63] proposes an approach to decompose global QoS constraints into local constraints with conservative upper and lower bounds. These local constraints are resolved by using an efficient distributed local selection strategy.

All of the aforementioned approaches only consider the service composition problems in small-scale scenarios. These linear programming approaches are not suitable to handle large-scale scenarios problems, e.g. service composition in cloud

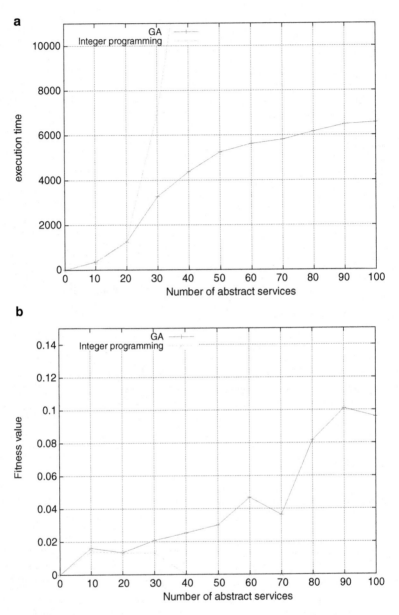

Fig. 8.11 GA vs Integer programming approach. (**a**) GA vs Integer programming on time. (**b**) GA vs Integer programming on fitness

computing. [93] was the first to use GA for optimization of QoS-aware compositions in SOC. The results show that their GA implementation scales better than linear programming. [135] presents a GA and a Culture Algorithm (CA) for Web service compositions. The first algorithm is similar to [93], the latter uses a global belief space and an influence function that accelerate the convergence of the population. [202] presents a mutation operator which consider both the local and global constraints to accelerate the converge of the population.

Existing GA-based approaches are solely focus on service composition in application level, which do not consider the computing resources composition. Service composition in cloud computing involves application service composition and computing resources matching and scheduling. In this chapter, a genetic algorithm based approach is proposed to compose services in cloud computing, by combining QoS-aware service composition approaches and resources matching and scheduling approaches.

8.5 Conclusion

A genetic algorithm based approach is presented for service compositions in cloud computing. Service compositions in cloud computing involve the selections of application services and utility computing services. The chromosome size is bound to the number of n of abstract services. The number of possible application services and utility computing services only augments the search space. For small-scale scenarios, the proposed approach finds optimal solutions. For larger-scale problems, it outperforms the integer programming approach. This is a beginning to propose robust service composition approaches in cloud computing. Future work may focus to eliminate several assumptions: (1) QoS values for each component are known in this research. Calculating the QoS values at runtime is one direction; (2) penalty factor in the fitness function is static. More dynamic fitness functions can be used to improve the performance of the approach. (3) novel crossover and mutation operators may accelerate the converge.

Chapter 9
Big Data Processing Systems

In the last two decades, the continuous increase of computational power has produced an overwhelming flow of data which has called for a paradigm shift in the computing architecture and large scale data processing mechanisms. MapReduce is a simple and powerful programming model that enables easy development of scalable parallel applications to process vast amounts of data on large clusters of commodity machines. It isolates the application from the details of running a distributed program such as issues on data distribution, scheduling and fault tolerance. However, the original implementation of the MapReduce framework had some limitations that have been tackled by many research efforts in several followup works after its introduction. This chapter provides a comprehensive survey for a *family* of approaches and mechanisms of large scale data processing mechanisms that have been implemented based on the original idea of the MapReduce framework and are currently gaining a lot of momentum in both research and industrial communities. We also cover a set of systems that have been implemented to provide declarative programming interfaces on top of the MapReduce framework. In addition, we review several large scale data processing systems that resemble some of the ideas of the MapReduce framework for different purposes and application scenarios. Finally, we discuss some of the future research directions for implementing the next generation of MapReduce-like solutions.

9.1 Introduction

Many enterprises continuously collect large datasets that record customer interactions, product sales, results from advertising campaigns on the Web, and other types of information. For example, Facebook collects 15 TeraBytes of data each day into a PetaByte-scale data warehouse [222]. In general, the growing demand for large-scale data processing and data analysis applications has spurred the development of novel solutions from both the industry (e.g., web-data analysis, click-stream analysis, network-monitoring log analysis) and the sciences (e.g., analysis of data

L. Zhao et al., *Cloud Data Management*, DOI 10.1007/978-3-319-04765-2_9,
© Springer International Publishing Switzerland 2014

produced by massive-scale simulations, sensor deployments, high-throughput lab equipment) [206]. Although parallel database systems [122] serve some of these data analysis applications (e.g. Teradata [45], SQL Server PDW [36], Vertica [51], Greenplum [25], ParAccel [40], Netezza [31], they are expensive, difficult to administer and lack fault-tolerance for long-running queries [194]. MapReduce [118] is a framework which is introduced by Google for programming commodity computer clusters to perform large-scale data processing in a single pass. The framework is designed such that a MapReduce cluster can scale to thousands of nodes in a fault-tolerant manner. One of the main advantages of this framework is its reliance on a simple and powerful programming model. In addition, it isolates the application developer from all the complex details of running a distributed program such as: issues on data distribution, scheduling and fault tolerance [193].

In principle, the success of many enterprises often rely on their ability to analyze expansive volumes of data. In general, cost-effective processing of large datasets is a nontrivial undertaking. Fortunately, MapReduce frameworks and cloud computing have made it easier than ever for everyone to step into the world of big data. This technology combination has enabled even small companies to collect and analyze terabytes of data in order to gain a competitive edge. For example, the Amazon Elastic Compute Cloud (EC2) [4] is offered as a commodity that can be purchased and utilised. In addition, Amazon has also provided the Amazon Elastic MapReduce [6] as an online service to easily and cost-effectively process vast amounts of data without the need to worry about time-consuming set-up, management or tuning of computing clusters or the compute capacity upon which they sit. Hence, such services enable third-parties to perform their analytical queries on massive datasets with minimum effort and cost by abstracting the complexity entailed in building and maintaining computer clusters.

The implementation of the basic MapReduce architecture had some limitations. Therefore, several research efforts have been triggered to tackle these limitations by introducing several advancements in the basic architecture in order to improve its performance. This chapter provides a comprehensive survey for a *family* of approaches and mechanisms of large scale data analysis mechanisms that have been implemented based on the original idea of the MapReduce framework and are currently gaining a lot of momentum in both research and industrial communities. In particular, the remainder of this chapter is organized as follows. Section 9.2 describes the basic architecture of the MapReduce framework. Section 9.3 discusses several techniques that have been proposed to improve the performance and capabilities of the MapReduce framework from different perspectives. Section 9.4 covers several systems that support a high level SQL-like interface for the MapReduce framework. In Sect. 9.5, we conclude the chapter and discuss some of the future research directions for implementing the next generation of MapReduce/Hadoop-like solutions.

9.2 MapReduce Framework: Basic Architecture

The MapReduce framework is introduced as a simple and powerful programming model that enables easy development of scalable parallel applications to process vast amounts of data on large clusters of commodity machines [118, 119]. In particular, the implementation described in the original paper is mainly designed to achieve high performance on large clusters of commodity PCs. One of the main advantages of this approach is that it isolates the application from the details of running a distributed program, such as issues on data distribution, scheduling and fault tolerance. In this model, the computation takes a set of key/value pairs input and produces a set of key/value pairs as output. The user of the MapReduce framework expresses the computation using two functions: *Map* and *Reduce*. The Map function takes an input pair and produces a set of intermediate key/value pairs. The MapReduce framework groups together all intermediate values associated with the same intermediate key I and passes them to the Reduce function. The Reduce function receives an intermediate key I with its set of values and merges them together. Typically just zero or one output value is produced per Reduce invocation. The main advantage of this model is that it allows large computations to be easily parallelized and re-executed to be used as the primary mechanism for fault tolerance. Figure 9.1 illustrates an example MapReduce program expressed in pseudo-code for counting the number of occurrences of each word in a collection of documents. In this example, the map function emits each word plus an associated count of occurrences while the reduce function sums together all counts emitted for a particular word. In principle, the design of the MapReduce framework has considered the following main principles [103]:

- *Low-cost unreliable commodity hardware*: Instead of using expensive, high-performance, reliable symmetric multiprocessing (SMP) or massively parallel processing (MPP) machines equipped with high-end network and storage subsystems, the MapReduce framework is designed to run on large clusters of commodity hardware. This hardware is managed and powered by open-source operating systems and utilities so that the cost is low.
- *Extremely scalable RAIN cluster*: Instead of using centralized RAID-based SAN or NAS storage systems, every MapReduce node has its own local off-the-shelf hard drives. These nodes are loosely coupled where they are placed in

```
map(String key, String value):          reduce(String key, Iterator values):
// key: document name                    // key: a word
// value: document contents              // values: a list of counts
for each word w in value:                int result = 0;
        EmitIntermediate(w, "1");        for each v in values:
                                                 result += ParseInt(v);
                                         Emit(AsString(result));
```

Fig. 9.1 An example MapReduce program

racks that can be connected with standard networking hardware connections. These nodes can be taken out of service with almost no impact to still-running MapReduce jobs. These clusters are called Redundant Array of Independent (and Inexpensive) Nodes (RAIN).

- *Fault-tolerant yet easy to administer*: MapReduce jobs can run on clusters with thousands of nodes or even more. These nodes are not very reliable as at any point in time, a certain percentage of these commodity nodes or hard drives will be out of order. Hence, the MapReduce framework applies straightforward mechanisms to replicate data and launch backup tasks so as to keep still-running processes going. To handle crashed nodes, system administrators simply take crashed hardware off-line. New nodes can be plugged in at any time without much administrative hassle. There is no complicated backup, restore and recovery configurations like the ones that can be seen in many DBMS.
- *Highly parallel yet abstracted*: The most important contribution of the MapReduce framework is its ability to automatically support the parallelization of task executions. Hence, it allows developers to focus mainly on the problem at hand rather than worrying about the low level implementation details such as memory management, file allocation, parallel, multi-threaded or network programming. Moreover, MapReduce's shared-nothing architecture [215] makes it much more scalable and ready for parallelization.

Hadoop [9] is an open source Java library [230] that supports data-intensive distributed applications by realizing the implementation of the MapReduce framework.[1] It has been widely used by a large number of business companies for production purposes.[2] On the implementation level, the Map invocations of a MapReduce job are distributed across multiple machines by automatically partitioning the input data into a set of M splits. The input splits can be processed in parallel by different machines. Reduce invocations are distributed by partitioning the intermediate key space into R pieces using a partitioning function (e.g. hash(key) mod R). The number of partitions (R) and the partitioning function are specified by the user. Figure 9.2 illustrates an example of the overall flow of a MapReduce operation which goes through the following sequence of actions:

1. The input data of the MapReduce program is split into M pieces and starts up many instances of the program on a cluster of machines.
2. One of the instances of the program is elected to be the *master* copy while the rest are considered as *workers* that are assigned their work by the master copy. In particular, there are M map tasks and R reduce tasks to assign. The master picks idle workers and assigns each one or more map tasks and/or reduce tasks.
3. A worker who is assigned a map task processes the contents of the corresponding input split and generates key/value pairs from the input data and passes each pair to the user-defined Map function. The intermediate key/value pairs produced by the Map function are buffered in memory.

---

[1]In the rest of this chapter, we use the two names: MapReduce and Hadoop, interchangeably.
[2]http://wiki.apache.org/hadoop/PoweredBy.

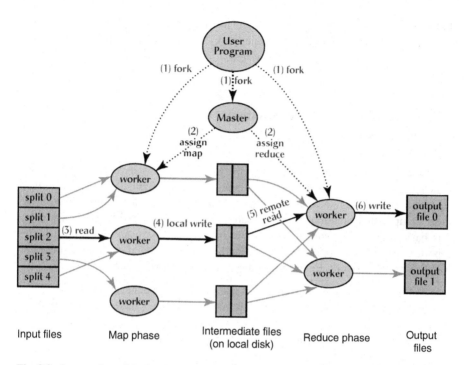

Fig. 9.2 An overview of the flow of execution a MapReduce operation

4. Periodically, the buffered pairs are written to local disk and partitioned into R regions by the partitioning function. The locations of these buffered pairs on the local disk are passed back to the master, who is responsible for forwarding these locations to the reduce workers.

5. When a reduce worker is notified by the master about these locations, it reads the buffered data from the local disks of the map workers which is then sorted by the intermediate keys so that all occurrences of the same key are grouped together. The sorting operation is needed because typically many different keys map to the same reduce task.

6. The reduce worker passes the key and the corresponding set of intermediate values to the user's Reduce function. The output of the Reduce function is appended to a final output file for this reduce partition.

7. When all map tasks and reduce tasks have been completed, the master program wakes up the user program. At this point, the MapReduce invocation in the user program returns the program control back to the user code.

During the execution process, the master pings every worker periodically. If no response is received from a worker within a certain amount of time, the master marks the worker as *failed*. Any map tasks marked *completed* or *in progress* by the worker are reset back to their initial idle state and therefore become eligible for scheduling by other workers. Completed map tasks are re-executed on a task failure because their output is stored on the local disk(s) of the failed machine and is therefore inaccessible. Completed reduce tasks do not need to be re-executed since their output is stored in a global file system.

9.3   Extensions and Enhancements of the MapReduce Framework

In practice, the basic implementation of the MapReduce is very useful for handling data processing and data loading in a heterogenous system with many different storage systems. Moreover, it provides a flexible framework for the execution of more complicated functions than that can be directly supported in SQL. However, this basic architecture suffers from some limitations. Dean and Ghemawa [120] reported about some possible improvements that can be incorporated into the MapReduce framework. Examples of these possible improvements include:

- MapReduce should take advantage of natural indices whenever possible.
- Most MapReduce output can be left unmerged since there is no benefit of merging them if the next consumer is just another MapReduce program.
- MapReduce users should avoid using inefficient textual formats.

In the following subsections we discuss some research efforts that have been conducted in order to deal with these challenges and the different improvements that has been made on the basic implementation of the MapReduce framework in order to achieve these goals.

Processing Join Operations

One main limitation of the MapReduce framework is that it does not support the joining of multiple datasets in one task. However, this can still be achieved with additional MapReduce steps. For example, users can map and reduce one dataset and read data from other datasets on the fly. Blanas et al. [82] have reported about a study that evaluated the performance of different distributed join algorithms using the MapReduce framework. In particular, they have evaluated the following implementation strategies of distributed join algorithms:

- *Standard repartition join*: The two input relations are dynamically partitioned on the join key and the corresponding pairs of partitions are joined using the standard partitioned sort-merge join approach.
- *Improved repartition join*: One potential problem with the standard repartition join is that all the records for a given join key from both input relations have to be buffered. Therefore, when the key cardinality is small or when the data is highly skewed, all the records for a given join key may not fit in memory. The

improved repartition join strategy fixes the buffering problem by introducing the following key changes:

- In the map function, the output key is changed to a composite of the join key and the table tag. The table tags are generated in a way that ensures records from one input relation will be sorted ahead of those from the other input relation on a given join key.
- The partitioning function is customized so that the hashcode is computed from just the join key part of the composite key. This way records with the same join key are still assigned to the same reduce task.
- As records from the smaller input are guaranteed to be ahead of those from L for a given join key, only the records from the smaller input are buffered and the records of the larger input are streamed to generate the join output.

• *Broadcast join*: Instead of moving both input relations across the network as in the repartition-based joins, the broadcast join approach moves only the smaller input relation so that it avoids the preprocessing sorting requirement of both input relations and more importantly avoids the network overhead for moving the larger relation.
• *Semi-join*: This join approach tries to avoid the problem of the broadcast join approach where it is possible to send many records of the smaller input relation across the network while they may not be actually referenced by any records in the other relation. It achieves this goal at the cost of an extra scan of the smaller input relation where it determines the set of unique join keys in the smaller relation, send them to the other relation to specify the list of the actual referenced join keys and then send only these records across the network for executing the real execution of the join operation.
• *Per-split semi-join*: This join approach tries to improve the semi-join approach with a further step to address the fact that not every record in the filtered version of the smaller relation will join with a particular split of the larger relation. Therefore, an extra process step is executed to determine the target split(s) of each filtered join key.

Figure 9.3 illustrates a decision tree that summarizes the tradeoffs of the studied join strategies according to the results of that study. Based on statistics, such as the relative data size and the fraction of the join key referenced, this decision tree tries to determine what is the right join strategy for a given circumstance. If data is not preprocessed, the right join strategy depends on the size of the data transferred via the network. If the network cost of broadcasting an input relation R to every node is less expensive than transferring both R and projected L, then the broadcast join algorithm should be used. When preprocessing is allowed, semi-join, per-split semi-join and directed join with sufficient partitions are the best choices. Semi-join and per-split semi-join offer further flexibility since their preprocessing steps are insensitive to how the log table is organized, and thus suitable for any number of reference tables. In addition, the preprocessing steps of these two algorithms are cheaper since there is no shuffling of the log data.

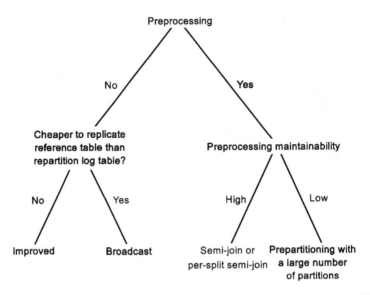

Fig. 9.3 Decision tree for choosing between various join strategies on the MapReduce framework

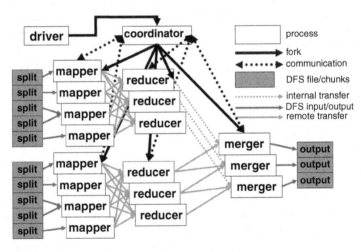

Fig. 9.4 An overview of the Map-Reduce-Merge framework

To tackle the limitation of the extra processing requirements for performing join operations in the MapReduce framework, the *Map-Reduce-Merge* model [103] have been introduced to enable the processing of multiple datasets. Figure 9.4 illustrates the framework of this model where the map phase transforms an input key/value pair $(k1, v1)$ into a list of intermediate key/value pairs $[(k2, v2)]$. The reduce function aggregates the list of values $[v2]$ associated with $k2$ and produces a list of values $[v3]$ which is also associated with k2. Note that inputs and outputs of both functions belong to the same lineage (α). Another pair of map and reduce functions produce the intermediate output $(k3, [v4])$ from another lineage (β). Based on keys $k2$ and $k3$, the merge function combines the two reduced outputs from different lineages into a list of key/value outputs $[(k4, v5)]$. This final output becomes a new lineage (γ). If $\alpha = \beta$ then this merge function does a self-merge which is similar to self-join in relational algebra. The main differences between the processing model of this framework and the original MapReduce is the production of a key/value list from the reduce function instead of just that of values. This change is introduced because the merge function requires input datasets to be organized (partitioned, then either sorted or hashed) by keys and these keys have to be passed into the function to be merged. In the original framework, the reduced output is final. Hence, users pack whatever is needed in $[v3]$ while passing $k2$ for the next stage is not required. Figure 9.5 illustrates a sample execution of the Map-Reduce-Merge framework. In this example, there are two datasets *Employee* and *Department* where Employee's key attribute is emp-id and the Department's key is dept-id. The execution of this example query aims to join these two datasets and compute employee bonuses. On the left hand side of Fig. 9.5, a mapper reads Employee entries and computes a bonus for each entry. A reducer then sums up these bonuses for every employee and sorts them by dept-id, then emp-id. On the right hand side, a mapper reads Department entries and computes bonus adjustments. A reducer then sorts these department entries. At the end, a merger matches the output records from the two reducers on dept-id and applies a department-based bonus adjustment on employee bonuses. Yang et al. [104] have also proposed an approach for improving the Map-Reduce-Merge framework by adding a new primitive called *Traverse*. This primitive can process index file entries recursively, select data partitions based on query conditions and feed only selected partitions to other primitives.

The *Map-Join-Reduce* [154] represents another approach that has been introduced with a filtering-join-aggregation programming model as an extension of the standard MapReduce's filtering-aggregation programming model. In particular, in addition to the standard mapper and reducer operation of the standard MapReduce framework, they introduce a third operation, join (called joiner), to the framework. Hence, to join multiple datasets for aggregation, users specify a set of *join()* functions and the join order between them. Then, the runtime system automatically joins the multiple input datasets according to the join order and invoke *join()* functions to process the joined records. They have also introduced a one-to-many shuffling strategy which shuffles each intermediate key/value pair to many joiners at one time. Using a tailored partition strategy, they can utilize the one-to-many shuffling scheme to join multiple datasets in one phase instead of a sequence of MapReduce jobs. The runtime system for executing a Map-Join-Reduce job launches two kinds of processes: *MapTask*, and *ReduceTask*. Mappers run inside the MapTask process while joiners and reducers are invoked inside the ReduceTask process. Therefore, Map-Join-Reduce's process model allows for the pipelining of intermediate results between joiners and reducers since joiners and reducers are run inside the same ReduceTask process.

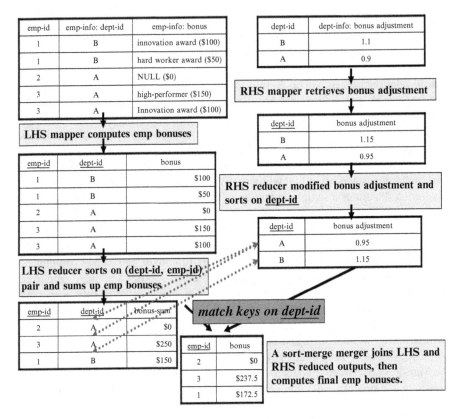

Fig. 9.5 A sample execution of the Map-Reduce-Merge framework

Afrati and Ullman [60, 61] have presented another approach to improve the join phase in the MapReduce framework. The approach aims to optimize the communication cost by focusing on selecting the most appropriate attributes that are used to partition and replicate the data among the reduce process. Therefore, it begins by identifying the *map-key*, the set of attributes that identify the Reduce process to which a Map process must send a particular tuple. Each attribute of the map-key gets a "*share*" which is the number of buckets into which its values are hashed, to form a component of the identifier of a Reduce process. Relations have their tuples replicated in limited fashion of which the degree of replication depends on the shares for those map-key attributes that are missing from their schema. The approach considers two important special join cases: *chain* joins (represents a sequence of two-way join operations where the output of one operation in this sequence is used as an input to another operation in a pipelined fashion) and *star* joins (represents joining of a large fact table with several smaller dimension tables). In each case, the proposed algorithm is able to determine the map-key and determine the shares that yield the least replication. The proposed approach is not always superior to the conventional way of using map-reduce to implement joins. However, there are some cases where the proposed approach results in clear wins such as:

- Analytic queries in which a very large fact table is joined with smaller dimension tables.
- Queries involving paths through graphs with high out-degree, such as the Web or a social network.

Li et al. [175] have proposed a data analysis platform, based on MapReduce, that is geared for *incremental* one-pass analytics. In particular, they replace the sort-merge implementation in the standard MapReduce framework with a purely hash-based framework, which is designed to address the computational and I/O bottlenecks as well as the blocking behavior of the sort-merge algorithm. Therefore, they devised two hash techniques to suit different user reduce functions, depending on whether the reduce function permits incremental processing. Besides eliminating the sorting cost from the map tasks, these hash techniques enable fast in-memory processing of the reduce function when the memory reaches a sufficient size as determined by the workload and algorithm. In addition, in order to bring the benefits of fast in-memory processing to workloads that require a large key-state space that far exceeds available memory, they presented a special technique to identify frequent keys and then update their states using a full in-memory processing path, both saving I/Os and also enabling early answers for these keys.

Supporting Iterative Processing

Many data analysis techniques (e.g. PageRank algorithm, recursive relational queries, social network analysis) require iterative computations. These techniques have a common requirement which is that data are processed iteratively until the computation satisfies a convergence or stopping condition. The basic MapReduce framework does not directly support these iterative data analysis applications. Instead, programmers must implement iterative programs by manually issuing multiple MapReduce jobs and orchestrating their execution using a driver program. In practice, there are two key problems with manually orchestrating an iterative program in MapReduce:

- Even though much of the data may be unchanged from iteration to iteration, the data must be re-loaded and re-processed at each iteration, wasting I/O, network bandwidth and CPU resources.
- The termination condition may involve the detection of when a fixpoint has been reached. This condition may itself require an extra MapReduce job on each iteration, again incurring overhead in terms of scheduling extra tasks, reading extra data from disk and moving data across the network.

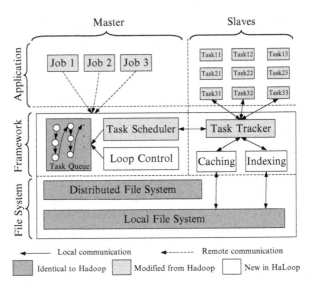

Fig. 9.6 An overview of HaLoop architecture

The *HaLoop* system [87, 88] is designed to support iterative processing on the MapReduce framework by extending the basic MapReduce framework with two main functionalities:

1. Caching the invariant data in the first iteration and then reusing them in later iterations.
2. Caching the reducer outputs, which makes checking for a fixpoint more efficient, without an extra MapReduce job.

Figure 9.6 illustrates the architecture of HaLoop as a modified version of the basic MapReduce framework. In order to accommodate the requirements of iterative data analysis applications, HaLoop has incorporated the following changes to the basic Hadoop MapReduce framework:

- It exposes a new application programming interface to users that simplifies the expression of iterative MapReduce programs.
- HaLoop's master node contains a new loop control module that repeatedly starts new map-reduce steps that compose the loop body until a user-specified stopping condition is met.
- It uses a new task scheduler that leverages data locality.
- It caches and indices application data on slave nodes. In principle, the task tracker not only manages task execution but also manages caches and indices on the slave node and redirects each task's cache and index accesses to local file system.

In principle, HaLoop relies on the same file system and has the same task queue structure as Hadoop but the task scheduler and task tracker modules are modified, and the loop control, caching, and indexing modules are newly introduced to the architecture. The task tracker not only manages task execution but also manages caches and indices on the slave node, and redirects each task's cache and index accesses to local file system.

In the MapReduce framework, each map or reduce task contains its portion of the input data and the task runs by performing the map/reduce function on its input data records where the life cycle of the task ends when finishing the processing of all the input data records has been completed. The *iMapReduce* framework [240] supports the feature of iterative processing by keeping alive each map and reduce task during the whole iterative process. In particular, when all of the input data of a persistent task are parsed and processed, the task becomes dormant, waiting for the new updated input data. For a map task, it waits for the results from the reduce tasks and is activated to work on the new input records when the required data from the reduce tasks arrive. For the reduce tasks, they wait for the map tasks' output and are activated synchronously as in MapReduce. Jobs can terminate their iterative process in one of two ways:

1. *Defining fixed number of iterations*: Iterative algorithm stops after it iterates n times.
2. *Bounding the distance between two consecutive iterations*: Iterative algorithm stops when the distance is less than a threshold.

The iMapReduce runtime system does the termination check after each iteration. To terminate the iterations by a fixed number of iterations, the persistent map/reduce task records its iteration number and terminates itself when the number exceeds a threshold. To bound the distance between the output from two consecutive iterations, the reduce tasks can save the output from two consecutive iterations and compute the distance. If the termination condition is satisfied, the master will notify all the map and reduce tasks to terminate their execution.

Other projects have been implemented for supporting iterative processing on the MapReduce framework. For example, *Twister* [50] is a MapReduce runtime with an extended programming model that supports iterative MapReduce computations efficiently [125]. It uses a publish/subscribe messaging infrastructure for communication and data transfers, and supports long running map/reduce tasks. In particular, it provides programming extensions to MapReduce with broadcast and scatter type data transfers. Microsoft has also developed a project that provides an iterative MapReduce runtime for Windows Azure called *Daytona* [37].

Data and Process Sharing

With the emergence of cloud computing, the use of an analytical query processing infrastructure (e.g., Amazon EC2) can be directly mapped to *monetary* value. Taking into account that different MapReduce jobs can perform similar work, there could be many opportunities for sharing the execution of their work. Thus, this sharing can reduce the overall amount of work which consequently leads to the reduction of the monetary charges incurred while utilizing the resources of the processing infrastructure. The *MRShare* system [187] have been presented as a sharing framework which is tailored to transform a batch of queries into a new batch that will be executed more efficiently by merging jobs into groups and evaluating each group as a single query. Based on a defined cost model, they described an optimization problem that aims to derive the optimal grouping of queries in order to avoid performing redundant work and thus resulting in significant savings on both processing time and money. In particular, the approach considers exploiting the following sharing opportunities:

- *Sharing scans.* To share scans between two mapping pipelines M_i and M_j, the input data must be the same. In addition, the key/value pairs should be of the same type. Given that, it becomes possible to merge the two pipelines into a single pipeline and scan the input data only once. However, it should be noted that such combined mapping will produce two streams of output tuples (one for each mapping pipeline M_i and M_j) . In order to distinguish the streams at the reducer stage, each tuple is tagged with a `tag()` part. This tagging part is used to indicate the origin mapping pipeline during the reduce phase.
- *Sharing map output.* If the map output key and value types are the same for two mapping pipelines M_i and M_j then the map output streams for M_i and M_j can be shared. In particular, if Map_i and Map_j are applied to each input tuple, then the map output tuples coming only from Map_i are tagged with `tag(i)` only. If a map output tuple was produced from an input tuple by both Map_i and Map_j, it is then tagged by `tag(i)+tag(j)`. Therefore, any overlapping parts of the map output will be shared. In principle, producing a smaller map output leads to savings on sorting and copying intermediate data over the network.
- *Sharing map functions.* Sometimes the map functions are identical and thus they can be executed once. At the end of the map stage, two streams are produced where each is tagged with its job tag. If the map output is shared, then clearly only one stream needs to be generated. Even if only some filters are common in both jobs, it is possible to share parts of the map functions.

In practice, sharing scans and sharing map-output yield I/O savings while sharing map functions (or parts of them) would yield additional CPU savings.

While the *MRShare* system focus on sharing the processing between queries that are executed concurrently, the *ReStore* system [126, 127] has been introduced so that it can enable the queries that are submitted at different times to share the intermediate results of previously executed jobs and reusing them for future submitted jobs to the system. In particular, each MapReduce job produces output that is stored in the distributed file system used by the MapReduce system (e.g. HDFS). These intermediate results are kept (for a defined period) and managed so that it can be used as input by subsequent jobs. ReStore can make use of whole jobs or sub-jobs reuse opportunities. To achieve this goal, the ReStore consists of two main components:

- *Repository of MapReduce job outputs*: It stores the outputs of previously executed MapReduce jobs and the physical plans of these jobs.
- *Plan matcher and rewriter*: Its aim is to find physical plans in the repository that can be used to rewrite the input jobs using the available matching intermediate results.

In principle, the approach of the *ReStore* system can be viewed as analogous to the steps of building and using materialized views for relational databases [145].

Support of Data Indices and Column Storage

One of the main limitations of the original implementation of the MapReduce framework is that it is designed in a way that the jobs can only scan the input data in a sequential-oriented fashion. Hence, the query processing performance of the MapReduce framework is unable to match the performance of a well-configured parallel DBMS [194]. In order to tackle this challenge, Dittrich et al. [123] have presented the *Hadoop++* system which aims to boost the query performance of the Hadoop system without changing any of the system internals. They achieved this goal by injecting their changes through user-defined function (UDFs) which only affect the Hadoop system from inside without any external effect. In particular, they introduce the following main changes:

- *Trojan index*: The original Hadoop implementation does not provide index access due to the lack of a priori knowledge of schema and the MapReduce jobs being executed. Hence, the Hadoop++ system is based on the assumption that if we know the schema and the anticipated MapReduce jobs, then we can create appropriate indices for the Hadoop tasks. In particular, trojan index is an approach to integrate indexing capability into Hadoop in a non-invasive way. These indices are created during the data loading time and thus have no penalty at query time. Each trojan index provides an optional index access path which can be used for selective MapReduce jobs. The scan access path can still be used for other MapReduce jobs. These indices are created by injecting appropriate UDFs inside the Hadoop implementation. Specifically, the main features of trojan indices can be summarized as follows:

  - *No external library or engine*: Trojan indices integrate indexing capability natively into the Hadoop framework without imposing a distributed SQL-query engine on top of it.
  - *Non-invasive*: They do not change the existing Hadoop framework. The index structure is implemented by providing the right UDFs.
  - *Optional access path*: They provide an optional index access path which can be used for selective MapReduce jobs. However, the scan access path can still be used for other MapReduce jobs.

- *Seamless splitting*: Data indexing adds an index overhead for each data split. Therefore, the logical split includes the data as well as the index as it automatically splits the indexed data at logical split boundaries.
- *Partial index*: Trojan Index need not be built on the entire split. However, it can be built on any contiguous subset of the split as well.
- *Multiple indexes*: Several Trojan Indexes can be built on the same split. However, only one of them can be the primary index. During query processing, an appropriate index can be chosen for data access based on the logical query plan and the cost model.

- *Trojan join*: Similar to the idea of the trojan index, the Hadoop++ system assumes that if we know the schema and the expected workload, then we can co-partition the input data during the loading time. In particular, given any two input relations, they apply the same partitioning function on the join attributes of both the relations at data loading time and place the co-group pairs, having the same join key from the two relations, on the same split and hence on the same node. As a result, join operations can be then processed locally within each node at query time. Implementing the trojan joins do not require any changes to be made to the existing implementation of the Hadoop framework. The only changes are made on the internal management of the data splitting process. In addition, trojan indices can be freely combined with trojan joins.

The design and implementation of a column-oriented and binary backend storage format for Hadoop has been presented in [132]. In general, a straightforward way to implement a column-oriented storage format for Hadoop is to store each column of the input dataset in a separate file. However, this raises two main challenges:

- It requires generating roughly equal sized splits so that a job can be effectively parallelized over the cluster.
- It needs to ensure that the corresponding values from different columns in the dataset are co-located on the same node running the map task.

The first challenge can be tackled by horizontally partitioning the dataset and storing each partition in a separate subdirectory. The second challenge is harder to tackle because of the default three-way block-level replication strategy of HDFS that provides fault tolerance on commodity servers but does not provide any co-location guarantees. Floratou et al. [132] tackle this challenge by implementing a modified HDFS block placement policy which guarantees that the files corresponding to the different columns of a split are always co-located across replicas. Hence, when reading a dataset, the column input format can actually assign one or more split-directories to a single split and the column files of a split-directory are scanned sequentially and the records are reassembled using values from corresponding positions in the files. A lazy record construction technique is used to mitigate the deserialization overhead in Hadoop, as well as eliminate unnecessary disk I/O. The basic idea behind lazy record construction is to deserialize only those columns of a record that are actually accessed in a map function. Each column of the input dataset can be compressed using one of the following compression schemes:

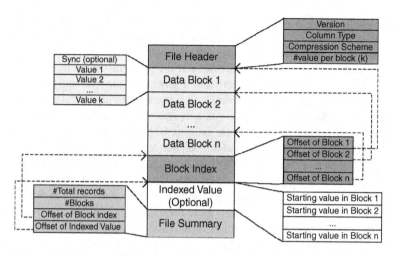

Fig. 9.7 An example structure of *CFile*

1. *Compressed blocks*: This scheme uses a standard compression algorithm to compress a block of contiguous column values. Multiple compressed blocks may fit into a single HDFS block. A header indicates the number of records in a compressed block and the block's size. This allows the block to be skipped if no values are accessed in it. However, when a value in the block is accessed, the entire block needs to be decompressed.
2. *Dictionary compressed skip list*: This scheme is tailored for map-typed columns. It takes advantage of the fact that the keys used in maps are often strings that are drawn from a limited universe. Such strings are well suited for dictionary compression. A dictionary is built of keys for each block of map values and store the compressed keys in a map using a skip list format. The main advantage of this scheme is that a value can be accessed without having to decompress an entire block of values.

One advantage of this approach is that adding a column to a dataset is not an expensive operation. This can be done by simply placing an additional file for the new column in each of the split-directories. On the other hand, a potential disadvantage of this approach is that the available parallelism may be limited for smaller datasets. Maximum parallelism is achieved for a MapReduce job when the number of splits is at least equal to the number of map tasks.

The *Llama* system [177] have introduced another approach of providing column storage support for the MapReduce framework. In this approach, each imported table is transformed into column groups where each group contains a set of files representing one or more columns. Llama introduced a column-wise format for Hadoop, called *CFile*, where each file can contain multiple data blocks and each block of the file contains a fixed number of records (Fig. 9.7). However, the size of each logical block may vary since records can be variable-sized. Each file includes a block index, which is stored after all data blocks, stores the offset of each block and is used to locate a specific block. In order to achieve storage efficiency, Llama uses block-level compression by using any of the well-known compression schemes. In order to improve the query processing and the performance of join operations, Llama columns are formed into correlation groups to provide the basis for the vertical partitioning of tables. In particular, it creates multiple vertical groups where each group is defined by a collection of columns, one of them is specified as the sorting column. Initially, when a new table is imported into the system, a basic vertical group is created which contains all the columns of the table and sorted by the table's primary key by default. In addition, based on statistics of query patterns, some auxiliary groups are dynamically created or discarded to improve the query performance. The *Clydesdale* system [73, 157], a system which has been implemented for targeting workloads where the data fits a star schema, uses *CFile* for storing its fact tables. It also relies on tailored join plans and block iteration mechanism [243] for optimizing the execution of its target workloads.

RCFile [146] (Record Columnar File) is another data placement structure that provides column-wise storage for Hadoop file system (HDFS). In RCFile, each table is firstly stored as horizontally partitioned into multiple row groups where each row group is then vertically partitioned so that each column is stored independently (Fig. 9.8). In particular, each table can have multiple HDFS blocks where each block organizes records with the basic unit of a row group. Depending on the row group size and the HDFS block size, an HDFS block can have only one or multiple row groups. In particular, a row group contains the following three sections:

1. The *sync marker* which is placed in the beginning of the row group and mainly used to separate two continuous row groups in an HDFS block.
2. A metadata header which stores the information items on how many records are in this row group, how many bytes are in each column and how many bytes are in each field in a column.
3. The table data section which is actually a column-store where all the fields in the same column are stored continuously together.

RCFile utilizes a column-wise data compression within each row group and provides a lazy decompression technique to avoid unnecessary column decompression during query execution. In particular, the metadata header section is compressed using the *RLE* (Run Length Encoding) algorithm. The table data section is not compressed as a whole unit. However, each column is independently compressed with the *Gzip* compression algorithm. When processing a row group, RCFile does not need to fully read the whole content of the row group into memory. It only reads the metadata header and the needed columns in the row group for a given query and thus it can skip unnecessary columns and gain the I/O advantages of a column-store. The metadata header is always decompressed and held in memory until RCFile processes the next row group. However, RCFile does not decompress all the loaded columns and uses a lazy decompression technique where a column will not be decompressed in memory until RCFile has determined that the data in the column will be really useful for query execution.

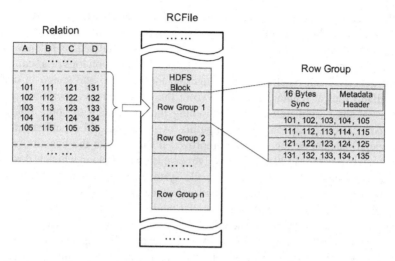

Fig. 9.8 An example structure of *RCFile*

The notion of *Trojan Data Layout* has been coined in [156] which exploits the existing data block replication in HDFS to create different Trojan Layouts on a per-replica basis. This means that rather than keeping all data block replicas in the same layout, it uses *different* Trojan Layouts for each replica which is optimized for a different subclass of queries. As a result, every incoming query can be scheduled to the most suitable data block replica. In particular, Trojan Layouts change the internal organization of a data block and not among data blocks. They co-locate attributes together according to query workloads by applying a column grouping algorithm which uses an interestingness measure that denotes how well a set of attributes speeds up most or all queries in a workload. The column groups are then packed in order to maximize the total interestingness of data blocks. At query time, an incoming MapReduce job is transparently adapted to query the data block replica that minimizes the data access time. The map tasks are then routed of the MapReduce job to the data nodes storing such data block replicas.

Effective Data Placement

In the basic implementation of the Hadoop project, the objective of the data placement policy is to achieve good load balance by distributing the data evenly across the data servers, independently of the intended use of the data. This simple data placement policy works well with most Hadoop applications that access just a *single* file. However, there are some other applications that process data from *multiple* files which can get a significant boost in performance with customized strategies. In these applications, the absence of data colocation increases the data shuffling costs, increases the network overhead and reduces the effectiveness of data partitioning. For example, log processing is a very common usage scenario for Hadoop framework. In this scenario, data are accumulated in batches from event logs such as: clickstreams, phone call records, application logs or a sequences of transactions. Each batch of data is ingested into Hadoop and stored in one or more HDFS files at regular intervals. Two of the most common operations in log analysis of these applications are (1) joining the log data with some reference data and (2) sessionization, i.e., computing user sessions. The performance of such operations can be significantly improved if they utilize the benefits of data colocation. *CoHadoop* [129] is a lightweight extension to Hadoop which is designed to enable colocating related files at the file system level while at the same time retaining the good load balancing and fault tolerance properties. It introduces a new file property to identify related data files and modify the data placement policy of Hadoop to colocate copies of those related files in the same server. These changes are designed in a way to retain the benefits of Hadoop, including load balancing and fault tolerance. In principle, CoHadoop provides a generic mechanism that allows applications to control data placement at the file-system level. In particular, a new file-level property called a *locator* is introduced and the Hadoop's data placement policy is modified so that it makes use of this locator property. Each locator is represented by a unique value (ID) where each file in HDFS is assigned to at most one locator and many files can be assigned to the same locator. Files with the same locator are placed on the same set of datanodes, whereas files with no locator are placed via Hadoop's default strategy. It should be noted that this colocation process involves all data blocks, including replicas. Figure 9.9 shows an example of colocating two files, *A* and *B*, via a common locator. All of *A*'s two HDFS blocks and *B*'s three blocks are stored on the same set of datanodes. To manage the locator information and keep track of collocated files, CoHadoop introduces a new data structure, *the locator table*, which stores a mapping of locators to the list of files that share this locator. In practice, the CoHadoop extension enables a wide variety of applications to exploit data colocation by simply specifying related files such as: colocating log files with reference files for joins, collocating partitions for grouping and aggregation, colocating index files with their data files and colocating columns of a table.

Pipelining and Streaming Operations

The original implementation of the MapReduce framework has been designed in a way that the entire output of each map and reduce task to be *materialized* into a local file before it can be consumed by the next stage. This materialization step allows for the implementation of a simple and elegant checkpoint/restart fault tolerance mechanism. The *MapReduce Online* approach [108, 109] has been proposed as a modified architecture of the MapReduce framework in which intermediate data is *pipelined* between operators while preserving the programming interfaces and fault

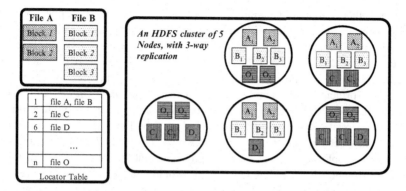

Fig. 9.9 Example file colocation in CoHadoop

tolerance models of previous MapReduce frameworks. This pipelining approach provides important advantages to the MapReduce framework such as:

- The reducers can begin their processing of the data as soon as it is produced by mappers. Therefore, they can generate and refine an approximation of their final answer during the course of execution. In addition, they can provide initial estimates of the results several orders of magnitude faster than the final results.
- It widens the domain of problems to which MapReduce can be applied. For example, it facilitates the ability to design MapReduce jobs that run continuously, accepting new data as it arrives and analyzing it immediately (continuous queries). This allows MapReduce to be used for applications such as event monitoring and stream processing.
- Pipelining delivers data to downstream operators more promptly, which can increase opportunities for parallelism, improve utilization and reduce response time.

In this approach, each reduce task contacts every map task upon initiation of the job and opens a TCP socket which will be used to pipeline the output of the map function. As each map output record is produced, the mapper determines which partition (reduce task) the record should be sent to, and immediately sends it via the appropriate socket. A reduce task accepts the pipelined data it receives from each map task and stores it in an in-memory buffer. Once the reduce task learns that every map task has completed, it performs a final merge of all the sorted runs. In addition, the reduce tasks of one job can optionally pipeline their output directly to the map tasks of the next job, sidestepping the need for expensive fault-tolerant storage in HDFS for what amounts to a temporary file. However, the computation of the reduce function from the previous job and the map function of the next job cannot be overlapped as the final result of the reduce step cannot be produced until all map tasks have completed, which prevents effective pipelining. Therefore, the reducer treats the output of a pipelined map task as *tentative* until the *JobTracker* informs the reducer that the map task has committed successfully. The reducer can merge together spill files generated by the same uncommitted mapper, but will not combine those spill files with the output of other map tasks until it has been notified that the map task has committed. Thus, if a map task fails, each reduce task can ignore any tentative spill files produced by the failed map attempt. The *JobTracker* will take care of scheduling a new map task attempt, as in standard Hadoop. In principle, the main limitation of the *MapReduce Online* approach is that it is based on HDFS. Therefore, it is not suitable for streaming applications, in which data streams have to be processed without any disk involvement. A similar approach has been presented by Logothetis and Yocum [179] which defines an *incremental* MapReduce job as one that processes data in large batches of tuples and runs continuously according to a specific window range and slide of increment. In particular, it produces a MapReduce result that includes all data within a window (of time or data size) of every slide and considers landmark MapReduce jobs where the trailing edge of the window is fixed and the system incorporates new data into the existing result. Map functions are trivially continuous, and process data on a tuple-by-tuple basis. However, before the reduce function may process the mapped data, the data must be partitioned across the reduce operators and sorted. When the map operator first receives a new key-value pair, it calls the map function and inserts the result into the latest increment in the map results. The operator then assigns output key-value pairs to reduce tasks, grouping them according to the partition function. Continuous reduce operators participate in the sort as well, grouping values by their keys before calling the reduce function.

The *Incoop* system [81] has been introduced as a MapReduce implementation that has been adapted for incremental computations which detects the changes on the input datasets and enables the automatic update of the outputs of the MapReduce jobs by employing a fine-grained result reuse mechanism. In particular, it allows MapReduce programs which are not designed for incremental processing to be executed transparently in an incremental manner. To achieve this goal, the design of Incoop introduces new techniques that are incorporated into the Hadoop MapReduce framework. For example, instead of relying on HDFS to store the input to MapReduce jobs, Incoop devises a file system called *Inc-HDFS* (Incremental HDFS) that provides mechanisms to identify similarities in the input data of consecutive job runs. In particular, Inc-HDFS splits the input into chunks whose boundaries depend on the file contents so that small changes to input do not change all chunk boundaries. Therefore, this partitioning mechanism can maximize the opportunities for reusing results from previous computations, while preserving compatibility with HDFS by offering the same interface and semantics. In addition, Incoop controls the granularity of tasks so that large tasks can be divided into smaller subtasks that can be re-used even when the large tasks cannot. Therefore, it introduces a new *Contraction phase* that leverages *Combiner* functions to reduce the network traffic by anticipating a small part of the processing done by the Reducer tasks and control their granularity. Furthermore, Incoop improves the effectiveness of memoization by implementing an affinity-based scheduler that applies a work stealing algorithm to minimize the amount of data movement across machines. This modified scheduler strikes a balance between exploiting the locality of previously computed results and executing tasks on any available machine to prevent straggling effects. On the runtime, instances of incremental Map tasks take advantage of previously stored results by querying the memoization server. If they find that the result has already been computed, they fetch the result from the location of their memoized output and conclude. Similarly, the results of a Reduce task are remembered by storing them persistently and locally where a mapping from a collision-resistant hash of the input to the location of the output is inserted in the memoization server.

Since a Reduce task receives input from n Map tasks, the key stored in the memoization server consists of the hashes of the outputs from all n Map task that collectively form the input to the Reduce task. Therefore, when executing a Reduce task, instead of immediately copying the output from the Map tasks, the Reduce task consults Map tasks for their respective hashes to determine if the Reduce task has already been computed in previous run. If so, that output is directly fetched from the location stored in the memoization server, which avoids the re-execution of that task.

The M^3 system [64] has been proposed to support the answering of continuous queries over streams of data bypassing the HDFS so that data gets processed only through a main-memory-only data-path and totally avoids any disk access. In this approach, Mappers and Reducers never terminate where there is only one MapReduce job per query operator that is continuously executing. In M^3, query processing is incremental where only the new input is processed, and the change in the query answer is represented by three sets of inserted ($+ve$), deleted ($-ve$) and updated (u) tuples. The query issuer receives as output a stream that represents the deltas (incremental changes) to the answer. Whenever an input tuple is received, it is transformed into a modify operation ($+ve$, $-ve$ or u) that is propagated in the query execution pipeline, producing the corresponding set of modify operations in the answer. Supporting incremental query evaluation requires that some intermediate state be kept at the various operators of the query execution pipeline. Therefore, Mappers and Reducers run continuously without termination, and hence can maintain main-memory state throughout the execution. In contrast to splitting the input data based on its size as in Hadoops Input Split functionality, M^3 splits the streamed data based on arrival rates where the Rate Split layer, between the main-memory buffers and the Mappers, is responsible for balancing the stream rates among the Mappers. This layer periodically receives rate statistics from the Mappers and accordingly redistributes the load of processing amongst Mappers. For instance, a fast stream that can overflow one Mapper should be distributed among two or more Mappers. In contrast, a group of slow streams that would underflow their corresponding Mappers should be combined to feed into only one Mapper. To support fault tolerance, input data is replicated inside the main memory buffers and an input split is not overwritten until the corresponding Mapper commits. When a Mapper fails, it re-reads its corresponding input split from any of the replica inside the buffers. A Mapper writes its intermediate key-value pairs in its own main-memory, and does not overwrite a set of key-value pairs until the corresponding reducer commits. When a reducer fails, it re-reads its corresponding sets of intermediate key-value pairs from the Mappers.

The *DEDUCE* system [166] has been presented as a middleware that attempts to combine real-time stream processing with the capabilities of a large scale data analysis framework like MapReduce. In particular, it extends the *IBM's System S* stream processing engine and augments its capabilities with those of the MapReduce framework. In this approach, the input data set to the MapReduce operator can be either pre-specified at compilation time or could be provided at runtime as a punctuated list of files or directories. Once the input data is available, the MapReduce operator spawns a MapReduce job and produces a list of punctuated list of files or directories, which point to the output data. Therefore, a MapReduce operator can potentially spawn multiple MapReduce jobs over the application lifespan but such jobs are spawned only when the preceding job (if any) has completed its execution. Hence, multiple jobs can be cascaded together to create a data-flow of MapReduce operators where the output from the MapReduce operators can be read to provide updates to the stream processing operators.

System Optimizations

Several studies have been conducted to evaluate the performance characteristics of the MapReduce framework. For example, Gu and Grossman [141] have reported the following lessons which they have learned from their experiments with the MapReduce framework:

- *The importance of data locality.* Locality is a key factor especially when relying on inexpensive commodity hardware.
- *Load balancing and the importance of identifying hot spots.* With poor load balancing, the entire system can be waiting for a single node. It is important to eliminate any "hot spots" which can be caused by data access (accessing data from a single node) or network I/O (transferring data into or out of a single node).
- *Fault tolerance comes with a price.* In some cases, fault tolerance introduces extra overhead in order to replicate the intermediate results. For example, in the cases of running on small to medium sized clusters, it might be reasonable to favor performance and re-run any failed intermediate task when necessary.
- *Streams are important.* Streaming is important in order to reduce the total running time of MapReduce jobs.

Jiang et al. [155] have conducted an in-depth performance study of MapReduce using its open source implementation, Hadoop. As an outcome of this study, they identified some factors that can have significant performance impact on the MapReduce framework. These factors are described as follows:

- Although MapReduce is independent of the underlying storage system, it still requires the storage system to provide efficient I/O modes for scanning data. The experiments of the study on HDFS show that direct I/O outperforms streaming I/O by 10–15 %.

- The MapReduce can utilize three kinds of indices (range-indices, block-level indices and database indexed tables) in a straightforward way. The experiments of the study show that the range-index improves the performance of MapReduce by a factor of 2 in the selection task and a factor of 10 in the join task when selectivity is high.
- There are two kinds of decoders for parsing the input records: mutable decoders and immutable decoders. The study claim that only immutable decoders introduce performance bottleneck. To handle database-like workloads, MapReduce users should strictly use mutable decoders. A mutable decoder is faster than an immutable decoder by a factor of 10, and improves the performance of selection by a factor of 2. Using a mutable decoder, even parsing the text record is efficient.
- Map-side sorting exerts negative performance effect on large aggregation tasks which require nontrivial key comparisons and produce millions of groups. Therefore, fingerprinting-based sort can significantly improve the performance of MapReduce on such aggregation tasks. The experiments show that fingerprinting-based sort outperforms direct sort by a factor of 4 to 5, and improves overall performance of the job by 20–25 %.
- Scheduling strategy affects the performance of MapReduce as it can be sensitive to the processing speed of slave nodes, and slows down the execution time of the entire job by 25–35 %.

The experiments of the study show that with proper engineering for these factors, the performance of MapReduce can be improved by a factor of 2.5 to 3.5 and approaches the performance of Parallel Databases. Therefore, several low-level system optimization techniques have been introduced to improve the performance of the MapReduce framework.

In general, running a single program in a MapReduce framework may require tuning a number of parameters by users or system administrators. The settings of these parameters control various aspects of job behavior during execution such as memory allocation and usage, concurrency, I/O optimization, and network bandwidth usage. The submitter of a Hadoop job has the option to set these parameters either using a program-level interface or through XML configuration files. For any parameter whose value is not specified explicitly during job submission, default values, either shipped along with the system or specified by the system administrator, are used [69]. Users can run into performance problems because they do not know how to set these parameters correctly, or because they do not even know that these parameters exist. Herodotou and Babu [148] have focused on the optimization opportunities presented by the large space of configuration parameters for these programs. They introduced a *Profiler* component to collect detailed statistical information from unmodified MapReduce programs and a *What-if* Engine for fine-grained cost estimation. In particular, the Profiler component is responsible for the following two main aspects:

1. Capturing information at the fine granularity of phases within the map and reduce tasks of a MapReduce job execution. This information is crucial to the accuracy of decisions made by the What-if Engine and the Cost-based Optimizer components.

2. Using dynamic instrumentation to collect run-time monitoring information from unmodified MapReduce programs. The dynamic nature means that monitoring can be turned on or off on demand.

The What-if Engine's accuracy come from how it uses a mix of simulation and model-based estimation at the phase level of the MapReduce job execution [147, 149, 150]. For a given MapReduce program, the role of the cost-based optimizer component is to enumerate and search efficiently through the high dimensional space of configuration parameter settings, making appropriate calls to the What-if Engine. In order for the program to find a good configuration setting, it clusters parameters into lower-dimensional subspaces such that the globally-optimal parameter setting in the high-dimensional space can be generated by composing the optimal settings found for the subspaces. *Stubby* [176] has been presented as a cost-based optimizer for MapReduce workflows that searches through the subspace of the full plan space that can be enumerated correctly and costed based on the information available in any given setting. Stubby enumerates the plan space based on plan-to-plan transformations and an efficient search algorithm.

The *Manimal* system [92, 153] is designed as a static analysis-style mechanism for detecting opportunities for applying relational style optimizations in MapReduce programs. Like most programming-language optimizers, it is a best-effort system where it does not guarantee that it will find every possible optimization and it only indicates an optimization when it is entirely safe to do so. In particular, the analyzer component of the system is responsible for examining the MapReduce program and sends the resulting optimization descriptor to the optimizer component. In addition, the analyzer also emits an index generation program that can yield a B+Tree of the input file. The optimizer uses the optimization descriptor, plus a catalog of pre-computed indexes, to choose an optimized execution plan, called an execution descriptor. This descriptor, plus a potentially-modified copy of the user's original program, is then sent for execution on the Hadoop cluster. These steps are performed transparently from the user where the submitted program does not need to be modified by the programmer in any way. In particular, the main task of the analyzer is to produce a set of optimization descriptors which enable the system to carry out a phase roughly akin to logical rewriting of query plans in a relational database. The descriptors characterize a set of potential modifications that remain logically identical to the original plan. The catalog is a simple mapping from a filename to zero or more (X, O) pairs where X is an index file and O is an optimization descriptor. The optimizer examines the catalog to see if there is any entry for input file. If not, then it simply indicates that Manimal should run the unchanged user program without any optimization. If there is at least one entry for the input file, and a catalog-associated optimization descriptor is compatible with analyzer-output, then the optimizer can choose an execution plan that takes advantage of the associated index file.

A key feature of MapReduce is that it automatically handles failures, hiding the complexity of fault-tolerance from the programmer. In particular, if a node crashes, MapReduce automatically restarts the execution of its tasks. In addition, if a node is available but is performing poorly, MapReduce runs a speculative copy of its task (backup task) on another machine to finish the computation faster. Without this mechanism of speculative execution, a job would be as slow as the misbehaving task. This situation can arise for many reasons, including faulty hardware and system misconfiguration. On the other hand, launching too many speculative tasks may take away resources from useful tasks. Therefore, the accuracy in estimating the progress and time-remaining long running jobs is an important challenge for a runtime environment like the MapReduce framework. In particular, this information can play an important role in improving resource allocation, enhancing the task scheduling, enabling query debugging or tuning the cluster configuration. The *Para-Timer* system [184, 185] has been proposed to tackle this challenge. In particular, ParaTimer provides techniques for handling several challenges including failures and data skew. To handle unexpected changes in query execution times such as those due to failures, ParaTimer provides users with a set of time-remaining estimates that correspond to the predicted query execution times in different scenarios (i.e., a single worst-case failure, or data skew at an operator). Each of these indicators can be annotated with the scenario to which it corresponds, giving users a detailed picture of possible expected behaviors. To achieve this goal, ParaTimer estimates time-remaining by breaking queries into pipelines where the time-remaining for each pipeline is estimated by considering the work to be done and the speed at which that work will be performed, taking (time-varying) parallelism into account. To get processing speeds, ParaTimer relies on earlier debug runs of the same query on input data samples generated by the user. In addition, ParaTimer identifies the critical path in a query plan where it then estimates progress along that path, effectively ignoring other paths. Zaharia et al. [236] have presented an approach to estimate the progress of MapReduce tasks within environments of clusters with heterogenous hardware configurations. In these environments, choosing the node on which to run a speculative task is as important as choosing the task. They proposed an algorithm for speculative execution called *LATE* (Longest Approximate Time to End) which is based on three principles: prioritizing tasks to speculate, selecting fast nodes on which to run and capping speculative tasks to prevent thrashing. In particular, the algorithm speculatively execute the task that it suspects will finish farthest into the future, because this task provides the greatest opportunity for a speculative copy to overtake the original and reduce the job's response time. To really get the best chance of beating the original task with the speculative task, the algorithm only launches speculative tasks on fast nodes (and not the first available node). The *RAFT* (Recovery Algorithms for Fast-Tracking) system [197, 198] has been introduced, as a part of the *Hadoop++* system [123], for tracking and recovering MapReduce jobs under task or node failures. In particular, RAFT uses two main checkpointing mechanisms: *local checkpointing* and *query metadata checkpointing*. On the one hand, the main idea of local checkpointing is to utilize intermediate results, which are by default persisted by Hadoop, as checkpoints of ongoing task progress computation. In general, map tasks spill buffered intermediate results to local disk whenever the output buffer is on the verge to overflow. RAFT exploits this spilling phase to piggy-back checkpointing metadata on the latest spill of each map task. For each checkpoint, RAFT stores a triplet of metadata that includes the *taskID* which represents a unique task identifier, *spillID* which represents the local path to the spilled data and *offset* which specifies the last byte of input data that was processed in that spill. To recover from a task failure, the RAFT scheduler reallocates the failed task to the same node that was running the task. Then, the node resumes the task from the last checkpoint and reuses the spills previously produced for the same task. This simulates a situation where previous spills appear as if they were just produced by the task. In case that there is no local checkpoint available, the node recomputes the task from the beginning. On the other hand, the idea behind query metadata checkpointing is to push intermediate results to reducers as soon as map tasks are completed and to keep track of those incoming key-value pairs that produce local partitions and hence that are not shipped to another node for processing. Therefore, in case of a node failure, the RAFT scheduler can recompute local partitions.

In general, energy consumption and cooling are large components of the operational cost of datacenters [74]. Therefore, the cluster-level energy management of MapReduce framework is another interesting system optimization aspect. In principle, the energy efficiency of a cluster can be improved in two ways [174]:

1. By matching the number of active nodes to the current needs of the workload and placing the remaining nodes in low-power standby modes.
2. By engineering the compute and storage features of each node to match its workload and avoid energy wastage due to oversized components.

Lang and Patel [169] have investigated the approach to power down (and power up) nodes of a MapReduce cluster in order to save energy during periods of low utilization. In particular, they compared between the following two strategies for MapReduce energy management:

1. Covering Set (CS) strategy that keeps only a small fraction of the nodes powered up during periods of low utilization.
2. All-In Strategy (AIS) that uses all the nodes in the cluster to run a workload and then powers down the entire cluster.

The results from this comparison show that there are two crucial factors that affect the effectiveness of these two methods:

• The computational complexity of the workload.
• The time taken to transition nodes to and from a low power (deep hibernation) state to a high performance state.

The evaluation shows that *CS* is more effective than *AIS* only when the computational complexity of the workload is low (e.g., linear), and the time it takes for the hardware to transition a node to and from a low power state is a relatively large fraction of the overall workload time (i.e., the workload execution time is small). In all other cases, the *AIS* shows better performance over *CS* in terms of energy savings and response time performance.

9.4   Systems of Declarative Interfaces for the MapReduce Framework

For programmers, a key appealing feature in the MapReduce framework is that there are only two main high-level declarative primitives (*map* and *reduce*) that can be written in any programming language of choice and without worrying about the details of their parallel execution. However, the MapReduce programming model has its own limitations such as:

- Its one-input data format (key/value pairs) and two-stage data flow is extremely rigid. As we have previously discussed, to perform tasks that have a different data flow (e.g. joins or *n* stages) would require inelegant workarounds.
- Custom code has to be written for even the most common operations (e.g. projection and filtering) which leads to the fact that the code is usually difficult to reuse and maintain unless the users build and maintain their own libraries with the common functions they use for processing their data.

Moreover, many programmers could be unfamiliar with the MapReduce framework and they would prefer to use SQL (in which they are more proficient) as a high level declarative language to express their task while leaving all of the execution optimization details to the backend engine. In addition, it is beyond doubt that high level language abstractions enable the underlying system to perform automatic optimization. In the following subsection we discuss research efforts that have been proposed to tackle these problems and add SQL-like interfaces on top of the MapReduce framework.

Sawzall

Sawzall [195] is a scripting language used at Google on top of MapReduce. A Sawzall program defines the operations to be performed on a single record of the data. There is nothing in the language to enable examining multiple input records simultaneously, or even to have the contents of one input record influence the processing of another. The only output primitive in the language is the *emit* statement, which sends data to an external aggregator (e.g. Sum, Average, Maximum, Minimum) that gathers the results from each record after which the results are then correlated and processed. The authors argue that aggregation is done outside the language for a couple of reasons: (1) A more traditional language can use the language to correlate results but some of the aggregation algorithms are sophisticated and are best implemented in a native language and packaged in some form. (2) Drawing an explicit line between filtering and aggregation enables a high degree of parallelism and hides the parallelism from the language itself.

Figure 9.10 depicts an example Sawzall program where the first three lines declare the aggregators *count*, *total* and *sum of squares*. The keyword *table*

```
count: table sum of int;
total: table sum of float;
sumOfSquares: table sum of float;
x: float = input;
emit count $<$- 1;
emit total $<$- x;
emit sumOfSquares $<$- x * x;
```

Fig. 9.10 An example Sawzall program

introduces an aggregator type which are called tables in Sawzall even though they may be singletons. These particular tables are *sum* tables which add up the values emitted to them, *ints* or *floats* as appropriate. The Sawzall language is implemented as a conventional compiler, written in C++, whose target language is an interpreted instruction set, or byte-code. The compiler and the byte-code interpreter are part of the same binary, so the user presents source code to Sawzall and the system executes it directly. It is structured as a library with an external interface that accepts source code which is then compiled and executed, along with bindings to connect to externally-provided aggregators. The datasets of Sawzall programs are often stored in Google File System (GFS) [137]. The business of scheduling a job to run on a cluster of machines is handled by a software called *Workqueue* which creates a large-scale time sharing system out of an array of computers and their disks. It schedules jobs, allocates resources, reports status and collects the results.

Google has also developed *FlumeJava* [97], a Java library for developing and running data-parallel pipelines on top of MapReduce. FlumeJava is centered around a few classes that represent parallel collections. Parallel collections support a modest number of parallel operations which are composed to implement data-parallel computations where an entire pipeline, or even multiple pipelines, can be translated into a single Java program using the FlumeJava abstractions. To achieve good performance, FlumeJava internally implements parallel operations using *deferred* evaluation. The invocation of a parallel operation does not actually run the operation, but instead simply records the operation and its arguments in an internal execution plan graph structure. Once the execution plan for the whole computation has been constructed, FlumeJava optimizes the execution plan and then runs the optimized execution plan. When running the execution plan, FlumeJava chooses which strategy to use to implement each operation (e.g., local sequential loop vs. remote parallel MapReduce) based in part on the size of the data being processed, places remote computations near the data on which they operate and performs independent operations in parallel.

SQL
SELECT category, **AVG**(pagerank)
FROM urls
WHERE pagerank > 0.2
GROUP BY category
HAVING COUNT(*) > 10^6

Pig Latin
good_urls = **FILTER** urls **BY** pagerank > 0.2;
groups = **GROUP** good_urls **BY** category;
big_groups = **FILTER** groups **BY** COUNT(good_urls)>10^6;
output = **FOREACH** big_groups **GENERATE**
category, **AVG**(good_urls.pagerank);

Fig. 9.11 An example SQL query and its equivalent Pig Latin program

Pig Latin

Olston et al. [188] have presented a language called *Pig Latin* that takes a *middle* position between expressing task using the high-level declarative querying model in the spirit of SQL and the low-level/procedural programming model using MapReduce. Pig Latin is implemented in the scope of the *Apache Pig* project [12] and is used by programmers at Yahoo! for developing data analysis tasks. Writing a Pig Latin program is similar to specifying a query execution plan (e.g. a data flow graph). To experienced programmers, this method is more appealing than encoding their task as an SQL query and then coercing the system to choose the desired plan through optimizer hints. In general, automatic query optimization has its limits especially with uncataloged data, prevalent user-defined functions and parallel execution, which are all features of the data analysis tasks targeted by the MapReduce framework. Figure 9.11 shows an example SQL query and its equivalent Pig Latin program. Given a URL table with the structure $(url, category, pagerank)$, the task of the SQL query is to find each large category and its average pagerank of high-pagerank urls (> 0.2). A Pig Latin program is described as a sequence of steps where each step represents a single data transformation. This characteristic is appealing to many programmers. At the same time, the transformation steps are described using high-level primitives (e.g. filtering, grouping, aggregation) much like in SQL.

Pig Latin has several other features that are important for casual ad-hoc data analysis tasks. These features include support for a flexible, fully nested data model, extensive support for user-defined functions and the ability to operate over plain input files without any schema information [136]. In particular, Pig Latin has a simple data model consisting of the following four types:

1. *Atom*: An atom contains a simple atomic value such as a string or a number, e.g. "alice".
2. *Tuple*: A tuple is a sequence of fields, each of which can be any of the data types, e.g. ("alice", "lakers").
3. *Bag*: A bag is a collection of tuples with possible duplicates. The schema of the constituent tuples is flexible where not all tuples in a bag need to have the same number and type of fields

   e.g. $\left\{ \begin{array}{l} (\text{"alice", "lakers"}) \\ (\text{"alice", ("iPod", "apple")}) \end{array} \right\}$.

Fig. 9.12 Pig compilation
and execution steps

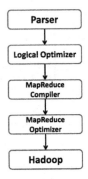

4. *Map*: A map is a collection of data items, where each item has an associated key
through which it can be looked up. As with bags, the schema of the constituent
data items is flexible However, the keys are required to be data atoms, e.g.
$$\left\{ \begin{array}{l} \text{``}k1\text{''} \rightarrow (\text{``}alice\text{''}, \text{``}lakers\text{''}) \\ \text{``}k2\text{''} \rightarrow \text{``}20\text{''} \end{array} \right\} .$$

To accommodate specialized data processing tasks, Pig Latin has extensive
support for user-defined functions (UDFs). The input and output of UDFs in Pig
Latin follow its fully nested data model. Pig Latin is architected such that the parsing
of the Pig Latin program and the logical plan construction is independent of the
execution platform. Only the compilation of the logical plan into a physical plan
depends on the specific execution platform chosen. Currently, Pig Latin programs
are compiled into sequences of MapReduce jobs which are executed using the
Hadoop MapReduce environment. In particular, a Pig Latin program goes through a
series of transformation steps [188] before being executed as depicted in Fig. 9.12.
The parsing steps verifies that the program is syntactically correct and that all
referenced variables are defined. The output of the parser is a canonical logical
plan with a one-to-one correspondence between Pig Latin statements and logical
operators which are arranged in a directed acyclic graph (DAG). The logical plan
generated by the parser is passed through a logical optimizer. In this stage, logical
optimizations such as projection pushdown are carried out. The optimized logical
plan is then compiled into a series of MapReduce jobs which are then passed
through another optimization phase. The DAG of optimized MapReduce jobs is
then topologically sorted and jobs are submitted to Hadoop for execution.

Hive

The *Hive* project [11] is an open-source data warehousing solution which has
been built by the Facebook Data Infrastructure Team on top of the Hadoop
environment [222]. The main goal of this project is to bring the familiar relational
database concepts (e.g. tables, columns, partitions) and a subset of SQL to the

```
FROM (
    MAP doctext USING 'python wc_mapper.py' AS (word, cnt)
    FROM docs
    CLUSTER BY word
) a
REDUCE word, cnt USING 'python wc_reduce.py';
```

Fig. 9.13   An example HiveQl query

unstructured world of Hadoop while still maintaining the extensibility and flexibility that Hadoop provides. Thus, it supports all the major primitive types (e.g. integers, floats, strings) as well as complex types (e.g. maps, lists, structs). Hive supports queries expressed in an SQL-like declarative language, *HiveQL* [29], and therefore can be easily understood by anyone who is familiar with SQL. These queries are compiled into MapReduce jobs that are executed using Hadoop. In addition, HiveQL enables users to plug in custom MapReduce scripts into queries [224]. For example, the canonical MapReduce word count example on a table of documents (Fig. 9.1) can be expressed in HiveQL as depicted in Fig. 9.13 where the *MAP* clause indicates how the input columns (*doctext*) can be transformed using a user program ('python wc_mapper.py') into output columns (*word* and *cnt*). The *REDUCE* clause specifies the user program to invoke ('python wc_reduce.py') on the output columns of the subquery.

HiveQL supports Data Definition Language (DDL) statements which can be used to create, drop and alter tables in a database [223]. It allows users to load data from external sources and insert query results into Hive tables via the load and insert Data Manipulation Language (DML) statements respectively. However, HiveQL currently does not support the update and deletion of rows in existing tables (in particular, INSERT INTO, UPDATE and DELETE statements) which allows the use of very simple mechanisms to deal with concurrent read and write operations without implementing complex locking protocols. The metastore component is the Hive's system catalog which stores metadata about the underlying table. This metadata is specified during table creation and reused every time the table is referenced in HiveQL. The metastore distinguishes Hive as a traditional warehousing solution when compared with similar data processing systems that are built on top of MapReduce-like architectures like Pig Latin [188].

Tenzing

The *Tenzing* system [100] has been presented by Google as an SQL query execution engine which is built on top of MapReduce and provides a comprehensive SQL92 implementation with some SQL99 extensions (e.g. ROLLUP() and CUBE() OLAP extensions). Tenzing also supports querying data in different formats such as: row stores (e.g. MySQL database), column stores, *Bigtable* (Google's built in key-value store) [99], *GFS* (Google File System) [137], text and protocol buffers. In particular, the Tenzing system has four major components:

- *The distributed worker pool*: Represents the execution system which takes a query execution plan and executes the MapReduce jobs. The pool consists of master and worker nodes plus an overall gatekeeper called the master watcher. The workers manipulate the data for all the tables defined in the metadata layer.
- *The query server*: Serves as the gateway between the client and the pool. The query server parses the query, applies different optimization mechanisms and sends the plan to the master for execution. In principle, the Tenzing optimizer applies some basic rule and cost-based optimizations to create an optimal execution plan.
- *Client interfaces*: Tenzing has several client interfaces including a command line client (CLI) and a Web UI. The CLI is a more powerful interface that supports complex scripting while the Web UI supports easier-to-use features such as query and table browsers tools. There is also an API to directly execute queries on the pool and a standalone binary which does not need any server side components but rather can launch its own MapReduce jobs.
- *The metadata server*: Provides an API to store and fetch metadata such as table names and schemas and pointers to the underlying data.

A typical Tenzing query is submitted to the query server (through the Web UI, CLI or API) which is responsible for parsing the query into an intermediate parse tree and fetching the required metadata from the metadata server. The query optimizer goes through the intermediate format, applies various optimizations and generates a query execution plan that consists of one or more MapReduce jobs. For each MapReduce, the query server finds an available master using the master watcher and submits the query to it. At this stage, the execution is physically partitioned into multiple units of work where idle workers poll the masters for available work. The query server monitors the generated intermediate results, gathers them as they arrive and streams the output back to the client. In order to increase throughput, decrease latency and execute SQL operators more efficiently, Tenzing has enhanced the MapReduce implementation with some main changes:

- *Streaming and in-memory chaining*: The implementation of Tenzing does not serialize the intermediate results of MapReduce jobs to GFS. Instead, it streams the intermediate results between the Map and Reduce tasks using the network and uses GFS only for backup purposes. In addition, it uses a memory chaining mechanism where the reducer and the mapper of the same intermediate results are co-located in the same process.
- *Sort avoidance*: Certain operators such as hash join and hash aggregation require shuffling but not sorting. The MapReduce API was enhanced to automatically turn off sorting for these operations, when possible, so that the mapper feeds data to the reducer which automatically bypasses the intermediate sorting step. Tenzing also implements a block-based shuffle mechanism that combines many

small rows into compressed blocks which is treated as one row in order to avoid reducer side sorting and avoid some of the overhead associated with row serialization and deserialization in the underlying MapReduce framework code.

Cheetah

The *Cheetah* system [101] has been introduced as a custom data warehouse solution which has been built on top of the MapReduce framework. In particular, it defines a virtual view on top of the common star or snowflake data warehouse schema and applies a stack of optimization techniques on top of the MapReduce framework including: data compression, optimized access methods, multi-query optimization and the exploiting materialized views. Cheetah provides an SQL-like and a non-SQL interface for applications to directly access the raw data which enables seamless integration of MapReduce and Data Warehouse tools so that the developers can take full advantage of the power of both worlds. For example, it has a JDBC interface such that a user program can submit query and iterate through the output results. If the query results are too big for a single program to consume, the user can write a MapReduce job to analyze the query output files which are stored on HDFS.

Cheetah stores data in the compressed columnar format. The choice of compression type for each column set is dynamically determined based on the data in each cell. During the *ETL* (extract-transfer-load) phase of a data warehousing project, the statistics of each column is maintained and the best compression method is chosen. During the query execution, Cheetah applies different optimization techniques. For example, the map phase uses a *shared scanner* which shares the scan of the fact tables and joins to the dimension tables where a selection pushup approach is applied in order to share the joins among multiple queries. Each scanner attaches a *query ID* to each output row, indicating which query this row qualifies. The reduce phase splits the input rows based on their query IDs and then sends them to the corresponding query operators. Cheetah also makes use of materialized view and applies a straightforward view matching and query rewriting process where the query must refer the virtual view that corresponds to the same fact table upon which the materialized view is defined. The non-aggregate columns referred in the SELECT and WHERE clauses in the query must be a subset of the materialized view's group by columns.

SQL/MapReduce

In general, a user-defined function (UDF) is a powerful database feature that allows users to customize database functionality. Friedman et al. [134] introduced the SQL/MapReduce (SQL/MR) UDF framework which is designed to facilitate parallel computation of procedural functions across hundreds of servers working

Fig. 9.14 Basic syntax of
SQL/MR query function

```
SELECT ...
FROM functionname(
   ON table-or-query
   [PARTITION BY expr, ...]
   [ORDER BY expr, ...]
   [clausename(arg, ...) ...]
   )
```

together as a single relational database. The framework is implemented as part of the *Aster Data Systems* [13] nCluster shared-nothing relational database. The framework leverages ideas from the MapReduce programming paradigm to provide users with a straightforward API through which they can implement a UDF in the language of their choice. Moreover, it allows maximum flexibility as the output schema of the UDF is specified by the function itself at query plan-time. This means that a SQL/MR function is polymorphic as it can process arbitrary input because its behavior as well as output schema are dynamically determined by information available at query plan-time. This also increases reusability as the same SQL/MR function can be used on inputs with many different schemas or with different user-specified parameters. In particular, SQL/MR allows the user to write custom-defined functions in any programming language and insert them into queries that leverage traditional SQL functionality. A SQL/MR function is defined in a manner that is similar to MapReduce's map and reduce functions.

The syntax for using a SQL/MR function is depicted in Fig. 9.14 where the SQL/MR function invocation appears in the SQL *FROM* clause and consists of the function name followed by a set of clauses that are enclosed in parentheses. The *ON* clause specifies the input to the invocation of the SQL/MR function. It is important to note that the input schema to the SQL/MR function is specified implicitly at query plan-time in the form of the output schema for the query used in the ON clause.

In practice, a SQL/MR function can be either a mapper (*Row* function) or a reducer (*Partition* function). The definitions of row and partition functions ensure that they can be executed in parallel in a scalable manner. In the *Row Function*, each row from the input table or query will be operated on by exactly one instance of the SQL/MR function. Semantically, each row is processed independently, allowing the execution engine to control parallelism. For each input row, the row function may emit zero or more rows. In the *Partition Function*, each group of rows as defined by the *PARTITION BY* clause will be operated on by exactly one instance of the SQL/MR function. If the *ORDER BY* clause is provided, the rows within each partition are provided to the function instance in the specified sort order. Semantically, each partition is processed independently, allowing parallelization by the execution engine at the level of a partition. For each input partition, the SQL/MR partition function may output zero or more rows.

HadoopDB

Parallel database systems have been commercially available for nearly two decades and there are now about a dozen of different implementations in the marketplace (e.g. Teradata [45], Aster Data [13], Netezza [31], Vertica [51], ParAccel [40], Greenplum [25]). The main aim of these systems is to improve performance through the parallelization of various operations such as loading data, building indices and evaluating queries. These systems are usually designed to run on top of a shared-nothing architecture [215] where data may be stored in a distributed fashion and input/output speeds are improved by using multiple CPUs and disks in parallel. On the other hand, there are some key reasons that make MapReduce a more preferable approach over a parallel RDBMS in some scenarios such as [82]:

- Formatting and loading a huge amount of data into a parallel RDBMS in a timely manner is a challenging and time-consuming task.
- The input data records may not always follow the same schema. Developers often want the flexibility to add and drop attributes and the interpretation of an input data record may also change over time.
- Large scale data processing can be very time consuming and therefore it is important to keep the analysis job going even in the event of failures. While most parallel RDBMSs have fault tolerance support, a query usually has to be restarted from scratch even if just one node in the cluster fails. In contrast, MapReduce deals with failures in a more graceful manner and can redo only the part of the computation that was lost due to the failure.

There has been a long debate on the comparison between the MapReduce framework and parallel database systems[3] [217]. Pavlo et al. [194] have conducted a large scale comparison between the Hadoop implementation of MapReduce framework and parallel SQL database management systems in terms of performance and development complexity. The results of this comparison have shown that parallel database systems displayed a significant performance advantage over MapReduce in executing a variety of data intensive analysis tasks. On the other hand, the Hadoop implementation was very much easier and more straightforward to set up and use in comparison to that of the parallel database systems. MapReduce have also shown to have superior performance in minimizing the amount of work that is lost when a hardware failure occurs. In addition, MapReduce (with its open source implementations) represents a very cheap solution in comparison to the very financially expensive parallel DBMS solutions (the price of an installation of a parallel DBMS cluster usually consists of seven figures of U.S. Dollars) [217].

The *HadoopDB* project [27] is a hybrid system that tries to combine the scalability advantages of MapReduce with the performance and efficiency advantages of parallel databases [58]. The basic idea behind HadoopDB is to connect

---

[3]http://databasecolumn.vertica.com/database-innovation/mapreduce-a-major-step-backwards/.

multiple single node database systems (PostgreSQL) using Hadoop as the task coordinator and network communication layer. Queries are expressed in SQL but their execution are parallelized across nodes using the MapReduce framework, however, as much of the single node query work as possible is pushed inside of the corresponding node databases. Thus, HadoopDB tries to achieve fault tolerance and the ability to operate in heterogeneous environments by inheriting the scheduling and job tracking implementation from Hadoop. Parallely, it tries to achieve the performance of parallel databases by doing most of the query processing inside the database engine. Figure 9.15 illustrates the architecture of HadoopDB which consists of two layers: (1) A data storage layer or the Hadoop Distributed File System (HDFS) [26]. (2) A data processing layer or the MapReduce Framework. In this architecture, HDFS is a block-structured file system managed by a central *NameNode*. Individual files are broken into blocks of a fixed size and distributed across multiple *DataNodes* in the cluster. The NameNode maintains metadata about the size and location of blocks and their replicas. The MapReduce Framework follows a simple master-slave architecture. The master is a single *JobTracker* and the slaves or worker nodes are *TaskTrackers*. The *JobTracker* handles the runtime scheduling of MapReduce jobs and maintains information on each TaskTracker's load and available resources. The *Database Connector* is the interface between independent database systems residing on nodes in the cluster and TaskTrackers. The Connector connects to the database, executes the SQL query and returns results as key-value pairs. The *Catalog* component maintains metadata about the databases, their location, replica locations and data partitioning properties. The *Data Loader* component is responsible for globally repartitioning data on a given partition key upon loading and breaking apart single node data into multiple smaller partitions or chunks. The *SMS planner* extends the HiveQL translator [222] (Sect. 9.4) and transforms SQL into MapReduce jobs that connect to tables stored as files in HDFS. Abouzeid et al. [59] have demonstrated HadoopDB in action running the following two different application types:

1. A semantic web application that provides biological data analysis of protein sequences.
2. A classical business data warehouse.

Jaql

Jaql [32] is a query language which is designed for Javascript Object Notation (JSON),[4] a data format that has become popular because of its simplicity and modeling flexibility. JSON is a simple, yet flexible way to represent data that ranges from flat, relational data to semi-structured, XML data. Jaql is primarily

---

[4]http://www.json.org/.

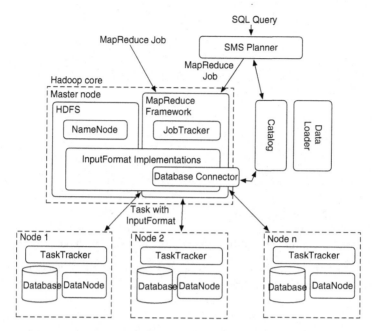

Fig. 9.15 The architecture of HadoopDB

used to analyze large-scale semi-structured data. It is a functional, declarative query language which rewrites high-level queries when appropriate into a low-level query consisting of Map-Reduce jobs that are evaluated using the Apache Hadoop project. Core features include user extensibility and parallelism. Jaql consists of a scripting language and compiler, as well as a runtime component [80]. It is able to process data with no schema or only with a partial schema. However, Jaql can also exploit rigid schema information when it is available, for both type checking and improved performance.

Jaql uses a very simple data model, a *JDM value* is either an atom, an array or a record. Most common atomic types are supported, including strings, numbers, nulls and dates. Arrays and records are compound types that can be arbitrarily nested. In more detail, an array is an ordered collection of values and can be used to model data structures such as vectors, lists, sets or bags. A record is an unordered collection of name-value pairs and can model structs, dictionaries and maps. Despite its simplicity, JDM is very flexible. It allows Jaql to operate with a variety of different data representations for both input and output, including delimited text files, JSON files, binary files, Hadoop's sequence files, relational databases, key-value stores or XML documents. Functions are first-class values in Jaql. They can be assigned to a variable and are high-order in that they can be passed as parameters or used as a return value. Functions are the key ingredient for reusability as any Jaql expression can be encapsulated in a function, and a function can be parameterized in powerful ways. Figure 9.16 depicts an example of a Jaql script that consists of a

Fig. 9.16 Sample Jaql script

```
import myrecord;

countFields = fn(records)(
  records
  -> transform myrecord::names($)
  -> expand
  -> group by fName = $ as occurrences
     into { name: fName, num: count(occurrences) }
);

read(hdfs("docs.dat"))
-> countFields()
-> write(hdfs("fields.dat"));
```

sequence of operators. The read operator loads raw data, in this case from Hadoop's
Distributed File System (HDFS), and converts it into Jaql values. These values are
processed by the countFields subflow, which extracts field names and computes
their frequencies. Finally, the write operator stores the result back into HDFS. In
general, the core expressions of the Jaql scripting language include:

1. *Transform*: The transform expression applies a function (or projection) to every
   element of an array to produce a new array. It has the form e1->transform
   e2, where e1 is an expression that describes the input array and e2 is applied to
   each element of e1.
2. *Expand*: The expand expression is most often used to unnest its input array. It
   differs from transform in two primary ways: (1) e2 must produce a value v that
   is an array type, and (2) each of the elements of v is returned to the output array,
   thereby removing one level of nesting.
3. *Group by*: Similar to SQL's GROUP BY, Jaql's group by expression partitions
   its input on a grouping expression and applies an aggregation expression to each
   group.
4. *Filter*: The filter expression, e− >filter p, retains input values from e for
   which predicate p evaluates to true.
5. *Join*: The join expression supports equijoin of 2 or more inputs. All of the options
   for inner and outer joins are also supported.
6. *Union*: The union expression is a Jaql function that merges multiple input arrays
   into a single output array. It has the form: union($e_1,\ldots$) where each e_i is an
   array.
7. *Control-flow*: The two most commonly used control-flow expressions in Jaql are
   if-then-else and block expressions. The if-then-else expression
   is similar to conditional expressions found in most scripting and programming
   languages. A block establishes a local scope where zero or more local variables
   can be declared and the last statement provides the return value of the block.

At a high-level, the Jaql architecture depicted in Fig. 9.17 is similar to most
database systems. Scripts are passed into the system from the interpreter or an
application, compiled by the parser and rewrite engine, and either explained
or evaluated over data from the I/O layer. The storage layer is similar to a
federated database. It provides an API to access data of different systems including

Fig. 9.17 Jaql system architecture

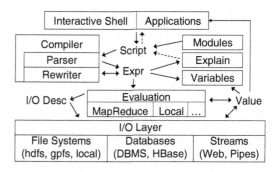

local or distributed file systems (e.g., Hadoop's HDFS), database systems (e.g., DB2, Netezza, HBase), or from streamed sources like the Web. Unlike federated databases, however, most of the accessed data is stored within the same cluster and the I/O API describes data partitioning, which enables parallelism with data affinity during evaluation. Jaql derives much of this flexibility from Hadoop's I/O API. It reads and writes many common file formats (e.g., delimited files, JSON text, Hadoop sequence files). Custom adapters are easily written to map a data set to or from Jaql's data model. The input can even simply be values constructed in the script itself. The Jaql interpreter evaluates the script locally on the computer that compiled the script, but spawns interpreters on remote nodes using MapReduce. The Jaql compiler automatically detects parallelization opportunities in a Jaql script and translates it to a set of MapReduce jobs.

9.5 Conclusions

The database community has been always focusing on dealing with the challenges of *Big Data* management, although the meaning of *"Big"* has been evolving continuously to represent different scales over the time [84]. According to IBM, we are currently creating 2.5 quintillion bytes of data, everyday. This data comes from many different sources and in different formats including digital pictures, videos, posts to social media sites, intelligent sensors, purchase transaction records and cell phone GPS signals. This is a new scale of *Big Data* which is attracting a huge interest from both the industrial and research communities with the aim of creating the best means to process and analyze this data in order to make the best use of it. In the last decade, the MapReduce framework has emerged as a popular mechanism to harness the power of large clusters of computers. It allows programmers to think in a *data-centric* fashion where they can focus on applying transformations to sets of data records while the details of distributed execution and fault tolerance are transparently managed by the MapReduce framework.

In this chapter, we presented a survey of the MapReduce family of approaches for developing scalable data processing systems and solutions. In general we notice that although the MapReduce framework, and its open source implementation of Hadoop, are now considered to be sufficiently mature such that they are widely used for developing many solutions by academia and industry in different application domains. We believe that it is unlikely that MapReduce will completely replace database systems even for data warehousing applications. We expect that they will always coexist and complement each others in different scenarios. We are also convinced that there is still room for further optimization and advancement in different directions on the spectrum of the MapReduce framework that is required to bring forward the vision of providing large scale data analysis as a commodity for novice end-users. For example, energy efficiency in the MapReduce is an important problem which has not attracted sufficient attention from the research community, yet. The traditional challenge of debugging large scale computations on distributed system has not been given sufficient consideration by the MapReduce research community. Related with the issue of the power of expressiveness of the programming model, we feel that this is an area that requires more investigation. We also noticed that the over simplicity of the MapReduce programming model have raised some key challenges on dealing with complex data models (e.g., nested models, XML and hierarchical model , RDF and graphs) efficiently. This limitation has called for the need of next-generation of big data architectures and systems that can provide the required scale and performance attributes for these domain. For example, Google has created the *Dremel* system [182, 183], commercialized under the name of *BigQuery* [22], to support interactive analysis of nested data. Google has also presented the *Pregel* system [180], open sourced by *Apache Giraph* and *Apache Hama* projects, that uses a BSP-based programming model for efficient and scalable processing of massive graphs on distributed cluster of commodity machines. Recently, *Twitter* has announced the release of the *Storm* [47] system as a distributed and fault-tolerant platform for implementing continuous and realtime processing applications of streamed data. We believe that more of these domain-specific systems will be introduced in the future to form the new generation of big data systems. Defining the right and most convenient programming abstractions and declarative interfaces of these domain-specific Big Data systems is another important research direction that will need to be deeply investigated.

Chapter 10
Conclusions

The advantages of the cloud computing paradigm opens up new avenues for deploying novel applications which were not economically feasible in a traditional enterprise infrastructure setting. Therefore, the cloud has become an increasingly popular platform for hosting software applications in a variety of domains such as e-retail, finance, news and social networking. Thus, we are witnessing a proliferation in the number of applications with a tremendous increase in the scale of the data generated as well as being consumed by such applications. Cloud-hosted database systems powering these applications form a critical component in the software stack of these applications. They play an important role in ensuring the smooth deployment or migration of software applications from the traditional enterprise infrastructures and on-premise data centers to the new cloud platforms and infrastructures. In the previous chapter, we presented an overview of the state-of-the-art of existing technologies for hosting the database tier of software applications in cloud environments. We crystallized the design choices, strengths, weaknesses of each technology. In this chapter, we shed the lights on a set of research challenges, that have been introduced by the new wave of cloud-hosted data storage systems that need to be addressed in order to ensure that the vision of designing and implementing successful scalable data management solutions can be achieved.

10.1 True Elasticity

A common characteristic of internet scale applications and services is that they can be used by large numbers of end-users and highly variable load spikes in the demand for services which can occur depending on the day and the time of year, and the popularity of the application [204]. In addition, the workload characteristic could vary significantly from one application type to another where possible fluctuations on the workload characteristics which could be of several orders of magnitude on the same business day may also occur [83]. In principle, elasticity and horizontal

scalability are considered to be of the most important features which are provided
by NoSQL systems [218]. In practice, both of the commercial NoSQL offerings
(e.g. Amazon SimpleDB) and commercial DaaS offerings (e.g. Amazon RDS,
Microsoft SQL Azure) do not provide their users with any flexibility to dynamically
increase or decrease the allocated computing resources of their applications. While
NoSQL offerings claim to provide elastic services of their tenants, they do not
provide any guarantee that their provider-side elasticity management will provide
scalable performance with increasing workloads [75]. Moreover, commercial DaaS
pricing models require their users to pre-determine the computing capacity that
will be allocated to their database instance as they provide standard packages of
computing resources (e.g. *Micro, Small, Large* and *Extra Large* DB Instances). In
practice, predicting the workload behavior (e.g. arrival pattern, I/O behavior, service
time distribution) and consequently accurate planning of the computing resource
requirements with consideration of their monetary costs are very challenging tasks.
Therefore, the user might still tend to over-provision the allocated computing
resources for the database tier of their application in order to ensure satisfactory
performance for their workloads. As a result of this, the software application is
unable to fully utilize the elastic feature of the cloud environment.

Xiong et al. [234] have presented an provider-centric approach for intelligently
managing the computing resources in a shared multi-tenant database system at the
virtual machine level. The proposed approach consists of two main components:

1. The system modeling module that uses machine learning techniques to learn
   a model that describes the potential profit margins for each tenant under
   different resource allocations. The learned model considers many factors of the
   environment such as SLA cost, client workload, infrastructure cost and action
   cost.
2. The resource allocation decision module dynamically adjusts the resource allocations, based on the information of the learned model, of the different tenants in
   order to achieve the optimum profits.

Tatemura et al. [220] proposed a declarative approach for achieving elastic
OLTP workloads. The approach is based on defining the following two main
components:

1. The transaction classes required for the application.
2. The actual workload with references to the transaction classes.

Using this information, a formal model can be defined to analyze elasticity of the
workload with transaction classes specified. In general, we believe that there is a
lack of flexible and powerful consumer-centric elasticity mechanisms that enable
software application to have more control on allocating the computing resources for
the database tier of their applications over the application running time and make
the best use of the elasticity feature of the cloud computing environments. More
attention from the research community is required to address these issues in the
future work.

10.2 Data Replication and Consistency Management

In general, stateless services are easy to scale since any new *replicas* of these services can operate completely independently of other instances. In contrast, scaling stateful services, such as a *database system*, needs to guarantee a consistent view of the system for users of the service. However, the cost of maintaining several database replicas that are always strongly consistent is very high. As we have previously described, according to the *CAP* theorem, most of the NoSQL systems overcome the difficulties of distributed replication by relaxing the consistency guarantees of the system and supporting various forms of weaker consistency models (e.g. eventual consistency [226]). In practice, a common feature of the *NoSQL* and *DaaS* cloud offerings is the creation and management of multiple replicas (usually 3) of the stored data while a replication architecture is running behind-the-scenes to enable automatic failover management and ensure high availability of the service. In general, replicating for performance differs significantly from replicating for availability or fault tolerance. The distinction between the two situations is mainly reflected by the higher degree of replication, and as a consequence the need for supporting weak consistency when scalability is the motivating factor for replication [95].

Several studies have been presented as an attempt to quantify the consistency guarantees of cloud storage services. Wada et al. [228] presented an approach for measuring time-based staleness by writing timestamps to a key from one client, reading the same key and computing the difference between the reader's local time and the timestamp read. Bermbach and Tai [78] have tried to address a side of these limitations by extending original the experiments of [228] using a number of readers which are geographically distributed. They measure the consistency window by calculating the difference between the latest read timestamp of version n and the write timestamp of version $n + 1$. Their experiments with Amazon S3 showed that the system frequently violates monotonic read consistency. Anderson et al. [65] presented an offline algorithm that analyzes the trace of interactions between the client machines and the underlying key-value store, and reports how many violations for consistent reads are there in the trace. This approach is useful for checking the safety of running operations and detecting any violation on the semantics of the executed operations. However, it is not useful for any system that require online monitoring for their data staleness or consistency grantees. Zellag and Kemme [237] have proposed an approach for real-time detection of consistency anomalies for arbitrary cloud applications accessing various types of cloud datastores in transactional or non-transactional contexts. In particular, the approach builds the dependency graph during the execution of a cloud application and detect cycles in the graph at the application layer and independently of the underlying datastore. Bailis et al. [71] presented an approach that provides expected bounds on staleness by predicting the behavior of eventually consistent quorum-replicated data stores using Monte Carlo simulations and an abstract model of the storage system including details such as the distribution of latencies for network links.

Kraska et al. [163] have argued that finding the right balance between cost, consistency and availability is not a trivial task. High consistency implies high cost per transaction and, in some situations, reduced availability but avoids penalty costs. Low consistency leads to lower costs per operation but might result in higher penalty costs. Hence, they presented a mechanism that not only allows designers to define the consistency guarantees on the data instead at the transaction level but also allows them to automatically switch consistency guarantees at runtime. They described a dynamic consistency strategy, called *Consistency Rationing*, to reduce the consistency requirements when possible (i.e., the penalty cost is low) and raise them when it matters (i.e., the penalty costs would be too high). The adaptation is driven by a cost model and different strategies that dictate how the system should behave. In particular, they divide the data items into three categories (A, B, C) and treat each category differently depending on the consistency level provided. The A category represents data items for which we need to ensure strong consistency guarantees as any consistency violation would result in large penalty costs, the C category represents data items that can be treated using session consistency as temporary inconsistency is acceptable while the B category comprises all the data items where the consistency requirements vary over time depending on the actual availability of an item. Therefore, the data of this category is handled with either strong or session consistency depending on a statistical-based policy for decision making. Keeton et al. [106, 159] have proposed a similar approach in a system called *LazyBase* that allows users to trade off query performance and result freshness. LazyBase breaks up metadata processing into a pipeline of ingestion, transformation, and query stages which can be parallelized to improve performance and efficiency. By breaking up the processing, LazyBase can independently determine how to schedule each stage for a given set of metadata, thus providing more flexibility than existing monolithic solutions. LazyBase uses models of transformation and query performance to determine how to schedule transformation operations to meet users' freshness and performance goals and to utilize resources efficiently.

In general, the simplicity of key-value stores comes at a price when higher levels of consistency are required. In these cases, application programmers need to spend extra time and exert extra effort to handle the requirements of their applications with no guarantee that all corner cases are handled which consequently might result in an error-prone application. In practice, data replication across different data centers is expensive. Inter-datacenter communication is prone to variation in Round-Trip Times (RTTs) and loss of packets. For example, RTTs are in the order of hundreds of milliseconds. Such large RTTs causes the communication overhead that dominates the commit latencies observed by users. Therefore, systems often sacrifice strong consistency guarantees to maintain acceptable response times. Hence, many solutions either rely on asynchronous replication mechanism and weaker consistency guarantees. Some systems have been recently proposed to tackle these challenges. For example, *Google Megastore* [72] has been presented as a scalable and highly available datastore which is designed to meet the storage requirements of large scale interactive Internet services. It relies on the *Paxos* protocol [98], a proven optimal fault-tolerant consensus algorithm with no requirement for a distinguished master, for achieving synchronous wide area replication. Megastore's replication mechanism provides a single, consistent view of the data stored in its underlying database replicas. Megastore replication semantics is done on *entity group* basis, a priori grouping of data for fast operations, basis by synchronously replicating the group's transaction log to a quorum of replicas. In particular, it uses a write-ahead log replication mechanism over a group of symmetric peers where any node can initiate reads and writes. Each log append blocks on acknowledgments from a majority of replicas, and replicas in the minority catch up as they are able. Kraska et al. [164] have proposed the *MDCC* (*M*ulti-*D*ata *C*enter *C*onsistency) commit protocol for providing strongly consistent guarantees at a cost that is comparable to eventually consistent protocols. In particular, in contrast to transactional consistency two-phase commit protocol (2PC), MDCC is designed to commit transactions in a single round-trip across data centers in the normal operational case. It also does not require a master node so that apply reads or updates from any node in any data center by ensuring that every commit has been received by a quorum of replicas. It does not also impose any database partitioning requirements. The MDCC commit protocol can be combined with different read guarantees where the default configuration is to guarantee read committed consistency without any lost updates. In principle, we believe that the problem of data replication and consistency management across different data centers in the cloud environment has, thus far, not attracted sufficient attention from the research community, and it represents a rich direction of future research and investigation. Nawab et al. [186] presented *Message Futures*, a distributed multi-datacenter transaction management system that provides strong consistency guarantees while maintaining low commit latency. It achieves an average commit latency of around one Round-Trip Times (RTT). In this approach, a transaction is committed when a commit condition on mutual information is met. The commit condition is designed to be true, at any point in time, for any single object in at most one datacenter. The protocol utilizes a Replicated Log (RLog) [233] to continuously share transactions and state information among datacenters which allows a datacenter to commit transactions without initiating a new wide-area message exchange with other datacenters and improves the protocol's resilience to node and communication failures.

The *COPS* system (Clusters of Order-Preserving Servers) [178] has been designed to provide geo-replicated and distributed data stores that support complex online applications, such as social networks, which must provide an *always on* facility where operations always complete with low latency. In particular, it provides causal + consistency where it executes all *put* and *get* operations in the local datacenter in a linearizable fashion, and it then replicates data across datacenters in a causal + consistent order in the background.COPS achieves the causal + consistency by tracking and explicitly checking that causal dependencies are satisfied before exposing writes in each cluster.

10.3   SLA Management

An SLA is a contract between a service provider and its customers. *Service Level Agreements* (SLAs) capture the agreed upon guarantees between a service provider and its customer. They define the characteristics of the provided service including service level objectives (SLOs) (e.g. maximum response times) and define penalties if these objectives are not met by the service provider. In practice, flexible and reliable management of SLA agreements is of paramount importance for both of cloud service providers and consumers. For example, Amazon found that every 100 ms of latency costs them 1% in sales and Google found that an extra 500 ms in search page generation time dropped traffic by 20%. In addition, large enterprise web applications (e.g., eBay and Facebook) need to provide high assurances in terms of SLA metrics such as response times and service availability to their users. Without such assurances, service providers of these applications stand to lose their user base, and hence their revenues.

In general, SLA management is a common general problem for the different types of software systems which are hosted in cloud environments for different reasons such as the unpredictable and bursty workloads from various users in addition to the performance variability in the underlying cloud resources [112,208]. In practice, resource management and SLA guarantee falls into two layers: the *cloud service providers* and the *cloud consumers* (users of cloud services). In particular, the cloud service provider is responsible for the efficient utilization of the physical resources and guarantee their availability for their customers (cloud consumers). The cloud consumers are responsible for the efficient utilization of their allocated resources in order to satisfy the SLA of their customers (application end users) and achieve their business goals. The state-of-the-art cloud databases do not allow the specification of SLA metrics at the application nor at the end-user level. In practice, cloud service providers guarantee only the availability (uptime guarantees), but not the performance, of their services [68, 75, 124]. In addition, sometimes the granularity of the uptime guarantees is also weak. For example, the uptime guarantees of Amazon EC2 is on a per data center basis where a data center is considered to be unavailable if a customer can not access any of its instances or can not launch replacement instances for a contiguous interval of 5 min. In practice, traditional cloud monitoring technologies (e.g. *Amazon CloudWatch*) focus on low-level computing resources (e.g. *CPU speed, CPU utilization, I/O disk speed*). In general, translating the SLO of software application to the thresholds of utilization for low-level computing resources is a very challenging task and is usually done in an ad-hoc manner due to the complexity and dynamism inherent in the interaction between the different tiers and components of the system. Furthermore, cloud service providers do not automatically detect SLA violation and leave the burden of providing the violation proof on the customer [75].

In the multi-tenancy environment of DaaS, it is an important goal for DaaS providers to promise high performance to their tenants. However, this goal normally conflicts with another goal of minimizing the overall running servers and thus operating costs by tenant consolidation. In general, increasing the *degree* of multi-tenancy (number of tenants per server) is normally expected to decrease per-tenant allocated resources and thus performance, but on the other hand, it also reduces the overall operating cost for the DaaS provider and vice versa. Therefore, it is necessary, but challenging for the DaaS providers to balance between the performance that they can deliver to their tenants and the data center's operating costs. Several provider-centric approaches have been proposed to tackle this challenge. Chi et al. [102] have proposed a cost-aware query scheduling algorithm, called *iCBS*, that takes the query costs derived from the service level agreements (SLA) between the service provider and its customers (in terms of response time) into account to make cost-aware scheduling decisions that aims to minimize the total expected cost. *SLA-tree* is another approach that have been proposed to efficiently support profit-oriented decision making of query scheduling. SLA-tree uses the information about the buffered queries which are waiting to be executed in addition to the SLA for each query that indicates the different profits for the query for varying query response times and provides support for the answering of certain profit-oriented *what if* type of questions. Lang et al. [170] presented a framework that takes as input the tenant workloads, their performance SLA, and the server hardware that is available to the DaaS provider, and produces server characterizing models that can be used to provide constraints into an optimization module. By solving this optimization problem, the framework provides a cost-effective hardware provisioning policy and a tenant scheduling policy on each hardware resource. The main limitation of this approach is that the input information of the tenant workloads is not always easy to specify and model accurately. *PIQL* [67] (Performance *I*nsightful *Q*uery *L*anguage) is a declarative language that has been proposed with a SLA compliance prediction model. The PIQL query compiler uses static analysis to select only query plans where it can calculate the number of operations to be performed at every step in their execution. In particular, PIQL extends SQL to allow developers to provide extra bounding information to the compiler. In contrast to traditional query optimizers, the objective of the query compiler is not to find the fastest plan but to avoid performance degradation. Thus, the compiler choose a potentially slower bounded plan over an unbounded plan that happens to be faster given the current database statistics. If the PIQL compiler cannot create a bounded plan for a query, it warns the developer and suggests possible ways to bound the computation.

In general, adequate SLA monitoring strategies and timely detection of SLA violations represent challenging research issues in the cloud computing environments. Salman [75] has suggested that it may be necessary, in the future, for cloud providers to offer performance based SLAs for their services with a tiered pricing model, and charge a premium for guaranteed performance. While this could be one of the directions to solve this problem, we believe that it is a very challenging goal to delegate the management of the fine-granular SLA requirements of the consumer applications to the side of the cloud service provider due to the wide heterogeneity in the workload characteristics, details and granularity of SLA requirements, and cost management objectives of the very large number of consumer applications (tenants) that can be running simultaneously in a cloud environment. Therefore, it becomes a significant issue for the cloud consumers to be able to monitor and adjust the deployment of their systems if they intend to offer viable service level agreements (SLAs) to their customers (end users). It is an important requirement for cloud service providers to enable the cloud consumers with a set of facilities, tools and framework that ease their job of achieving this goal effectively.

10.4   Transaction Support

A transaction is a core concept in the data management world that represents a set of operations which are required to be executed *atomically* on a single consistent view of a database [140]. In general, the expertise gained from building distributed database systems by researchers and practitioners have shown that supporting distributed transactions hinder the ability of building scalable and available systems [189]. Therefore, to satisfy the scalability requirements of large scale internet services, many systems have sacrificed the ability to support distributed transactions. For example, most of the NoSQL systems (e.g. Bigtable, Dynamo, SimpleDB) supports atomic access only at the granularity of single keys. This design choice allows these systems to horizontally partition the tables, without worrying about the need for distributed synchronization and transaction support. While many web applications can live with single key access patterns [99, 121], many other applications (e.g. payment, auction services, online gaming, social networks, collaborative editing) would require atomicity guarantee on multi key accesses patterns. In practice, leaving the burden of ensuring transaction support to the application programmer normally leads to increased code complexity, slower application development, and low-performance client-side transaction management. Therefore, one of the main challenges of cloud-hosted database systems that has been considered is to support transactional guarantees for their applications without compromising the scalability property as one of the main advantages of the cloud environments.

The *G-Store* system [117] has been presented as a scalable data store which provides transactional multi key access guarantees over non-overlapping groups of keys using a key-value store. The main idea of GStore is the *Key Group* abstraction that defines a relationship between a group of keys and represents the granule for on-demand transactional access. This abstraction allows the Key Grouping protocol to collocate control for the keys in the group to allow efficient access to the group of keys. In particular, the Key Grouping protocol enables the transfer of ownership for all keys in a group to a single node which then efficiently executes the operations on the Key Group. At any instance of time, each key can only belong to a single group and the Key Group abstraction does not define a relationship between two groups. Thus, groups are guaranteed to be independent of each other and the transactions on a group guarantee consistency only within the confines of a group. The Key Grouping protocol ensures that the ownership of the members of a group reside with a single node. Thus, the implementation of the transaction manager component does not require any distributed synchronization and is similar to the transaction manager of any single node relational database management systems. The key difference is that in G-Store, transactions are limited to smaller logical entities (key groups). A similar approach has been followed by the *Google Megastore* system [72]. It implements a transactional record manager on top of the BigTable data store [99] and provides transaction support across multiple data items where programmers have to manually link data items into hierarchical groups and each transaction can only access a single group. Megastore partitions the data into a collection of *entity groups*, a priori user-defined grouping of data for fast operations, where each group is independently and synchronously replicated over a wide area. In particular, Megastore tables are either entity group root tables or child tables. Each child table must declare a single distinguished foreign key referencing a root table. Thus, each child entity references a particular entity in its root table (called the root entity). An entity group consists of a root entity along with all entities in child tables that reference it. Entities within an entity group are mutated with single- phase ACID transactions (for which the commit record is replicated via Paxos). Operations across entity groups could rely on expensive two-phase commit operations but they could leverage the built-in Megastore's efficient asynchronous messaging to achieve these operations. Google's *Spanner* [113] has been presented as a scalable and globally-distributed database that shards data across many sets of Paxos state machines in datacenters which are spread all over the world. Spanner automatically reshards data across machines as the amount of data or the number of servers changes, and it automatically migrates data across machines (even across datacenters) to balance load and in response to failures. It supports general-purpose transactions, and provides a SQL-based query language.

  Deuteronomy [173] have presented a radically different approach towards scaling databases and supporting transactions in the cloud by *unbundling* the database into two components: (1) The *transactional component* (TC) that manages transactions and their concurrency control and undo/redo recovery but knows nothing about physical data location. (2) The *data component* (DC) that maintains a data cache and uses access methods to support a record-oriented interface with atomic operations but knows nothing about transactions. Applications submit requests to the TC which uses a lock manager and a log manager to logically enforce transactional concurrency control and recovery. The TC passes requests to the appropriate Data Component (DC). The DC, guaranteed by the TC to never receive conflicting concurrent operations, needs to only support atomic record operations, without concern for transaction properties that are already guaranteed by the TC. In this architecture, data can be stored anywhere (e.g., local disk, in the cloud, etc) as the TC functionality in no way depends on where the data is located. The TC and DC can be deployed in a number of ways. Both can be located within the client, and that is helpful in providing fast transactional access to closely held data. The TC could be located with the client while the DC could be in the cloud, which is helpful in case a user would like to use its own subscription at a TC service or wants to perform transactions that involve manipulating data in multiple locations. Both TC and DC can be in the cloud, which is helpful if a cloud data storage provider would like to localize transaction services for some of its data to a TC component. There can be multiple DCs serviced by one TC, where transactions spanning multiple DCs are naturally supported because a TC does not depend on where data items are stored. Also, there can be multiple TCs, yet, a transaction is serviced by one specific TC.

The *Calvin* system [221] has been designed to run alongside a non-transactional storage system with the aim of transforming it into a shared-nothing (near-)linearly scalable database system that provides high availability and full ACID transactions. These transactions can potentially span multiple partitions spread across the shared-nothing cluster. Calvin accomplishes this goal by providing a layer above the storage system that handles the scheduling of distributed transactions, as well as replication and network communication in the system. The key technical feature of Calvin is that it relies on a deterministic locking mechanism that enables the elimination of distributed commit protocols. In particular, the essence of Calvin lies in separating the system into three separate layers of processing:

- *The sequencing layer* which intercepts transactional inputs and places them into a global transactional input sequence which represents the order of transactions to which all replicas will ensure serial equivalence during their execution.
- *The scheduling layer* that orchestrates transaction execution using a deterministic locking scheme to guarantee equivalence to the serial order specified by the sequencing layer while allowing transactions to be executed concurrently by a pool of transaction execution threads.
- *The storage layer* which handles all physical data layout. Calvin transactions access data using a simple CRUD interface. Therefore, any storage engine supporting a similar interface can be directly plugged into Calvin.

Each node in a Calvin deployment typically runs one partition of each layer. It supports horizontal scalability of the database and unconstrained ACID-compliant distributed transactions by supporting both asynchronous and Paxos-based synchronous replication, both within a single data center and across geographically separated data centers.

10.5   Summary

In this chapter, we discussed a set of research challenges, that have been brought on by the reliance on cloud computing platforms and faced by application developers and designers of cloud database systems, and pointed out alternative research directions for tackling them. Table 10.1 summarizes some of the open research challenges along with the key related factors which could influence the design of their solutions. For user of cloud database services, we can draw the following recommendations:

Table 10.1 Open research challenges of cloud-hosted database systems

Research aspect	Related factors	Open research challenges
Elasticity management	– Application workload – SLA satisfaction – Monetary Cost – Side of control (provider or consumer)	– Designing accurate models for characterizing and predicting Internet scale application workloads – Designing flexible dynamic provisioning mechanisms that carefully consider the target consumer application SLA and the target monetary costs – Enabling the consumer applications with powerful and flexible tools (admission controllers) to declaratively define and control their elasticity policies
Data replication and consistency management	– CAP theorem – Levels of consistency guarantee – Replica locations	– Designing adaptable consistency mechanisms that can be flexibly configured on the runtime according to the application context . – Designing efficient data replication and consistency management protocols across different data centers in the cloud environment – Further understanding to the practical limits of the CAP theorem
Live migration	– Down time – Migration time – SLA effect – Triggering of migration need (when to migrate?)	– Optimizing the down time and migration time metrics of the live migration techniques – Minimizing the performance effect and SLA degradation of the co-located tenants during the migration process – Designing partitioning-aware live database migration techniques – Designing intelligent schedulers for the activities of the migration processes – Designing intelligent techniques for deciding the optimal source and destination tenants and servers with aim of optimizing the overall system performance and the overall utilization of the computing resources
SLA management	– Side of control – SLA granularity – Monetary cost	– Designing efficient mechanisms for monitoring and timely detecting SLA violations in cloud environments – Providing fine-granular SLA guarantees for cloud hosting database services – Designing cost-aware SLA management techniques – Enabling the consumer applications with flexible mechanisms to declaratively define, monitor and control their SLA requirements

Table 10.1 (continued)

Research aspect	Related factors	Open research challenges
Transaction support	– Granularity of atomicity – Distributed transactions – Performance	– Providing efficient multi row atomicity guarantees on NoSQL systems – Designing intelligent workload-aware and transaction-aware database partitioning mechanisms for cloud-hosted databases – Providing scalable transactional guarantees over multiple partitions for distributed database (across different data centers) in cloud environments

- NoSQL systems are viable solutions for applications that require scalable data stores which can easily scale out over multiple servers and support flexible data model and storage scheme. However, the access pattern of these applications should not require much join operations and can work with limited transaction support and weaker consistency guarantees. In general, NoSQL systems are recommended for newly developed applications but not for migrating existing applications which are written on top of traditional relational database systems. For example, Amazon Web Services describe the anti-patterns for using its cloud-hosted NoSQL solution, SimpleDB, to include: pre-developed software applications which are tied to traditional relational database or applications that may require many join operations and complex transactions.[1] In addition, with the wide options and variety of currently available NoSQL systems, software developers need to well understand the requirements of their application to choose the NoSQL system with adequate design decisions of their applications.
- Database-as-a-Service solutions are recommended for software applications which are built on top of relational databases. They can be easily migrated to cloud servers and alleviate the need to purchase expensive hardware, deal with software upgrades and hire professionals for administrative and maintenance tasks. However, these application should have the ability to accurately predict their application workloads and provision the adequate computing resources that can achiever their performance requirements. Unfortunately, these applications should be ready to not automatically leverage the elasticity and scalability promises of cloud services.
- Virtualized database servers are recommended for software applications which require to leverage the full elasticity and scalability promises of cloud services and need to have full control on the performance of their applications. However, these application need to build and configure their admission control for managing the database tier of their applications.

---

[1]http://aws.amazon.com/whitepapers/storage-options-aws-cloud/.

For designers and developers, it is clear that there is no single perfect technology or solution for hosting databases in cloud platforms. Different application target different aspects in the design space, and multiple open problems still remain. Therefore, they can use the challenges which are discussed above in order to effectively decide on the points which can be improved in order to make an effective contribution towards the vision of designing and implementing successful data management solutions in the cloud environment. We believe that there is still many opportunities for new innovations and optimizations in this area. For users of cloud database services, they often have the challenge of choosing the appropriate technology and system that can satisfy their specific set of application requirements. Therefore, a thorough understanding of current cloud database technologies is essential for dealing with this situation.

References

1. https://code.google.com/p/clouddb-replication/.
2. Amazon Auto Scaling Web Service. http://aws.amazon.com/autoscaling/s.
3. Amazon Cloud Watch. http://aws.amazon.com/cloudwatch/.
4. Amazon EC2 Cloud Service. http://aws.amazon.com/ec2/.
5. Amazon Elastic Load Balancing. http://aws.amazon.com/elasticloadbalancing/.
6. Amazon Elastic MapReduce (Amazon EMR). http://aws.amazon.com/elasticmapreduce/.
7. Apache Cassandra database - Project Webpage. http://cassandra.apache.org/.
8. Apache CouchDB database - Project Webpage. http://couchdb.apache.org/.
9. Apache Hadoop - Project Webpage. http://hadoop.apache.org/.
10. Apache HBase database - Project Webpage. http://hbase.apache.org/.
11. Apache Hive: Project Webpage. http://hive.apache.org/.
12. Apache Pig: Project Webpage. http://pig.apache.org/.
13. Aster Data Systems. http://www.asterdata.com/.
14. DEX: a distributed key-value storage system. http://www.dama.upc.edu/technology-transfer/dex.
15. Dynomite: a distributed key-value storage system. http://wiki.github.com/cliffmoon/dynomite/dynomite-framework.
16. Eucalyptus: Open Source AWS Compatible Private Clouds. http://www.eucalyptus.com/.
17. GoGrid Cloud Hosting. http://www.gogrid.com/.
18. GoGrid Load Balncer. http://www.gogrid.com/cloud-hosting/load-balancers.php.
19. Google App Engine. http://developers.google.com/appengine/.
20. Google AppEngine datastore. http://code.google.com/appengine/docs/python/datastore/.
21. Google Apps for Business. http://www.google.com/apps/.
22. Google BigQuery. https://developers.google.com/bigquery/.
23. Google Cloud SQL. https://developers.google.com/cloud-sql/.
24. GQL: Google Data Store Query Language. http://code.google.com/appengine/docs/python/datastore/gqlreference.html.
25. Greenplum Inc. http://www.greenplum.com/.
26. Hadoop Distributed Filesystem (HDFS). http://hadoop.apache.org/hdfs/.
27. HadoopDB Project Webpage. http://db.cs.yale.edu/hadoopdb/hadoopdb.html.
28. Heroku Cloud Application Platform. http://www.heroku.com/.
29. HiveQL: Language Manual. https://cwiki.apache.org/confluence/display/Hive/LanguageManual.
30. HyperTable: A high performance, scalable, distributed storage and processing system for structured and unstructured data. http://hypertable.org/.
31. IBM Netezza Data Warehouse Appliances. http://www-01.ibm.com/software/data/netezza/.

32. Jaql: Query Language for JavaScript(r) Object Notation (JSON). http://code.google.com/p/jaql/.
33. KVM (Kernel-based Virtual Machine). http://www.linux-kvm.org/.
34. List of NoSQL Databases. http://NoSQL-database.org/.
35. Memcached: a distributed memory object caching system. http://memcached.org/.
36. Microsoft Appliance: Parallel Data Warehouse (PDW). http://www.microsoft.com/sqlserver/en/us/solutions-technologies/data-warehousing/pdw.aspx.
37. Microsoft Windows Azure). http://www.windowsazure.com/.
38. MongoDB: an open-source document database. http://www.mongodb.org/.
39. Neo4J: Graph Database System. http://neo4j.org/.
40. ParAccel Big Data Analytics Platform. http://www.paraccel.com/.
41. Riak: a distributed key-value storage system. http://wiki.basho.com/display/RIAK/Riak.
42. RUBiS: Rice University Bidding System. http://rubis.ow2.org/.
43. SalesForce Cloud Solutions. http://salesforce.com/.
44. SQL Azure Database. http://www.windowsazure.com/en-us/services/data-management/.
45. Teradata Inc. http://teradata.com/.
46. The DZero Experiment. http://www-d0.fnal.gov/.
47. The Storm Project. https://github.com/nathanmarz/storm/.
48. The Xen Project). http://xen.org/.
49. TPC-W: a transactional web e-Commerce benchmark. http://www.tpc.org/tpcw/.
50. Twister: Iterative MapReduce. http://www.iterativemapreduce.org/.
51. Vertica Systems Inc. http://www.vertica.com/.
52. Voldemort: a distributed key-value storage system. http://project-voldemort.com/.
53. YCSB++ Benchmark - Project Webpage. http://www.pdl.cmu.edu/ycsb++/index.shtml.
54. YCSB: Yahoo! Cloud Serving Benchmark . http://wiki.github.com/brianfrankcooper/YCSB/.
55. Zoho Suite of Online Web Applications. http://www.zoho.com/.
56. Daniel Abadi. Data management in the cloud: Limitations and opportunities. *Data Eng. Bull.*, 32(1):3–12, March 2009.
57. Daniel Abadi. Consistency tradeoffs in modern distributed database system design: CAP is only part of the story. *Computer*, 45(2):37–42, February 2012.
58. Azza Abouzeid, Kamil Bajda-Pawlikowski, Daniel Abadi, Avi Silberschatz, and Alexander Rasin. HadoopDB: an architectural hybrid of MapReduce and DBMS technologies for analytical workloads. *Proc. VLDB Endow.*, 2(1):922–933, August 2009.
59. Azza Abouzied, Kamil Bajda-Pawlikowski, Jiewen Huang, Daniel J. Abadi, and Avi Silberschatz. HadoopDB in action: Building real world applications. In *Proceedings of the 2010 ACM SIGMOD International Conference on Management of Data*, SIGMOD '10, pages 1111–1114, New York, NY, USA, 2010. ACM.
60. Foto N. Afrati and Jeffrey D. Ullman. Optimizing joins in a map-reduce environment. In *EDBT*, pages 99–110, 2010.
61. Foto N. Afrati and Jeffrey D. Ullman. Optimizing Multiway Joins in a Map-Reduce Environment. *IEEE TKDE*, 23(9):1282–1298, 2011.
62. Divyakant Agrawal, Amr El Abbadi, Fatih Emekci, and Ahmed Metwally. Database management as a service: Challenges and opportunities. In *Proceedings of the 25th IEEE International Conference on Data Engineering*, ICDE '09, pages 1709–1716, Shanghai, China, March 2009. IEEE Computer Society.
63. Mohammad Alrifai and Thomas Risse. Combining global optimization with local selection for efficient QoS-aware service composition. In *Proceedings of the 18th international conference on World wide web*, WWW '09, pages 881–890, New York, NY, USA, 2009. ACM.
64. Ahmed M. Aly, Asmaa Sallam, Bala M. Gnanasekaran, Long-Van Nguyen-Dinh, Walid G. Aref, Mourad Ouzzaniy, and Arif Ghafoor. M^3: Stream Processing on Main-Memory MapReduce. In *ICDE*, 2012.
65. Eric Anderson, Xiaozhou Li, Mehul A. Shah, Joseph Tucek, and Jay J. Wylie. What consistency does your key-value store actually provide? In *HotDep*, 2010.

66. Danilo Ardagna and Barbara Pernici. Adaptive service composition in flexible processes. *IEEE Trans. Softw. Eng.*, 33(6):369–384, June 2007.

67. Michael Armbrust, Kristal Curtis, Tim Kraska, Armando Fox, Michael J. Franklin, and David A. Patterson. PIQL: Success-Tolerant Query Processing in the Cloud. *PVLDB*, 5(3):181–192, 2011.

68. Michael Armbrust, Armando Fox, Rean Griffith, Anthony D. Joseph, Randy Katz, Andy Konwinski, Gunho Lee, David Patterson, Ariel Rabkin, Ion Stoica, and Matei Zaharia. A view of cloud computing. *Commun. ACM*, 53(4):50–58, April 2010.

69. Shivnath Babu. Towards automatic optimization of MapReduce programs. In *SoCC*, pages 137–142, 2010.

70. Peter Bailis, Alan Fekete, Ali Ghodsi, Joseph M. Hellerstein, , and Ion Stoica. The Potential Dangers of Causal Consistency and an Explicit Solution. In *SoCC*, 2012.

71. Peter Bailis, Shivaram Venkataraman, Michael J. Franklin, Joseph M. Hellerstein, and Ion Stoica. Probabilistically bounded staleness for practical partial quorums. *PVLDB*, 5(8), 2012.

72. Jason Baker, Chris Bond, James C. Corbett, JJ Furman, Andrey Khorlin, James Larson, Jean-Michel Leon, Yawei Li, Alexander Lloyd, and Vadim Yushprakh. Megastore: Providing scalable, highly available storage for interactive services. In *Proceedings of the 5th Biennial Conference on Innovative Data Systems Research*, CIDR '11, pages 223–234, Asilomar, California, USA, January 2011.

73. Andrey Balmin, Tim Kaldewey, and Sandeep Tata. Clydesdale: structured data processing on Hadoop. In *Proceedings of the 2012 ACM SIGMOD International Conference on Management of Data*, SIGMOD '12, pages 705–708, New York, NY, USA, 2012. ACM.

74. Luiz André Barroso and Urs Hölzle. The Case for Energy-Proportional Computing. *IEEE Computer*, 40(12):33–37, 2007.

75. Salman A. Baset. Cloud SLAs: present and future. *SIGOPS Oper. Syst. Rev.*, 46(2):57–66, July 2012.

76. G. Bell, J. Gray, and A. Szalay. Petascale computational systems. *IEEE Computer*, 39(1):110–112, 2006.

77. Michel Berkelaar, Kjell Eikland, and Peter Notebaert. lpsolve: Open source (mixed-integer) linear programming system. Technical report, Eindhoven U. of Technology.

78. David Bermbach and Stefan Tai. Eventual consistency: How soon is eventual? an evaluation of Amazon S3's consistency behavior. In *Proceedings of the 6th Workshop on Middleware for Service Oriented Computing*, MW4SOC '11, pages 1:1–1:6, Lisboa, Portugal, 2011. ACM.

79. Philip A. Bernstein, Istvan Cseri, Nishant Dani, Nigel Ellis, Ajay Kalhan, Gopal Kakivaya, David B. Lomet, Ramesh Manne, Lev Novik, and Tomas Talius. Adapting Microsoft SQL server for cloud computing. In *Proceedings of the 27th IEEE International Conference on Data Engineering*, ICDE '11, pages 1255–1263, Hannover, Germany, 2011. IEEE Computer Society.

80. Kevin S. Beyer, Vuk Ercegovac, Rainer Gemulla, Andrey Balmin, Mohamed Y. Eltabakh, Carl-Christian Kanne, Fatma Özcan, and Eugene J. Shekita. Jaql: A scripting language for large scale semistructured data analysis. *Proc. VLDB Endow.*, 4(12):1272–1283, August 2011.

81. Pramod Bhatotia, Alexander Wieder, Rodrigo Rodrigues, Umut A. Acar, and Rafael Pasquin. Incoop: MapReduce for incremental computations. In *Proceedings of the 2nd ACM Symposium on Cloud Computing*, SOCC '11, pages 7:1–7:14, New York, NY, USA, 2011. ACM.

82. Spyros Blanas, Jignesh M. Patel, Vuk Ercegovac, Jun Rao, Eugene J. Shekita, and Yuanyuan Tian. A comparison of join algorithms for log processing in MapReduce. In *Proceedings of the 2010 ACM SIGMOD International Conference on Management of Data*, SIGMOD '10, pages 975–986, New York, NY, USA, 2010. ACM.

83. Peter Bodík, Armando Fox, Michael J. Franklin, Michael I. Jordan, and David A. Patterson. Characterizing, modeling, and generating workload spikes for stateful services. In *Proceedings of the 1st ACM Symposium on Cloud computing*, SoCC '10, pages 241–252, Indianapolis, IN, USA, 2010. ACM.

84. Vinayak Borkar, Michael J. Carey, and Chen Li. Inside "Big Data management": ogres, onions, or parfaits? In *Proceedings of the 15th International Conference on Extending Database Technology*, EDBT '12, pages 3–14, New York, NY, USA, 2012. ACM.

85. Matthias Brantner, Daniela Florescu, David Graf, Donald Kossmann, and Tim Kraska. Building a database on S3. In *Proceedings of the 2008 ACM SIGMOD International Conference on Management of Data*, SIGMOD '08, pages 251–264, Vancouver, BC, Canada, 2008. ACM.

86. Eric Brewer. Towards robust distributed systems (abstract). In *Proceedings of the 19th Annual ACM Symposium on Principles of Distributed Computing*, PODC '00, page 7, Portland, OR, USA, 2000. ACM.

87. Yingyi Bu, Bill Howe, Magdalena Balazinska, and Michael D. Ernst. HaLoop: efficient iterative data processing on large clusters. *Proc. VLDB Endow.*, 3(1–2):285–296, September 2010.

88. Yingyi Bu, Bill Howe, Magdalena Balazinska, and Michael D. Ernst. The HaLoop approach to large-scale iterative data analysis. *VLDB J.*, 21(2):169–190, 2012.

89. Chris Bunch, Navraj Chohan, Chandra Krintz, Jovan Chohan, Jonathan Kupferman, Puneet Lakhina, Yiming Li, and Yoshihide Nomura. An evaluation of distributed datastores using the AppScale cloud platform. In *Proceedings of the 3rd IEEE International Conference on Cloud Computing*, CLOUD '10, pages 305–312, Washington, DC, USA, 2010. IEEE Computer Society.

90. Mike Burrows. The Chubby lock service for loosely-coupled distributed systems. In *Proceedings of the 7th Symposium on Operating Systems Design and Implementation*, OSDI '06, pages 335–350, Seattle, WA, USA, 2006. USENIX Association.

91. Rajkumar Buyya, Chee Shin Yeo, Srikumar Venugopal, James Broberg, and Ivona Brandic. Cloud computing and emerging it platforms: Vision, hype, and reality for delivering computing as the 5th utility. *Future Gener. Comput. Syst.*, 25(6):599–616, June 2009.

92. Michael J. Cafarella and Christopher Ré. Manimal: Relational Optimization for Data-Intensive Programs. In *WebDB*, 2010.

93. Gerardo Canfora, Massimiliano Di Penta, Raffaele Esposito, and Maria Luisa Villani. An approach for qos-aware service composition based on genetic algorithms. In *Proceedings of the 2005 Conference on Genetic and Evolutionary Computation*, GECCO '05, pages 1069–1075, New York, NY, USA, 2005. ACM.

94. Rick Cattell. Scalable SQL and NoSQL data stores. *SIGMOD Rec.*, 39(4):12–27, May 2011.

95. Emmanuel Cecchet, George Candea, and Anastasia Ailamaki. Middleware-based database replication: the gaps between theory and practice. In *SIGMOD Conference*, pages 739–752, 2008.

96. Emmanuel Cecchet, Rahul Singh, Upendra Sharma, and Prashant Shenoy. Dolly: virtualization-driven database provisioning for the cloud. In *Proceedings of the 7th ACM SIGPLAN/SIGOPS International Conference on Virtual Execution Environments*, VEE '11, pages 51–62, Newport Beach, CA, USA, 2011. ACM.

97. Craig Chambers, Ashish Raniwala, Frances Perry, Stephen Adams, Robert R. Henry, Robert Bradshaw, and Nathan Weizenbaum. FlumeJava: easy, efficient data-parallel pipelines. *SIGPLAN Not.*, 45(6):363–375, June 2010.

98. Tushar Deepak Chandra, Robert Griesemer, and Joshua Redstone. Paxos made live: an engineering perspective. In *PODC*, pages 398–407, 2007.

99. Fay Chang, Jeffrey Dean, Sanjay Ghemawat, Wilson C. Hsieh, Deborah A. Wallach, Mike Burrows, Tushar Chandra, Andrew Fikes, and Robert E. Gruber. Bigtable: A distributed storage system for structured data. *ACM Trans. Comput. Syst.*, 26(2):4:1–4:26, June 2008.

100. Biswapesh Chattopadhyay, Liang Lin, Weiran Liu, Sagar Mittal, Prathyusha Aragonda, Vera Lychagina, Younghee Kwon, and Michael Wong. Tenzing A SQL Implementation On The MapReduce Framework. *PVLDB*, 4(12):1318–1327, 2011.

101. Songting Chen. Cheetah: a high performance, custom data warehouse on top of MapReduce. *Proc. VLDB Endow.*, 3(1–2):1459–1468, September 2010.

102. Yun Chi, Hyun Jin Moon, and Hakan Hacigümüş. iCBS: incremental cost-based scheduling under piecewise linear SLAs. *Proc. VLDB Endow.*, 4(9):563–574, June 2011.
103. Hung chih Yang, Ali Dasdan, Ruey-Lung Hsiao, and D. Stott Parker. Map-reduce-merge: simplified relational data processing on large clusters. In *SIGMOD*, pages 1029–1040, 2007.
104. Hung chih Yang and D. Stott Parker. Traverse: Simplified indexing on large map-reduce-merge clusters. In *DASFAA*, pages 308–322, 2009.
105. Navraj Chohan, Chris Bunch, Sydney Pang, Chandra Krintz, Nagy Mostafa, Sunil Soman, and Rich Wolski. AppScale: Scalable and open AppEngine application development and deployment. In Dimiter R. Avresky, Michel Diaz, Arndt Bode, Bruno Ciciani, and Eliezer Dekel, editors, *Proceedings of the 1st International Conference on Cloud Computing*, volume 34 of *CloudComp '09*, pages 57–70, Munich, Germany, October 2009. Springer Berlin Heidelberg.
106. James Cipar, Greg Ganger, Kimberly Keeton, Charles B. Morrey, III, Craig A.N. Soules, and Alistair Veitch. LazyBase: trading freshness for performance in a scalable database. In *Proceedings of the 7th ACM European Conference on Computer Systems*, EuroSys '12, pages 169–182, Bern, Switzerland, April 2012. ACM.
107. Carlos A. Coello Coello. Theoretical and Numerical Constraint-Handling Techniques used with Evolutionary Algorithms: A Survey of the State of the Art. *Computer methods in applied mechanics and engineering*, 191(11–12):1245–1287, 2002.
108. Tyson Condie, Neil Conway, Peter Alvaro, Joseph M. Hellerstein, Khaled Elmeleegy, and Russell Sears. Mapreduce online. In *NSDI*, 2010.
109. Tyson Condie, Neil Conway, Peter Alvaro, Joseph M. Hellerstein, John Gerth, Justin Talbot, Khaled Elmeleegy, and Russell Sears. Online aggregation and continuous query support in MapReduce. In *SIGMOD Conference*, pages 1115–1118, 2010.
110. Brian F. Cooper, Eric Baldeschwieler, Rodrigo Fonseca, James J. Kistler, P. P. S. Narayan, Chuck Neerdaels, Toby Negrin, Raghu Ramakrishnan, Adam Silberstein, Utkarsh Srivastava, and Raymie Stata. Building a cloud for yahoo! *IEEE Data Eng. Bull.*, 32(1):36–43, 2009.
111. Brian F. Cooper, Raghu Ramakrishnan, Utkarsh Srivastava, Adam Silberstein, Philip Bohannon, Hans-Arno Jacobsen, Nick Puz, Daniel Weaver, and Ramana Yerneni. PNUTS: Yahoo!'s hosted data serving platform. *Proc. VLDB Endow.*, 1(2):1277–1288, August 2008.
112. Brian F. Cooper, Adam Silberstein, Erwin Tam, Raghu Ramakrishnan, and Russell Sears. Benchmarking cloud serving systems with YCSB. In *Proceedings of the 1st ACM Symposium on Cloud Computing*, SoCC '10, pages 143–154, Indianapolis, IN, USA, 2010. ACM.
113. James C. Corbett, Jeffrey Dean, Michael Epstein, Andrew Fikes, Christopher Frost, J. J. Furman, Sanjay Ghemawat, Andrey Gubarev, Christopher Heiser, Peter Hochschild, Wilson Hsieh, Sebastian Kanthak, Eugene Kogan, Hongyi Li, Alexander Lloyd, Sergey Melnik, David Mwaura, David Nagle, Sean Quinlan, Rajesh Rao, Lindsay Rolig, Yasushi Saito, Michal Szymaniak, Christopher Taylor, Ruth Wang, and Dale Woodford. Spanner: Google's globally-distributed database. In *Proceedings of the 10th USENIX conference on Operating Systems Design and Implementation*, OSDI '12, pages 251–264, Berkeley, CA, USA, 2012. USENIX Association.
114. Thomas H. Cormen, Charles E. Leiserson, Ronald L. Rivest, and Clifford Stein. *Introduction to Algorithms*. MIT press, 3rd edition, September 2009.
115. ´italo S. Cunha, Jussara M. Almeida, Virgilio Almeida, and Marcos Santos. Self-adaptive capacity management for multi-tier virtualized environments. In *Integrated Network Management*, pages 129–138, 2007.
116. Carlo Curino, Evan Jones, Yang Zhang, Eugene Wu, and Sam Madde. Relational Cloud: The Case for a Database Service. In *CIDR*, 2011.
117. Sudipto Das, Divyakant Agrawal, and Amr El Abbadi. G-Store: a scalable data store for transactional multi key access in the cloud. In *Proceedings of the 1st ACM Symposium on Cloud computing*, SoCC '10, pages 163–174, New York, NY, USA, 2010. ACM.
118. Jeffrey Dean and Sanjay Ghemawat. Mapreduce: Simplified data processing on large clusters. In *OSDI*, pages 137–150, 2004.

119. Jeffrey Dean and Sanjay Ghemawat. Mapreduce: simplified data processing on large clusters. *Commun. ACM*, 51(1):107–113, 2008.

120. Jeffrey Dean and Sanjay Ghemawat. Mapreduce: a flexible data processing tool. *Commun. ACM*, 53(1):72–77, 2010.

121. Giuseppe DeCandia, Deniz Hastorun, Madan Jampani, Gunavardhan Kakulapati, Avinash Lakshman, Alex Pilchin, Swaminathan Sivasubramanian, Peter Vosshall, and Werner Vogels. Dynamo: Amazon's highly available key-value store. *SIGOPS Oper. Syst. Rev.*, 41(6):205–220, October 2007.

122. David J. DeWitt and Jim Gray. Parallel Database Systems: The Future of High Performance Database Systems. *Commun. ACM*, 35(6):85–98, 1992.

123. Jens Dittrich, Jorge-Arnulfo Quiané-Ruiz, Alekh Jindal, Yagiz Kargin, Vinay Setty, and Jörg Schad. Hadoop++: making a yellow elephant run like a cheetah (without it even noticing). *Proc. VLDB Endow.*, 3(1–2):515–529, September 2010.

124. Dave Durkee. Why cloud computing will never be free. *Commun. ACM*, 53(5):62–69, May 2010.

125. Jaliya Ekanayake, Hui Li, Bingjing Zhang, Thilina Gunarathne, Seung-Hee Bae, Judy Qiu, and Geoffrey Fox. Twister: a runtime for iterative MapReduce. In *HPDC*, pages 810–818, 2010.

126. Iman Elghandour and Ashraf Aboulnaga. ReStore: Reusing Results of MapReduce Jobs. *PVLDB*, 5(6):586–597, 2012.

127. Iman Elghandour and Ashraf Aboulnaga. ReStore: reusing results of MapReduce jobs in pig. In *SIGMOD Conference*, pages 701–704, 2012.

128. Aaron J. Elmore, Sudipto Das, Divyakant Agrawal, and Amr El Abbadi. Zephyr: live migration in shared nothing databases for elastic cloud platforms. In *Proceedings of the 2011 ACM SIGMOD International Conference on Management of Data*, SIGMOD '11, pages 301–312, Athens, Greece, 2011. ACM.

129. Mohamed Y. Eltabakh, Yuanyuan Tian, Fatma Özcan, Rainer Gemulla, Aljoscha Krettek, and John McPherson. CoHadoop: flexible data placement and its exploitation in Hadoop. *Proc. VLDB Endow.*, 4(9):575–585, June 2011.

130. Constantinos Evangelinos and C. N. Hill. Cloud computing for parallel scientific HPC applications: Feasibility of running coupled atmosphere-ocean climate models on Amazon's EC2. In *Proceedings of the 1st Workshop on Cloud Computing and Its Applications*, CCA '08, Chicago, IL, USA, 2008.

131. Avrilia Floratou, Jignesh M. Patel, Willis Lang, and Alan Halverson. When free is not really free: what does it cost to run a database workload in the cloud? In *Proceedings of the 3rd TPC Technology Conference on Topics in Performance Evaluation, Measurement and Characterization*, TPCTC '11, pages 163–179, Seattle, WA, USA, August 2011. Springer.

132. Avrilia Floratou, Jignesh M. Patel, Eugene J. Shekita, and Sandeep Tata. Column-oriented storage techniques for MapReduce. *Proc. VLDB Endow.*, 4(7):419–429, April 2011.

133. Daniela Florescu and Donald Kossmann. Rethinking cost and performance of database systems. *SIGMOD Rec.*, 38(1):43–48, June 2009.

134. Eric Friedman, Peter M. Pawlowski, and John Cieslewicz. SQL/MapReduce: A practical approach to self-describing, polymorphic, and parallelizable user-defined functions. *PVLDB*, 2(2):1402–1413, 2009.

135. Gaber and Bakouya. an affinity-driven clustering approach for service discovery and composition for pervasive computing. In *Proceedings of the 3rd ACS/IEEE International Conference on Pervasive Services*, PERSER '06, pages 277–280, Washington, DC, USA, 2006. IEEE Computer Society.

136. Alan Gates. *Programming Pig*. O'Reilly Media, 2011.

137. Sanjay Ghemawat, Howard Gobioff, and Shun-Tak Leung. The Google file system. *SIGOPS Oper. Syst. Rev.*, 37(5):29–43, October 2003.

138. Seth Gilbert and Nancy Lynch. Brewer's conjecture and the feasibility of consistent, available, partition-tolerant web services. *SIGACT News*, 33(2):51–59, June 2002.

139. Jim Gray. Distributed computing economics. *Queue*, 6(3):63–68, May 2008.

140. Jum Gray and Andreas Reuter. *Transaction Processing: Concepts and Techniques*. The Morgan Kaufmann Series in Data Management Systems, 1992.

141. Yunhong Gu and Robert L. Grossman. Lessons learned from a year's worth of benchmarks of large data clouds. In *Proceedings of the 2nd Workshop on Many-Task Computing on Grids and Supercomputers*, MTAGS '09, pages 3:1–3:6, New York, NY, USA, 2009. ACM.

142. Wei Guo, Weiqiang Sun, Yaohui Jin, Weisheng Hu, and Chunming Qiao. Demonstration of joint resource scheduling in an optical network integrated computing environment. *Comm. Mag.*, 48(5):76–83, May 2010.

143. I. W. Habib, Qiang Song, Zhaoming Li, and N. S.V. Rao. Deployment of the GMPLS control plane for grid applications in experimental high-performance networks. *Comm. Mag.*, 44(3):65–73, March 2006.

144. Hakan Hacigümüs, Sharad Mehrotra, and Balakrishna R. Iyer. Providing Database as a Service. In *ICDE*, 2002.

145. Alon Y. Halevy. Answering queries using views: A survey. *The VLDB Journal*, 10(4):270–294, December 2001.

146. Yongqiang He, Rubao Lee, Yin Huai, Zheng Shao, Namit Jain, Xiaodong Zhang, and Zhiwei Xu. RCFile: A fast and space-efficient data placement structure in MapReduce-based warehouse systems. In *ICDE*, pages 1199–1208, 2011.

147. Herodotos Herodotou. Hadoop performance models. Technical Report CS-2011-05, Duke University, February 2011.

148. Herodotos Herodotou and Shivnath Babu. Profiling, What-if Analysis, and Cost-based Optimization of MapReduce Programs. *PVLDB*, 4(11):1111–1122, 2011.

149. Herodotos Herodotou, Fei Dong, and Shivnath Babu. MapReduce Programming and Cost-based Optimization? Crossing this Chasm with Starfish. *PVLDB*, 4(12):1446–1449, 2011.

150. Herodotos Herodotou, Harold Lim, Gang Luo, Nedyalko Borisov, Liang Dong, Fatma Bilgen Cetin, and Shivnath Babu. Starfish: A Self-tuning System for Big Data Analytics. In *CIDR*, pages 261–272, 2011.

151. Tony Hey, Stewart Tansley, and Kristin M. Tolle, editors. *The Fourth Paradigm: Data-Intensive Scientific Discovery*. Microsoft Research, Redmond, Washington, USA, 2009.

152. Zach Hill and Marty Humphrey. A quantitative analysis of high performance computing with Amazon's EC2 infrastructure: The death of the local cluster? In *Proceedings of the 10th IEEE/ACM International Conference on Grid Computing*, pages 26–33, Banff, AB, Canada, October 2009. IEEE Computer Society.

153. Eaman Jahani, Michael J. Cafarella, and Christopher Ré. Automatic optimization for MapReduce programs. *Proc. VLDB Endow.*, 4(6):385–396, March 2011.

154. David Jiang, Anthony K. H. Tung, and Gang Chen. MAP-JOIN-REDUCE: Toward Scalable and Efficient Data Analysis on Large Clusters. *IEEE TKDE*, 23(9):1299–1311, 2011.

155. Dawei Jiang, Beng Chin Ooi, Lei Shi, and Sai Wu. The Performance of MapReduce: An In-depth Study. *PVLDB*, 3(1):472–483, 2010.

156. Alekh Jindal, Jorge-Arnulfo Quiane-Ruiz, and Jens Dittrich. Trojan Data Layouts: Right Shoes for a Running Elephant. In *SoCC*, 2011.

157. Tim Kaldewey, Eugene J. Shekita, and Sandeep Tata. Clydesdale: structured data processing on MapReduce. In *Proceedings of the 15th International Conference on Extending Database Technology*, EDBT '12, pages 15–25, New York, NY, USA, 2012. ACM.

158. David Karger, Eric Lehman, Tom Leighton, Rina Panigrahy, Matthew Levine, and Daniel Lewin. Consistent hashing and random trees: distributed caching protocols for relieving hot spots on the World Wide Web. In *Proceedings of the 29th Annual ACM Symposium on Theory of Computing*, STOC '97, pages 654–663, El Paso, TX, USA, May 1997. ACM.

159. Kimberly Keeton, Charles B. Morrey, III, Craig A.N. Soules, and Alistair Veitch. LazyBase: freshness vs. performance in information management. *SIGOPS Oper. Syst. Rev.*, 44(1):15–19, March 2010.

160. Bettina Kemme, Ricardo Jiménez Peris, and Marta Patiño-Martínez. *Database Replication*. Synthesis Lectures on Data Management. Morgan & Claypool, 1st edition, 2010.

161. Jeffrey O. Kephart and David M. Chess. The vision of autonomic computing. *Computer*, 36(1):41–50, January 2003.
162. Donald Kossmann, Tim Kraska, and Simon Loesing. An evaluation of alternative architectures for transaction processing in the cloud. In *Proceedings of the 2010 ACM SIGMOD International Conference on Management of Data*, SIGMOD '10, pages 579–590, Indianapolis, IN, USA, June 2010. ACM.
163. Tim Kraska, Martin Hentschel, Gustavo Alonso, and Donald Kossmann. Consistency rationing in the cloud: pay only when it matters. *Proc. VLDB Endow.*, 2(1):253–264, August 2009.
164. Tim Kraska, Gene Pang, Michael J. Franklin, and Samuel Madden. MDCC: Multi-Data Center Consistency. *CoRR*, abs/1203.6049, 2012.
165. Sriram Krishnan. *Programming Windows Azure: Programming the Microsoft Cloud*. O'Reilly Media, Sebastopol, CA, USA, 1st edition, 2010.
166. Vibhore Kumar, Henrique Andrade, Buğra Gedik, and Kun-Lung Wu. DEDUCE: at the intersection of MapReduce and stream processing. In *Proceedings of the 13th International Conference on Extending Database Technology*, EDBT '10, pages 657–662, New York, NY, USA, 2010. ACM.
167. Avinash Lakshman and Prashant Malik. Cassandra: a structured storage system on a p2p network. In *Proceedings of the 21st Annual Symposium on Parallelism in Algorithms and Architectures*, SPAA '09, pages 47–47, New York, NY, USA, 2009. ACM.
168. Avinash Lakshman and Prashant Malik. Cassandra: a decentralized structured storage system. *SIGOPS Oper. Syst. Rev.*, 44(2):35–40, April 2010.
169. Willis Lang and Jignesh M. Patel. Energy management for MapReduce clusters. *Proc. VLDB Endow.*, 3(1–2):129–139, September 2010.
170. Willis Lang, Srinath Shankar, Jignesh M. Patel, and Ajay Kalhan. Towards Multi-tenant Performance SLOs. In *ICDE*, pages 702–713, 2012.
171. Tom Lehman, Jerry Sobieski, and Bijan Jabbari. DRAGON: a framework for service provisioning in heterogeneous grid networks. *Comm. Mag.*, 44(3):84–90, March 2006.
172. Alexander Lenk, Michael Menzel, Johannes Lipsky, Stefan Tai, and Philipp Offermann. What are you paying for? performance benchmarking for Infrastructure-as-a-Service offerings. In *Proceedings of the 2011 IEEE 4th International Conference on Cloud Computing*, IEEE CLOUD '11, pages 484–491, Washington, DC, USA, July 2011. IEEE Computer Society.
173. Justin J. Levandoski, David Lomet, Mohamed F. Mokbel, and Kevin Keliang Zhao. Deuteronomy: Transaction support for cloud data. In *Proceedings of the 5th Biennial Conference on Innovative Data Systems Research*, CIDR '11, pages 123–133, Asilomar, California, USA, January 2011.
174. Jacob Leverich and Christos Kozyrakis. On the energy (in)efficiency of Hadoop clusters. *Operating Systems Review*, 44(1):61–65, 2010.
175. Boduo Li, Edward Mazur, Yanlei Diao, Andrew McGregor, and Prashant Shenoy. A platform for scalable one-pass analytics using MapReduce. In *Proceedings of the 2011 ACM SIGMOD International Conference on Management of Data*, SIGMOD '11, pages 985–996, New York, NY, USA, 2011. ACM.
176. Harold Lim, Herodotos Herodotou, and Shivnath Babu. Stubby: A Transformation-based Optimizer for MapReduce Workflows. *PVLDB*, 5(12), 2012.
177. Yuting Lin, Divyakant Agrawal, Chun Chen, Beng Chin Ooi, and Sai Wu. Llama: leveraging columnar storage for scalable join processing in the MapReduce framework. In *SIGMOD Conference*, pages 961–972, 2011.
178. Wyatt Lloyd, Michael J. Freedman, Michael Kaminsky, and David G. Andersen. Don't settle for eventual: Scalable causal consistency for wide-area storage with COPS. In *Proceedings of the 23rd ACM Symposium on Operating Systems Principles*, SOSP '11, pages 401–416, New York, NY, USA, 2011. ACM.
179. Dionysios Logothetis and Kenneth Yocum. Ad-hoc data processing in the cloud. *Proc. VLDB Endow.*, 1(2):1472–1475, August 2008.

180. Grzegorz Malewicz, Matthew H. Austern, Aart J. C. Bik, James C. Dehnert, Ilan Horn, Naty Leiser, and Grzegorz Czajkowski. Pregel: a system for large-scale graph processing. In *SIGMOD*, pages 135–146, 2010.

181. Peter M. Mell and Timothy Grance. Sp 800-145. the NIST definition of cloud computing. Technical report, National Institute of Standards and Technology, Gaithersburg, MD, USA, 2011.

182. Sergey Melnik, Andrey Gubarev, Jing Jing Long, Geoffrey Romer, Shiva Shivakumar, Matt Tolton, and Theo Vassilakis. Dremel: interactive analysis of web-scale datasets. *Proc. VLDB Endow.*, 3(1–2):330–339, September 2010.

183. Sergey Melnik, Andrey Gubarev, Jing Jing Long, Geoffrey Romer, Shiva Shivakumar, Matt Tolton, and Theo Vassilakis. Dremel: interactive analysis of web-scale datasets. *Commun. ACM*, 54(6):114–123, June 2011.

184. Kristi Morton, Magdalena Balazinska, and Dan Grossman. ParaTimer: a progress indicator for MapReduce DAGs. In *SIGMOD Conference*, pages 507–518, 2010.

185. Kristi Morton, Abram L. Friesen, Magdalena Balazinska, and Dan Grossman. Estimating the progress of mapreduce pipelines. In *Proceedings of the 26th IEEE International Conference on Data Engineering*, ICDE '10, pages 681–684, Long Beach, CA, USA, March 2010. IEEE Computer Society.

186. Faisal Nawab, Divyakant Agrawal, and Amr El Abbadi. Message Futures: Fast Commitment of Transactions in. Multi-datacenter Environments. In *CIDR*, 2013.

187. Tomasz Nykiel, Michalis Potamias, Chaitanya Mishra, George Kollios, and Nick Koudas. MRShare: Sharing Across Multiple Queries in MapReduce. *PVLDB*, 3(1):494–505, 2010.

188. Christopher Olston, Benjamin Reed, Utkarsh Srivastava, Ravi Kumar, and Andrew Tomkins. Pig latin: a not-so-foreign language for data processing. In *SIGMOD*, pages 1099–1110, 2008.

189. M. Tamer Özsu and Patrick Valduriez. *Principles of Distributed Database Systems*. Springer, New York, NY, USA, 3rd edition, March 2011.

190. Pradeep Padala, Kang G. Shin, Xiaoyun Zhu, Mustafa Uysal, Zhikui Wang, Sharad Singhal, Arif Merchant, and Kenneth Salem. Adaptive control of virtualized resources in utility computing environments. In *Proceedings of the 2nd ACM SIGOPS/EuroSys European Conference on Computer Systems*, EuroSys '07, pages 289–302, Lisboa, Portugal, March 2007. ACM.

191. Douglas F. Parkhill. *The challenge of the computer utility*. Addison-Wesley, 1966.

192. Swapnil Patil, Milo Polte, Kai Ren, Wittawat Tantisiriroj, Lin Xiao, Julio López, Garth Gibson, Adam Fuchs, and Billie Rinaldi. YCSB++: benchmarking and performance debugging advanced features in scalable table stores. In *SOCC*, 2011.

193. David A. Patterson. Technical perspective: the data center is the computer. *Commun. ACM*, 51(1):105, 2008.

194. Andrew Pavlo, Erik Paulson, Alexander Rasin, Daniel J. Abadi, David J. DeWitt, Samuel Madden, and Michael Stonebraker. A comparison of approaches to large-scale data analysis. In *Proceedings of the 2009 ACM SIGMOD International Conference on Management of Data*, SIGMOD '09, pages 165–178, New York, NY, USA, 2009. ACM.

195. Rob Pike, Sean Dorward, Robert Griesemer, and Sean Quinlan. Interpreting the data: Parallel analysis with sawzall. *Sci. Program.*, 13(4):277–298, October 2005.

196. Dan Pritchett. BASE: An ACID alternative. *Queue*, 6(3):48–55, May 2008.

197. Jorge-Arnulfo Quiané-Ruiz, Christoph Pinkel, Jörg Schad, and Jens Dittrich. RAFT at work: speeding-up mapreduce applications under task and node failures. In *SIGMOD Conference*, pages 1225–1228, 2011.

198. Jorge-Arnulfo Quiané-Ruiz, Christoph Pinkel, Jörg Schad, and Jens Dittrich. RAFTing MapReduce: Fast recovery on the RAFT. In *ICDE*, pages 589–600, 2011.

199. Thomas Ristenpart, Eran Tromer, Hovav Shacham, and Stefan Savage. Hey, you, get off of my cloud: exploring information leakage in third-party compute clouds. In *Proceedings of the 16th ACM Conference on Computer and Communications Security*, CCS '09, pages 199–212, Chicago, IL, USA, November 2009. ACM.

200. Jennie Rogers, Olga Papaemmanouil, and Ugur Çetintemel. A generic auto-provisioning framework for cloud databases. In *Proceedings of the 26th IEEE International Conference on Data Engineering Workshops*, ICDEW '10, pages 63–68, Long Beach, CA, USA, March 2010. IEEE Computer Society.

201. Florian Rosenberg, Predrag Celikovic, Anton Michlmayr, Philipp Leitner, and Schahram Dustdar. An end-to-end approach for QoS-aware service composition. In *Proceedings of the 13th IEEE International Enterprise Distributed Object Computing Conference*, EDOC '09, pages 151–160, Washington, DC, USA, 2009. IEEE Computer Society.

202. Florian Rosenberg, Max Benjamin Müller, Philipp Leitner, Anton Michlmayr, Athman Bouguettaya, and Schahram Dustdar. Metaheuristic Optimization of Large-Scale QoS-aware Service Compositions. In *IEEE SCC*, pages 97–104, 2010.

203. Sherif Sakr and Anna Liu. SLA-based and consumer-centric dynamic provisioning for cloud databases. In *Proceedings of the 5th IEEE International Conference on Cloud Computing*, IEEE CLOUD '12, pages 360–367, Honolulu, HI, USA, June 2012. IEEE Computer Society.

204. Sherif Sakr and Anna Liu. Is your cloud-hosted database truly elastic? In *Proceedings of the 9th IEEE World Congress on Services*, IEEE SERVICES '13. IEEE Computer Society, June 2013.

205. Sherif. Sakr, Anna. Liu, Daniel .M. Batista, and Mohammad. Alomari. A survey of large scale data management approaches in cloud environments. *IEEE Communications Surveys & Tutorials*, 13(3):311–336, 2011.

206. Sherif Sakr, Anna Liu, and Ayman G. Fayoumi. The Family of MapReduce and Large Scale Data Processing Systems. *CoRR*, abs/1302.2966, 2013.

207. Sherif Sakr, Liang Zhao, Hiroshi Wada, and Anna Liu. CloudDB AutoAdmin: Towards a truly elastic cloud-based data store. In *Proceedings of the 9th IEEE International Conference on Web Services*, ICWS '11, pages 732–733, Washington, DC, USA, July 2011. IEEE Computer Society.

208. Jörg Schad, Jens Dittrich, and Jorge-Arnulfo Quiané-Ruiz. Runtime measurements in the cloud: observing, analyzing, and reducing variance. *Proc. VLDB Endow.*, 3(1–2):460–471, September 2010.

209. Adam Silberstein, Jianjun Chen, David Lomax, B. McMillan, M. Mortazavi, P. P. S. Narayan, Raghu Ramakrishnan, and Russell Sears. PNUTS in Flight: Web-Scale Data Serving at Yahoo. *IEEE Internet Computing*, 16(1):13–23, 2012.

210. Will Sobel, Shanti Subramanyam, Akara Sucharitakul, Jimmy Nguyen, Hubert Wong, Arthur Klepchukov, Sheetal Patil, Armando Fox, and David Patterson. Cloudstone: Multi-platform, multi-language benchmark and measurement tools for web 2.0. In *Proceedings of the 1st Workshop on Cloud Computing and Its Applications*, CCA '08, Chicago, IL, USA, October 2008.

211. Ahmed A. Soror, Umar Farooq Minhas, Ashraf Aboulnaga, Kenneth Salem, Peter Kokosielis, and Sunil Kamath. Automatic virtual machine configuration for database workloads. *ACM Trans. Database Syst.*, 35(1):7:1–7:47, February 2008.

212. Yair Sovran, Russell Power, Marcos K. Aguilera, and Jinyang Li. Transactional storage for geo-replicated systems. In *Proceedings of the 23rd ACM Symposium on Operating Systems Principles*, SOSP '11, pages 385–400, New York, NY, USA, 2011. ACM.

213. M. Srinivas and Lalit M. Patnaik. Genetic algorithms: A survey. *Computer*, 27(6):17–26, June 1994.

214. James Staten, Simon Yates, Frank E. Gillett, and Walid Saleh. Is cloud computing ready for the enterprise? Technical report, Forrester Research, March 2008.

215. Michael Stonebraker. The case for shared nothing. *IEEE Database Eng. Bull.*, 9(1):4–9, 1986.

216. Michael Stonebraker. One size fits all: an idea whose time has come and gone. *Commun. ACM*, 51(12):76, 2008.

217. Michael Stonebraker, Daniel J. Abadi, David J. DeWitt, Samuel Madden, Erik Paulson, Andrew Pavlo, and Alexander Rasin. Mapreduce and parallel dbmss: friends or foes? *Commun. ACM*, 53(1):64–71, 2010.

218. Basem Suleiman, Sherif Sakr, Ross Jeffrey, and Anna Liu. On understanding the economics and elasticity challenges of deploying business applications on public cloud infrastructure. *Internet Services and Applications*, 3(2):173–193, 2012.

219. Andrew S. Tanenbaum and Maarten van Steen. *Distributed Systems: Principles and Paradigms*. Prentice Hall, Upper Saddle River, NJ, USA, 2nd edition, October 2006.

220. Jun'ichi Tatemura, Oliver Po, and Hakan Hacigümüs. Microsharding: a declarative approach to support elastic OLTP workloads. *Operating Systems Review*, 46(1):4–11, 2012.

221. Alexander Thomson, Thaddeus Diamond, Shu-Chun Weng, Kun Ren, Philip Shao, and Daniel J. Abadi. Calvin: fast distributed transactions for partitioned database systems. In *Proceedings of the 2012 ACM SIGMOD International Conference on Management of Data*, SIGMOD '12, pages 1–12, New York, NY, USA, 2012. ACM.

222. Ashish Thusoo, Joydeep Sen Sarma, Namit Jain, Zheng Shao, Prasad Chakka, Suresh Anthony, Hao Liu, Pete Wyckoff, and Raghotham Murthy. Hive: a warehousing solution over a map-reduce framework. *Proc. VLDB Endow.*, 2(2):1626–1629, August 2009.

223. Ashish Thusoo, Joydeep Sen Sarma, Namit Jain, Zheng Shao, Prasad Chakka, Ning Zhang, Suresh Anthony, Hao Liu, and Raghotham Murthy. Hive: a petabyte scale data warehouse using Hadoop. In *Proceedings of the 26th IEEE International Conference on Data Engineering*, ICDE '10, pages 996–1005, Long Beach, CA, USA, March 2010. IEEE Computer Society.

224. Ashish Thusoo, Zheng Shao, Suresh Anthony, Dhruba Borthakur, Namit Jain, Joydeep Sen Sarma, Raghotham Murthy, and Hao Liu. Data warehousing and analytics infrastructure at facebook. In *Proceedings of the 2010 ACM SIGMOD International Conference on Management of Data*, SIGMOD '10, pages 1013–1020, New York, NY, USA, 2010. ACM.

225. Luis M. Vaquero, Luis Rodero-Merino, Juan Caceres, and Maik Lindner. A break in the clouds: towards a cloud definition. *SIGCOMM Comput. Commun. Rev.*, 39(1):50–55, December 2008.

226. Werner Vogels. Eventually consistent. *Commun. ACM*, 52(1):40–44, January 2009.

227. Mladen A. Vouk. Cloud computing - issues, research and implementations. In *Proceedings of the 30th International Conference on Information Technology Interfaces*, ITI '08, pages 31–40, Dubrovnik, Croatia, June 2008.

228. Hiroshi Wada, Alan Fekete, Liang Zhao, Kevin Lee, and Anna Liu. Data consistency properties and the trade-offs in commercial cloud storage: the consumers' perspective. In *Proceedings of the 5th Biennial Conference on Innovative Data Systems Research*, CIDR '11, pages 134–143, Asilomar, California, USA, January 2011.

229. Lee Wang, Howard Jay Siegel, Vwani P. Roychowdhury, and Anthony A. Maciejewski. Task Matching and Scheduling in Heterogenous Computing Environments Using a Genetic-Algorithm-Based Approach. *J. Parallel Distrib. Comput.*, 47(1):8–22, 1997.

230. Tom White. *Hadoop: The Definitive Guide*. O'Reilly Media, 3rd edition, May 2012.

231. Darrell Whitley. The GENITOR algorithm and selection pressure: why rank-based allocation of reproductive trials is best. In *Proceedings of the third international conference on Genetic algorithms*, pages 116–121, San Francisco, CA, USA, 1989. Morgan Kaufmann Publishers Inc.

232. Timothy Wood, Prashant Shenoy, Arun Venkataramani, and Mazin Yousif. Black-box and gray-box strategies for virtual machine migration. In *Proceedings of the 4th USENIX Conference on Networked Systems Design & Implementation*, NSDI '07, pages 229–242, Cambridge, MA, USA, April 2007. USENIX Association.

233. Gene T.J. Wuu and Arthur J. Bernstein. Efficient solutions to the replicated log and dictionary problems. In *Proceedings of the 3rd Annual ACM Symposium on Principles of Distributed Computing*, PODC '84, pages 233–242, New York, NY, USA, 1984. ACM.

234. Pengcheng Xiong, Yun Chi, Shenghuo Zhu, Hyun Jin Moon, Calton Pu, and Hakan Hacigumus. Intelligent management of virtualized resources for database systems in cloud environment. In *Proceedings of the 27th IEEE International Conference on Data Engineering*, ICDE '11, pages 87–98, Washington, DC, USA, 2011. IEEE Computer Society.

235. Lamia Youseff, Maria Butrico, and Dilma Da Silva. Towards a unified ontology of cloud computing. In *GCE*, 2008.

236. Matei Zaharia, Andy Konwinski, Anthony D. Joseph, Randy Katz, and Ion Stoica. Improving MapReduce performance in heterogeneous environments. In *Proceedings of the 8th USENIX Conference on Operating Systems Design and Implementation*, OSDI '08, pages 29–42, Berkeley, CA, USA, 2008. USENIX Association.

237. Kamal Zellag and Bettina Kemme. How consistent is your cloud application? In *Proceedings of the 3rd ACM Symposium on Cloud Computing*, SoCC '12, pages 6:1–6:14, New York, NY, USA, 2012. ACM.

238. Liangzhao Zeng, Boualem Benatallah, Anne H. H. Ngu, Marlon Dumas, Jayant Kalagnanam, and Henry Chang. QoS-Aware Middleware for Web Services Composition. *IEEE Trans. Software Eng.*, 30(5):311–327, 2004.

239. Qi Zhang, Lu Cheng, and Raouf Boutaba. Cloud computing: state-of-the-art and research challenges. *J. Internet Serv. Appl.*, 1(1):7–18, May 2010.

240. Yanfeng Zhang, Qixin Gao, Lixin Gao, and Cuirong Wang. iMapReduce: A distributed computing framework for iterative computation. *J. Grid Comput.*, 10(1):47–68, March 2012.

241. Liang Zhao, Anna Liu, and Jacky Keung. Evaluating cloud platform architecture with the CARE framework. In *Proceedings of the 17th Asia Pacific Software Engineering Conference*, APSEC '10, pages 60–69, Washington, DC, USA, 2010. IEEE Computer Society.

242. Liang Zhao, Sherif Sakr, and Anna Liu. Application-managed replication controller for cloud-hosted databases. In *Proceedings of the 5th IEEE International Conference on Cloud Computing*, CLOUD '12, pages 922–929, Washington, DC, USA, 2012. IEEE Computer Society.

243. Marcin Zukowski, Peter A. Boncz, Niels Nes, and Sándor Héman. MonetDB/X100 - A DBMS In The CPU Cache. *IEEE Data Eng. Bull.*, 28(2):17–22, 2005.

Printed in the United States
By Bookmasters